LEADING FROM

THE AUTOBIOGRAPHY OF
MIKE GATTING

Angela Patmore, who wrote this book with Mike Gatting, has previously collaborated with snooker star Alex Higgins and squash champion Jonah Barrington. She is also the author of a book on pressure in top-class sport, *Sportsmen Under Stress*
She lives in London.

LEADING FROM THE FRONT
THE AUTOBIOGRAPHY OF MIKE GATTING

With Angela Patmore

Additional material by Angela Patmore

Futura
Queen Anne Press

A *Queen Anne Press/Futura* BOOK

First published in Great Britain in 1988 by
Queen Anne Press, a division of
Macdonald & Co (Publishers) Ltd
66–73 Shoe Lane
London
EC4P 4AB

A member of Maxwell Pergamon
Publishing Corporation plc

This edition published in Great
Britain in 1989 by Queen Anne
Press/Futura

Cover photograph: All-Sport
Designed by Dave Crook

ISBN 0-7088-37786

Typeset, printed and bound in Great Britain by
Hazell Watson & Viney Limited
Member of BPCC Limited
Aylesbury, Bucks, England

Contents

For Andrew and James from their absent father

CHAPTER ONE
The Bruiser
1957–70

My parents were living in a furnished flat in Kingsbury when I was born on 6 June, 1957. The landlady hadn't really wanted children on the premises and I used to wake up in the night, every night, crying and yelling. Mum's remedy was to feed me – I've always liked my food – but I didn't sleep much in the daytime either. Perhaps an hour here and there. After about eighteen months of this hyperactive yelling and feeding, and partly from concern for the landlady's sanity, we moved out of earshot to Willesden. The new Gatting home was 11 Church Lane. There was a hefty mortgage, and Mum and Dad soon found they needed two jobs each to make ends meet, as well as several babysitters.

By trade my Dad, Bill, was an aircraft fitter with Handley Page in Cricklewood, but he also worked as a steward in their sports club in Cool Oak Lane, Hendon, by the Welsh Harp reservoir. Even when Handley Page went into liquidation and the sports facilities were taken over by National Cash Registers, the place remained the focal point of Dad's work and of my childhood. If you wonder why my whole life has been consumed with sport, it dates back to that environment, where there was really very little else to do. Obviously, when you have such excellent facilities at an early age, you tend to get carried along, because there were always racquets and bats and balls and boots lying about, and tennis courts, and playing fields, and the great open air.

Mum and Dad were always working. My Mum, Vera, would bring home complicated tracing jobs, going over draftsmen's plans for Smiths, the instrument and clock-maker. I can still smell the drying powder she dusted on the prints. I used to admire her so much, sitting there for hours, tracing away. And when she wasn't doing that, she'd be helping Dad with the stewarding at Cool Oak Lane. It was all very hectic and happy. Then when I was two, 'something terrible' happened. My Mum suddenly disappeared in the middle of the night, and came back days later with a new baby. Of course, I wouldn't say hello to her or anything. She put him in my pram as well, though I managed to hurl him out on the floor once or twice. His name was Steve. I didn't know then that my new baby brother would grow up to be a professional footballer for Arsenal and Brighton, and play in a Wembley Cup Final. All I knew was, he was in my pram, and after that I became a very angry, naughty, stubborn little bloke, and very very determined.

Babysitter Yvonne Waller:

We lived opposite the Gattings; I'd look after Mike, and when Steve came along I'd mind the pair of them. Steve was a placid little boy, blond and blue-eyed. But he was regularly in the wars, and once had to go to hospital after running into a sightboard. There were these performances, when Mike would get in one of his tempers in the house. We'd go out of the room and shut the sliding doors and you'd hear him let rip. After it had gone quiet, we'd venture back in and his Mum would say, 'Have you finished now, Michael?'

He was a proper little bruiser, and always had a crewcut. He used to chase his mother with caterpillars. We'd see them running along the bottom of Church Lane, with his Mum in front shouting, 'Put it down, Michael!' Then there was the time he fell out of an upstairs bedroom window, and landed in the garden. We nearly died – his Mum was in the loo at the time – but he got up, brushed himself down, and toddled away. We took him to hospital – they said there was nothing wrong with him.

I remember that incident vaguely, because I'd always been

told about not going out on the balcony, but I was curious. There was this little ledge that ran round to the Sullivans' next door, and it was always inviting for an inquisitive child. I used to look up at it longingly from the garden and think, if I could get on top of that, I could see a lot of things from up there. But I overbalanced slightly getting out of the window. I can remember feeling winded as I came down. It was quite a drop for a three-year-old.

The window in question was in Steve's bedroom. Steve was very irritating at times. He was quiet, but he knew how to incense me. It wasn't a question of 'poor little Steve'. He'd take something and goad me – '*Mnea, mnea, mnea*!' – and then run off. He was quicker than me as well: he had to be. And, small as he was, with me exploding after him, he'd keep coming back for more, just to aggravate me. Our feuds were soon translated into sport, either in the garden or at Handley Page's club. We'd waddle about with pads on up to our waists, trying to play cricket in the driveway of our semi-detached. You had to whack the ball back past the bowler because if you played a crossbat shot, the ball would go through the garage window or into next door's garden. So you learned to play with a straight bat. It was a great help, though I didn't realize it at the time.

We used to play football in that same garage driveway and because I was bigger and stronger and heavier than Steve he had to learn quick footwork and manoeuvring skills to get the ball past me. So that probably helped him a bit as well, in later life! We'd play any game at all: tennis, table-tennis, bowls, even snooker, darts, cards and chess as we got older, to say nothing of swimming and diving. For his size, Steve was very good at everything. I got on at football because I was burlier than most boys of my own age, and wouldn't get knocked off the ball, whereas poor Steve would get kicked off and go flying. I was a little tank, and if somebody got me cross I'd just go charging in again. When Steve got whacked, he got hurt. So it was mainly through strength that I beat him at things, hitting the ball harder. He learned to use his brain, and hand-eye coordination, and because he was so quick, one thing he *could* beat me at was table-tennis. We used to keep out of trouble, as we got older, at Oxford and Kilburn Youth Club, where table-tennis was very keenly contested, but we'd play at home as well, as little kids.

Steve was especially good at table-tennis, and could probably have made a career of it, had it not been for his football and cricket. And because I always had to be the best, there would be scenes. Like the time I saved up for two months (washing cars and doing my paper rounds and my milk round) for a table-tennis bat which cost £2 10s, a lot of money in those days. And what happened? I lost this very tight game because I couldn't get the ball past him by brute strength, and I got so annoyed – not so much with Steve as with myself – that I smashed my expensive bat on the table and broke it in half. I'd only had it a week. If you ask Steve, he'll tell you how nasty I was to him. I don't know why – in fact I defended him once from the school bully and got caned for it. It's just that I didn't like losing to him. I didn't like losing to anybody.

Steve Gatting:

> Because our parents were so busy and both had jobs in the evening, we'd often be left alone. For some reason, we always ended up fighting. Always. And I'd be on the wrong end of it because he was bigger than me. Many's the time I'd be chased round the house, upstairs and down, with Mike hot on my heels.

As we got older, although we continued to argue, it got better. He learned not to taunt me and nip off round the corner, and I learned to control my temper – I very rarely lose it these days: somebody *really* has to upset me. Things gradually settled down, and Steve and I have a brilliant relationship now. But in his tender years I'd chase him with a cricket bat in my hand.

I can't remember my Dad playing sport with us much, though I'm told he was a good club cricketer and a useful batsman before the War intervened, and *his* father had been a considerable wicket-keeper. My very first away match, in fact, was the annual trip on the coach to Sittingbourne in Kent, to see my Dad play for National Cash Registers. I took my kit along, being the rather short twelfth man, but I was never called upon. My heart sank as the day dragged on – I've never been a great spectator, and I was *so* disappointed.

Steve and I very rarely saw my Dad in the house: he was gone before we got up, and home after our bedtime. But early Sunday mornings were happy hours because my Dad was there, pottering about. We'd get up and put Frankie Laine on the record player, and as 'Champion the Wonder Horse' and 'Cool Clear Water' drifted through the room, Steve and I cleared out the fireplace, putting the ashes on the compost heap – in between having an argument, probably. Dad never had a car, but he'd tinker with his motor-bike (Steve and he came off it on occasion). Bikes and pipes he liked, and sometimes we'd watch television together. *Lassie* or *The Avengers*. But usually, Dad was working. He had an ulcer, I remember, and was on a milk diet.

The times we spent as a family were basically holidays and at Handley Page's club, steeped in sport. I got run over by a car once, doing my milk round, and as I lay outside the off-licence with tyre marks over my waist and a dislocated shoulder, I managed to croak, 'Mum and Dad . . . Handley Page's . . .' before I expired. Each weekend, the Gattings, kids, pushchairs and food, would be piled on the bus – well, two buses if we couldn't get a 266 – and then it was the long walk down to Cool Oak Lane to our Home from Home.

Mum had to get the cricketers' teas and the footballers' steak and kidney pies – with brown sauce – and I would stick the pies in this huge old gas cooker, which exploded when you lit it – the first time, I jumped out of my skin and singed all my hair. When there were big dances on, Steve and I would collect glasses, and I'd help Dad behind the bar, pulling pints (2s 6d for a light and bitter) and the drummer

International Dance Teachers' Association Ltd.

AMATEUR DANCING TEST

School ....RIDGE DANCE STUDIOS........

Test to be taken ....BRONZE........ Branch ....(B)........
See over (1) *See over* (2)

Christian Name ....MICHAEL........ Surname ....GATTING........

State Junior (under 16) or Adult ....JUNIOR........ Date of Test ....25-2-68........

CAPITAL LETTERS OR TYPE, PLEASE

EXAMINER'S REPORT — For official use only

Dance........WALTZ........ Marks........90........

Excellent stance — good leads
— most promising action

Dance........Q.S........ Marks........90........

Good buoyant style
— very well trained for this test

Dance........................ Marks........................

Marks (in each dance). Pass 65%, Commended 75%, Highly Commended 90%.

Examiner........[illegible]........ Result........H.COMM........
(F, P, C, or H.C.)

would be going '*sshh-te-ke*' with a little fan on the drums, and they'd all waltz to songs and saxophones. Steve and I would sit on the bar, though we could both do proper ballroom dancing, if required, and got bronze medals at Neasden Ritz.

We grew up in a man's world – that's probably why I love doing childish things now; people do tell me, 'You grew up too fast to have a childhood.' I played football for National Cash Registers in a Sunday side, as well as for Edgware FC when I was a teenager, and found out how difficult it was to keep up with large, well-built men of six foot one. Long before that, Steve and I were pretending to be pint-size reserves for Handley Page's, turning up on the sidelines in our kit. Steve had Manchester United strip, or Chelsea (he would eventually be signed by Arsenal), and I had Manchester City because I liked the colours (I'm a lifelong Spurs supporter). We'd dive about in the mud behind the goal, keeping a wary eye on Les Elliott, the keeper, who was in charge of the Sports and Social Club and had three attractive daughters. Les became a pal and an Uncle to us, and later employed me as a plumber – more of which later.

When the footballers had finished, and had their huge bath, Steve and I would jump in the same scum-coated water in our kit, wring it out, and put it on the side to dry, so that it didn't get caked up. And there we would splosh for hours, until Dad dragged us out. Then we might play table-tennis – or darts or whist – with the grown-ups, or watch the International Cavaliers or *Dr Who* on the bar telly. There were tennis courts; there was a bowling green, even a sailing club down by the Reservoir, where once I fell off the pontoon and everything went very black before a man called Tony Hayes hauled me out. Lots to do. I remember it all: Con, the caretaker, stoking the boiler; the cage, where they stored the empties; the cellar, where Dad once locked me in after some uncontrollable outburst. I sat on the stone steps, staring at the light under the door, imagining an enormous daddy long legs was about to scuttle out of the gloom after me. And I remember Sheila Sumner who was about seventeen, and still bears a scar on her leg from having nets with us.

Sheila Sumner:

I used to play cricket in the nets with Mike, and it sounds ridiculous, but whenever I saw him, he always had a bat in his hand. He was a hyperactive little menace, but when he got hold of a cricket bat, he was a different person – the bat was his mate, his best friend. I don't think there was ever a 'before cricket'. If he could have had a bat in the womb with him, he would have done. He was a hundred per cent energy ball; always a little man, never a boy. I was giving him a shower once in the changing room and as I stood him on the side, he put his arms around me and kissed my neck – well, bit me actually. 'There you are, Sheila', he said, 'that's a love heart!' I think he was old before his time.

Sheila also saw the other side of me as well. There was a funny little sweetshop round the corner called Albert's, run by a grumpy old boy who used to watch us eagle-eyed in case we nicked anything (I never did). He had a big high glass counter with all the old candy shrimps and bullseyes on display, and we used to go in there for our favourite triangular ice-lollies, 'Jubblies'.

Sheila Sumner:

Mike came home from school and said, 'Can I have sixpence to go to Albert's?'

Vera said, 'Yes Michael, but go upstairs first and take off your school shoes and trousers and put your trainers on.'

'I want sixpence to go to Albert's,' repeated Mike, about five times.

Now, I was in the lounge, watching all this, and I thought, if he doesn't do as he's told in a minute I shall have to interfere. Eventually I couldn't bear it, so I grabbed him, took him upstairs and threw him on the bunk bed.

'Why can't you do as you're asked?' I yelled. 'You're a naughty little boy!' I threatened him loudly with a good hiding and lectured him, and his face came over all angelic.

'Sheila – talk to me,' he said, very sweetly. He was a menace, but he was a lovable menace. 'Now go downstairs at once,' I told him, 'and apologize to your mother!'

And he went down to her, and as God is my judge, you know what he said? 'I'm sorry, Mummy. Can I have sixpence to go to Albert's?'

Mrs Vera Gatting:

I used to have nightmares worrying about the children, and when I started waking up in the night shouting, 'Mike, *stop it!*' the doctor said I should get some specialist advice. It was as a result of the specialist's advice that we traced Bill's father: he suggested that because Mike's Dad was working and he didn't see much of him, it would be helpful if we could find his Grandad. You see, my husband was brought up in a London County Council home; his mother apparently died in childbirth and his father contracted TB and had to go into a sanatorium. After a lot of letters, and warnings not to build up our hopes, we finally traced Grandad Gatting: he was retired, remarried, and living down in Devon.

The first time I met him I was about nine: we went down in the coach, and Grandad collected us in an old Austin A40 with leather upholstery. I remember Dad giving Grandad a hug. Grandma was totally loving and soft with us, but Grandad was very strict – you could tell he was an old Army man. He didn't like Steve and myself playing football on his lawn in case we damaged his vegetables. They had a lovely bungalow down there at Galmpton, and two little doggies, Sookie and Tina, which we'd take for walks on the common, or play with in the house, much to Grandad's annoyance. I've always loved dogs and could never have one of my own because the family were working: the nearest I got was bathing Jimmy the spaniel, who belonged to our bus-conductress neighbour, Yvonne Cotrel. Sookie and Tina were a special attraction. We had some lovely, happy holidays down in Devon, playing cricket on the beach with Dad and Grandad. I was so elated that one day I apparently marched up to my grandfather and announced, 'I want to captain England one day, Grandad!' Sadly he and Grandma are both dead now, but Grandma lived to see me successful at cricket. She said, 'Grandad would have been *so* proud of you.'

Before this, our holidays would be spent at camps, like Warner's or Butlins, where I learned to swim and dive and won tankards, or at Ilfracombe, where one holiday was darkened when I saw a poor mongrel run over by a car, and got very upset, shouting at the driver – a thing I never did. We also used to go to Southend-on-Sea to see my Nanny Lucas, and on one occasion I ended up in an oxygen tent in hospital with a chest infection, I can't remember how. But Steve and I would save up our pocket money for the amusement arcades – even now I love things like this – and we'd lose all our money on the cranes and grabbers and ask Dad for an advance on next week's pocket money, to tide us over.

'That's it,' Dad would say. 'You can't have any more.' Of course, Mum and Dad had to work so hard for it, you had to learn the value. Ever since, I've always appreciated that lesson; it takes so much effort and hard work to come by money, I've always been a bit worried about how much goes where, for example on clothes. Me, I've never troubled about dressing fashionably. Steve has always been a snappy dresser and looks nice in off-the-peg suits because he's the right build; but I've never cared because so long as I've got trousers to fit me I'm happy. If I *find* trousers to fit me, I usually buy four pairs!

Having said that, I've always been very careful with my clothes, and kit and stuff, because when we were small, things were hard to come by and expensive. Which brings me to a story about the Scouts. Steve and I were both keen Scouts: I liked it better than the 72nd Boys' Brigade which had a lot of square bashing and brass bands. Steve was in the Cubs as well, which I wasn't: I was a Sea Scout. The man in charge was a big bluff chap called Fred Malcolm, who wore navy-blue long shorts and was known to us boys as 'Guv'.

'Guv' Malcolm:

I had three pet hates, disrespect for the flag, hands in pockets, and direct lies. If I caught any of them at any of these, it was instant paddle. Mike was never saucy or insubordinate at camp: whether he respected his elders or went in fear of the paddle, I don't know. But he hated

> losing, even then. If he was swimming team captain, he gave a hundred per cent and expected as much of the others. He went out like a torpedo for us in the relay race of the swimming gala: we had the smallest representative team but we walked the competition, really, with Steve and Mike. Yet although Mike was the best swimmer in the group, he yelled blue murder on his birthday when they gave him the traditional fully-clothed dunking in the river. Went home and told his mother!

I wasn't so much worried about being thrown in, as ruining my clothes, or losing something out of the pockets: I was always worried about losing things. My trainers were soaking, and I was dreading what Mum would say when I got home. I tried to look after all my gear at camp – clothes, knife, fork, billy can, enamel mug and plate. We did our own cooking, you see: you had to do proper meals (no packets), dig your own firepit, and fetch kindling. ('Guv' would torment us with the 'rubbing sticks' method and then give us a match.) We'd have canoe races and sit round the campfire singing, and sleep in our sleeping bags in a big hut with a pot-bellied stove, with everyone snoring. Scout camps were very happy: a mix of discipline and survival skills. They helped you grow up.

The other major childhood thing, of course, was school and as my dawning sports career and school are closely linked, I've left the subject till last. I went to Wykeham Primary (Steve's infant school as well, though I attended a nursery school near Neasden tube station). Wykeham was a mixed junior school, and when we went on trips to the Isle of Wight and so on, girls came too, housed in different parts of the hotel. I wasn't one of the brave lads who visited the girls' sleeping quarters in the small hours, either: I queued for my cocoa and went to bed. I respected authority and teachers. At school I was known chiefly for playing cricket and football, swimming, praising school-dinner ladies and rushing around. My nice fourth-form teacher, Mrs Collister, said I was a 'bull in a china shop'. I was only trying to be helpful, but I used to tear about because I wanted to be the first to do it, and then I'd knock the lot over and have to clear it all up, and be the last to finish.

I was the same at cricket, as well. Mrs Collister used to take us for 20-over matches, with springback stumps. I'd hit the ball for an hour, and then I'd want to do it just one more time, instead of trying to keep going and construct an innings and would usually get out. I remember getting my first hundred, though, on 3 July 1968, because it was against Stonebridge, our bitter rivals. We'd bowled them out for 101, and my little brother opened our account and untypically got out for 0, whereupon the innings folded around my ears. But I managed to get 102, out of 115 for 8. Technically, of course, we'd already won by that stage, but the teachers thought, that having got 86 I should be allowed to keep going and see if I can make my century. I had to go up on the stage at assembly the next day, which was very embarrassing, and they presented me with a bat. I went bright red, as I usually did in those days. Apart from being in the choir, this was my first taste of standing up in front of people.

Wykeham headmaster Arthur Powell:

> I remember Mike mostly for sport – he was an exceptionally good goalkeeper at football, as well as being a fine bowler, wicketkeeper and batsman. At the time I produced a school scorebook, and that shows how proficient Mike was, often winning matches on his own – it was, after all, very exceptional for a boy of his age to get a 100. What coaching did he get? There are certain fundamentals which can be taught, but one would never wish to regiment them so much that you destroy their natural ability.

Mr Powell also thinks it a great pity about the discouragement of competitive sport in school these days. It's nice to hear someone from his era as well as my own say how absolutely silly it is not to allow children to compete. As Mr Powell says, life is a competition anyway, and we enjoyed it. My days at Wykeham helped me no end.

From there I went to John Kelly Boys' High School in Cricklewood. The Eleven Plus had been abolished and as you know, I'm the first England captain to have gone fully comprehensive. By now I was pretty serious about sport. I'd already played for Brent schools both as a goalkeeper and wicketkeeper – I wasn't afraid to get hit so I was pretty good at stopping the ball. And I'm sure I did some representative bowling as well. At football I started playing out in the field when I was about fourteen, because I got bored watching everybody else rushing around, and I played centre-half for Brent Schools and then Middlesex Schools.

John Kelly deputy head, Harold Phillips:

> While Mike was there, I became deputy headmaster, in charge of school cricket, and served on the committee of the Schools Cricket Association of Middlesex. The first time Mike came to my notice was when his year head, Mr MacMillan, said, 'You ought to come down and see this little stocky boy Gatting hitting them all round the field!' This was true – he was going like a bomb. Although he was above average academically, we soon realized that he was almost undoubtedly going to be a professional sportsman, so we gave him every encouragement to concentrate on sport. Unfortunately John Kelly didn't have its own sports field and the council facilities were indifferent, with wickets tending from reasonable to potentially dangerous. However, Mike was an incredibly good little goalkeeper – both he and his brother were obviously gifted games players, and I think Mike, like Steve, would have made a first-class footballer. In fact, although nothing came of it, in his 5th year I recommended Mike to West Ham.

It didn't matter too much about the lack of cricket facilities at John Kelly, because by then I'd begun my 'adult' cricket career, if you like, as a club and county player, as I'll explain in Chapter 2. I had fun at school playing for the teachers' side (where the opposition would refer to me contemptuously as 'the ringer' until I started bowling at them) and going on marvellous school trips to the Dove Valley, Snowdonia and Dorset. I played for Middlesex Schools U-15s for two seasons, and at fourteen I was picked to play for the South of England and to take part in the Schools Festival at Rugby School. After some play-offs there, I was selected to play for the England Schools side against the Public Schools, G. H. G. Doggart's XI, and I got 100 in about 110 minutes. I remember being very nervous to start with, but I got off to such a good start, it was just a question of going for quick runs, which I managed to do and I think we ended up winning the game. I was even prouder when I graduated straight from the U-15 side to the U-19s – as only Alan Knott had done before me. It was a great honour to be linked in some way with Alan Knott, and I felt I must be getting somewhere.

I think it was for that 100 at Rugby that I was given the Sir Jack Hobbs Memorial Award for the best colt in my year, and had to go for the presentation at the Bloomsbury Centre Hotel in the West End. They said I would have to get up and say thank you for it, so I'd been panicking all week worrying about what I should say. I stood up for perhaps thirty seconds – it seemed like thirty minutes – and I started off slowly as I'd been instructed, but got quicker and quicker and sat down with a thump. I was fourteen and it was very frightening for me.

A little before this, at thirteen, I won a Wrigley Foundation Scholarship for a course at Lilleshall Sports Centre in Shropshire. About twenty or thirty kids had been selected from the whole of England. I was picked for my bowling, and I remember looking round and thinking, there are some good players here. We were put up in this big, creepy old mansion and it was like being at school, except that this was *cricket* school, with coaching, discussion, and films. I went on the course for two successive years, and got on famously with the Pakistani Test cricketer Khan Mohammad, who helped me really to understand swing bowling – how to practise it and how to play against it; he was such a lovely man.

From then on, I found myself in a lot of coaching schools and lots of representative sides. I played my first game of cricket with men in earnest, when I was thirteen, and of course I played for Middlesex Schools and other associations. There was a lot of head-hunting and inter-team poaching, and some bitter rows about who the best boys should be playing for. So far as I was concerned, I just wanted to play, never mind for whom. I didn't want to be home at weekends twiddling my thumbs. At football I had a trial at junior level for QPR, and myself and a chap called Phil Parkes were the goalkeepers – at fourteen. He was tall and blond and I was a little, short, round fellow, and they told me I was overweight. Unless I slimmed down, they weren't interested. Fine, I thought, I had other fish to fry.

Although my school years are mostly happy memories, I wasn't always the goody-goody sports prodigy. The time I got the cane commemorated the one and only fight I ever had at school. I've never been one for getting into punchups in later life either and ironically it happened because *Steve*, my usual adversary, got picked on by the school bully, who received his senior education in Borstal. I took the matter up with the bloke, and we set about one another in the bicycle shed. We were both caned by this very strict, braces-tugging teacher called Mr Hoish – 'Bummer Hoish' we used to call him. He had hands like shovels and when he smacked your legs, it really hurt. Mind you, he was quite right to expect a bit of discipline: I wish they had corporal punishment in schools today because I'm all in favour of law and order. I don't say you should beat kids, but respect is what's lacking in a lot of them now. Getting a smack never did *us* any harm.

CHAPTER TWO
The Colt
1970–73

I was just into my teens when I began playing not only colts' cricket, but senior cricket as well. I'm not sure if I was cocky; I don't *think* so. I was always me, which is hustling and bustling, so that probably gave the appearance of cockiness, and I may have been a bit noisy as well, as a kid.

Mike Brearley: He's noisy now!

I always seemed, on the surface, to be very confident, but I was really quite nervous. Every time I went out to bat, the tension would hit me, though everybody said, 'He looks bubbly and full of himself!' But I had to get over the initial twenty minutes of an innings before I could settle, and even then I couldn't really relax: it wasn't that other people were pushing me; I was pushing myself. I really wanted to do well, and get somewhere. I wanted to win. I enjoyed the cricket for its own sake, very very much, but this other impulse kept taking me forward. I always seemed to be playing an important game for somebody, or a trial, and it carried you along on a series of escalators, going up and up and up, in age, size and ability.

It was during the school holidays when I was eleven, and Mum was working part-time in an office in Petty France, London, that we saw the ad. Steve and I had been playing with the army kids just over the road in St James's Barracks, and we'd had our cheese and pickle sandwich lunch and a game of cards with the builders, and we were browsing through newspapers in Mum's office. The advertisement, in the *Willesden and Brent Chronicle,* said 'Colts required'. Budding young cricketers and their parents were invited along for a trial at Brondesbury Cricket Club in South Hampstead. (I don't know to this day why South Hampstead CC is in Brondesbury and Brondesbury CC is in South Hampstead, or at least Cricklewood.) The gentleman you had to apply to was a Mr Ted Jackson, so Mum typed out a letter for me, explaining about my 100 not out for Wykeham and my schoolboy cricket, and signing off, 'and my ambition is to play for England one day' – which it was.

I remember turning up at the trial with my parents, having arrived in magnificent style on the 260 bus up Cricklewood Lane. It was 5 pm, and assorted boys, some in whites and some not, were swinging bats in front of the oldest wooden pavilion I'd ever seen in my life. A man with a beard welcomed us. He was effervescent and bouncy, had a Cambridge accent, a Cambridge sweater, and transmitted pure enthusiasm about the game. This was Ted Jackson, CBE, a driving force in colts' cricket, with an evolving theory about finding the gaps in the field by angling the bat face instead of playing crossbat shots. (*Ted Jackson:* 'I believe in it as deeply as some believe in God'.) Of course, I wasn't to know this at the time.

As I went through my paces for Mr Jackson, I noticed behind his gesticulating arm another figure standing at a distance, an older, balding man, with a fag hanging out of the side of his mouth, which dripped ash on a derelict MCC sweater. It turned out to be W. L. 'Peter' Farara, or 'Curly' as we came to call him when even more of his hair had fallen out. In their contrasting styles, these two coaches were to nurture the colt Mike Gatting – and later the colt Steve Gatting – for the next three or four years, and impart all their knowledge of the game, which was considerable. But I'll always remember them as I saw them that day: Ted clapping his hands and shouting, 'Make sure you hit the ball *down*! *No*!!! Hit the ball along the *ground,* Michael! You hit that pull shot in the *air*!' and Curly, with his fag on, watching quietly but rather dangerously in the background. Of course, you wouldn't have called him 'Curly' to his face, or said 'boo' to him either for that matter. It was only later that we found out his bark was worse than his bite; that he was a bachelor, devoted all his waking hours to that club and to colts' cricket, had a heart of gold, and befriended stray dogs, like Bungey, who bit me on the thigh as I ran past the pavilion – and me a dog lover.

Ted Jackson:

Wholehearted involvement. These were the two words to decribe the young Gatt. He *loved* hitting the ball – he really could hit it – and he loved watching the ball, and there was a determination about it. Frequently people who like hitting the ball will lift their heads and slog. Not Michael. He kept his head still and watched the ball and – *bonk*! When he hit it, it stayed hit. That was the thing that impressed Peter Farara and impressed me no end. We never gave him any regimental coaching. Individuality is everything: you feed a young man's strengths and you work on what weaknesses he has. You can make suggestions, when the boy is a complete beginner, as to what he should do. But if he is following his own ability – as Peter Willey is, as Bradman did, as O'Reilly did – and it's working, you interfere at the peril of showing yourself to be a lunatic.

Thank goodness for that: I'm dead against regimented coaching for children: I think it's totally wrong. The main thing is surely to let the kids enjoy it and get used to hitting the ball; getting the coordination right. Because they learn a lot quicker that way: the brain accepts the fact and takes a lot more in. I think Brondesbury's altered a lot now, but when we were just starting out, there were just the two of them, Ted and Curly, setting up the colts' section which was one of the first in the country and setting standards for neighbouring clubs.

Curly was a good coach: he'd demonstrate, and he'd get me to demonstrate, and it was fun. He was utterly selfless and hard-working for the club, and also very rude, blunt, basic and to the point. There were no frills on Curly's coaching; he'd show you, and then let you develop. He'd draw on the ground with chalk, to indicate where your feet should go, and you'd start off with the pull shot because that was the easiest and the one kids instinctively enjoy, and then go to the forward defensive, and build up, week by week, until you'd assimilated every stroke (no, not the reverse-sweep – that came later). And then you'd have bowling practice, and Curly, a reasonable off-spinner, and Ted, a leg-spinner, would bowl at you in the nets. Ted used to bowl quick leg breaks at me, and the occasional wrong 'un, flipper and top-per. I class myself as a very fortunate Englishman to have had this tuition from the age of thirteen up, because the leg-break bowler poses special problems. As to my own bowling – Ted always thought very highly of me because I could bowl away-swingers but also produce a fair inswinger and once thumped him on the leg where his thigh-pad should have been – praise indeed. Early on, you know, *I* felt I could bowl a bit!

The facilities at Brondesbury were unusual. We had con-crete and rubberoid nets just inside the club gates, laid down in strips, and these were the newest thing about, so I suppose they were OK. But the dressing room facilities were rather amazing. They've refurbished the pavilion now, but it must be one of the oldest wooden ones about. The biggest draw-back were the outdoor loos. We had urinals in the changing rooms, but you had to go outside for anything else. Still, we had decent nets and good coaches, and these are the major factors for a club. Kids can change anywhere.

When I started, I batted number 6 or 7 in the 3rd XI. I was thirteen, and slightly lacking in stature, compared to my team-mates, but at least, with my little roly-poly build, I presented a solid front. Everybody's always called me fat – 'Fat Gatt' or 'Maxi' – but if you examine me close to, you'd be surprised at my modest dimensions. I look fat on television because it squares you up, and if you're short and wide with pads on, you fill the whole screen. It used to bother me a bit, being called fat when I was young, but I laugh about it now, because people come up to me and say, 'You're quite thin really, aren't you! You look *enormous* on television!'

I think what *might* have set me back slightly, as a young batsman, was not worrying about my girth, but that I always felt that scoring 30 was enough. Or that 30 was good for *me*. I felt that if I averaged 30 in a season at Brondesbury, playing in the first team with men, that would be a fairly realistic figure to aim at, and wouldn't put too much pressure on me. And that's exactly what I got in my first season in the 1st XI. I was only 14½, and I was playing football and other sports as well, competitively, and it was only when people began commenting on my 30s and 40s that I realized what was happening. They said, 'Look, you got yourself in, you got all the men back, and yet you still tried to hit it over their heads. Go for some singles.' They were right: it was a bit silly. I was being Mrs Collister's 'Bull in a china shop' again. But nobody at Brondesbury ever said, 'Right, Gatting – you've got to do *this* now!' – for which I'm eternally grateful. I think word reached my parents early on from this quarter, 'Don't push him. Let him be, and let him get on with it. He'll learn.' And that was the biggest help to me of all time.

Family friend Les Elliott:

I think Mike's dad has been a very good influence on both Mike and Steve, keeping them level-headed. I've known Bill since we worked at Handley Page before Mike was born, and I knew him when he worked behind the bar, first at the sports club, and later at the cricket school in Finchley. He told me that he's seen so many fathers ruin their boys, that he just likes to keep out of it. He's very proud of his sons, but you'd never think so, to listen to him, because he's so down-to-earth about it all.

I used to pick Mike up on Saturday mornings for his football; he'd play for Watford Juniors Saturday mornings, then for me at NCR in the afternoons, and then in the evenings he'd swim as well. And Bill would say, 'That boy's going to kill himself.' He'd never mention Mike's achievements, and Mike's the same.

I was playing for Brondesbury 2nd XI at cricket, and he came back from an away match and charged himself up at the club with bangers and mash, and he was sitting there talking about something, not cricket, and a club player came past and said, 'Well done, Mike!'

'Oh right, ta.'

So I asked him, 'What was that?'

'Oh, I got a few runs.'

He wouldn't tell you that he'd just scored 172 for Brondesbury at Reading.

During the football season, when Les would ferry us to our weekend games, sometimes the girls would come. Les's three daughters were Dawn, Joy and Janina, and they lived in Wembley, where Steve and I spent a bit of time in a back room listening to Carpenters records, because our families were always together. But it wasn't until I got to thirteen or fourteen that sitting in the back of the car with the girls took on a new significance. Dawn was tall, slender and good-looking. I was very naive about girls, but it got to the stage where I thought, it would be nice to see Dawn. I'm not sure, but I think she had a crush on Steve. Ten years later Steve ended up marrying Dawn's sister Joy. I never worried anyway: I was up to the gunnels in football, cricket, squash, tennis, table-tennis, basketball, swimming, life-saving, chess, darts, cards and snooker. And you were never ever lonely because there were always so many people around, especially grown-ups, willing to give you a game.

At Brondesbury, Steve and I galvanized people into playing table-tennis, and we managed to start up a team, beginning in the 8th division of the Willesden TT League and working its way up to the premier division, thanks to our best players, like Steve. It was quite an achievement for a club like us, and gave you a nice feeling of progress to have been in on it from the start.

Steve Gatting:

> It was very, very competitive. It had to be. I hated it. We played squash at Brondesbury as well. I used to run round like a lunatic and Mike would stand in the middle of the court smashing at either side. Then there was the cricket, of course. I think that's where Mike learned to drink, in the 1st XI at Brondesbury, when he was about fifteen. It was a very boozy team. They'd arrive back from an away match at about 10 pm and Mum would pick us up, and many's the time Mike would come back quite tipsy.

Mum would often collect us in her new car. She was quite fit and sporty herself – she'd have liked to have been a gym teacher – and she would chide me for not playing tennis with her at Brondesbury, as she was very keen. Once, I let her talk me into entering the mixed doubles tournament and I thought, now, if we reach the finals of this there could be problems because I've got to play cricket Saturday afternoon. Sure enough, we reached the finals. Poor Mum. That was the one and only time I've ever played any sort of competitive game with either of my parents.

At cricket, Ted and Curly actually got a very good colts' side together – the best in the area – and we won the Chairman's Cup, a knockout competition for Under-17 teams – from 1968 to 1973, under skipper Peter Kaufman. In fact, the only year we *didn't* win it was when I was captain, and we lost the semi-final against Enfield. As Ted says, it was a black night for him, coaching from the boundary and telling everybody to watch me when I went out to bat. You see, apart from playing for Brondesbury Colts in this Cup, I'd played for their 3rd XI at 13, and after just one game in their 2nd XI, where I scored 75 not out at Forest Hill, I'd gone straight into their 1st XI at 14½ and made my first 50 for them against an Oxford college. And I was playing for other representative teams as well.

Ted Jackson:

At the start of the match against Enfield, Mike had told the opposition skipper something like, 'I hope we can get this over fairly quickly as my old school mate, Ashok Patel, and I have to go and play for England' (meaning the English Schools Cricket Association).

We'd bowled pretty well, but they weren't a bad side either, and I came in at number 3, played across the line and got out cheaply, and we lost. It was very embarrassing. Steve was in the side keeping wicket, I remember, and I was cross about something when I went out to bat, which is why I didn't play a good shot.

Brother-in-law Mike Mabbott:

I was playing in that game, for Enfield Colts. When he came in, he hit the first 4 balls through the covers faster than anything I'd ever seen, but when he was out, as far as we were concerned, we'd won the match. Brondesbury fell apart.

You mustn't go out to bat cross: you have to have an even temperament, which I normally do. I can only think of one other occasion when I batted in anger: we were playing at a little club called Sawbridgeworth against Herts Schools and I'd bowled most of the morning without much luck, and I was cursing the batsman for getting about 70 streaky runs, playing and missing, and I said, bitterly, 'When I opened the batting I'll probably nick one and he'll catch it.' And that's exactly what happened, because I was in such a bad mood. You mustn't bat in a bad frame of mind. It's all right to have a bit of determination, but you mustn't ever go out there angry. You'll do something hasty, and get out.

So there are a few of my memories of club cricket. I don't know how other people at Brondesbury remember me.

Former chairman of Middlesex selectors, Mike Sturt:

I had heard of a boy called Gatting from Ted Jackson. The first time I saw him, I'd been playing in an away match for Brondesbury and returned to the club some time in the evening, where they were holding a little dance. There was this boy, who seemed as wide as he was tall, demanding money with menaces, saying in a squeaky voice, 'You've got to give me some money, Mr Sturt, Sir!' I said, 'You must be Gatting!' Because there could only be one Gatting; the other one hadn't appeared yet (and when he did we christened them 'Mini' and 'Maxi' Gatt to distinguish). Naturally I handed over the money. From then on it was always a great pleasure watching him thump the ball to all parts. I remember during an innings of 72 at Reading, he was batting with a quite senior player called John Evans. During the partnership, Evans wasn't playing particularly well, so at the end of an over, the 16-year-old told him, in his, by now, louder squeaky voice, 'You're not moving your shoulder into it', duly demonstrating the correct method. He could say and do the most outrageous things, without giving offence or appearing arrogant, which everyone accepted because it was Gatting and everyone knew and liked him.

Present 1st XI captain, Tony Ayre:

If you were cocky, you would have been slaughtered because there were some sharp customers at the club, and there was a lot of stick going about. Extrovert was OK, but you couldn't afford to be over-confident, or pompous, or full of yourself, because you'd very quickly be brought back to reality by sharp-tongued cynical comments. You couldn't dominate the group: not in that sort of company. Gatt was a very good team man, very enthusiastic, very brave. At Upton House school we had a good staff football side, with a lot of ex-professional players, and Mike also played for us there. It was social football, but a lot of the blokes were from the East End and very sharp, as you can imagine. I can also remember Mike playing for Fortune Green on Sunday mornings, demanding the ball and going through all these great hulking six-foot thugs trying to kick the hell out of him, and him not taking any notice at all, still smacking goals in.

Former 1st XI skipper, fixture secretary and treasurer, Martin Edney:

Mike was an absolutely honest, straightforward chap, and had a very good cricketing brain, even when he was 16. He and Ashok Patel between them would devise a plan to get somebody out, not by talking to him or by horrible psychology, but by actually bowling him out. He thought about the game far more deeply than most of the young players in the side. Earlier, though, when he was fourteen, I found out that he and two other boys, Monroe and Bunning, had been secretly playing for Paddington on Sundays. I used to be called 'The Führer' because of the way I controlled things at Brondesbury, and I summoned them for an interview to find out what was going on. I gave them a good dressing down and told them that this club gave them a lot, and we expected loyalty in return. And Monroe and Bunning both burst into tears. Gatt didn't!

One Easter, when I was about fourteen, Ted suggested I went on a coaching award course at Aylestone School (I'd already been to Lilleshall on the Wrigley Scholarship). Ted himself was teaching, and the examiner was David Fletcher of Surrey. The course lasted six weeks, and I was surrounded by men students thinking, what's going on here? But by the end of it I was asked to do quite a lot of demonstrating because I was fortunate enough to have the practical cricketing ability – whereas a lot of prospective coaches understand the theory but lack the coordination. To me, the toughest part was expressing myself in the written examination, but I managed to pass, and there followed an enormous argument about my being given the certificate because I was too young.

I remember Ted having rows and rows with the authorities. But that course was very useful to me, and I ended up coaching part-time at the MCC Cricket and Squash Centre in Finchley during school holidays.

It was in 1972 when I was brought to the attention of Middlesex County coach Don Bennett, and that happened basically through Ted as well.

Ted Jackson:

It was ironic. There was a young man called Andy Needham – he played for Surrey and he's now gone back to Middlesex, and a bigger contrast between two cricketers I would find it hard to imagine, because Needham is quiet and low-key, voltage about 110, quite unlike Mike. And I remember talking to Don Bennett about nine months before Mike was offered a contract, saying I thought there was a great future there for Gatt, and Don, so help me, said, 'Andy Needham's a better bat, any day of the week.' I froze with horror, and immediately got on the typewriter to Mike's father: 'Listen – at the moment he hasn't made his mark with Don Bennett, and what you must do is to get private lessons with him now. This is how Michael will persuade him that he should get a contract.'

Don Bennett:

I can remember saying I thought Andy Needham was technically a better batsman at the time, yes, but he hadn't got the quality Mike had, for which there isn't a word, really. Killer instinct perhaps. Almost a selfishness in the way they play. Savagery almost. I first saw Mike when he was about fourteen, playing in a Sunday match at Eastcote. I'd heard about him: Ted Jackson was always telling me about his young prospects but he mentioned Mike a lot, and when I saw him I thought, Blimey! He's big and strong for fourteen. He wouldn't be out of place playing Middlesex 2nd XI cricket if I was pushed.

I knew his father, and one day Bill Gatting said, 'I see

you've invited Michael up to the nets in January. Don't you think he's a bit young?'

'No, I think he's big enough and good enough.'

And Bill said, 'Well, I'm a bit apprehensive about it. Would you take him for a few weeks' private coaching beforehand?'

I said, 'Can do.'

So that October, heart beating, I went along for my first meeting with the County coach. Every Friday between 5.30 and 6, right up until Christmas, I'd go straight from school on the 112 bus up the North Circular Road to Finchley Cricket School in the East End Road, and have my lesson with Mr Bennett, who'd given up his tea breaks to see me. He was an ex-professional footballer and former Middlesex cricketer, a very neat, fit-looking man, with gunmetal hair and an air of authority.

After the first half-hour session he said, 'Mike, you're not very good playing on the on-side, are you? Do you feel comfortable round your legs? Not really, do you? You're a bit tucked up. Well, that's where we're going to work on it, not until I'm satisfied, but until you're satisfied.'

So then we set about the on-drive. He'd bowl the ball and I'd drive it through the off side all day long, and Don would say, 'No! Mid-on. Mid-on.' And I'd keep going *whack*! though square-leg, because I'd got into this bad habit.

Finally one night he got so exasperated that he shouted out, 'Right! That's it. If you can't ruddy well do it now you never will! Come out of the net' – and Don can be an awesome sight when he's cross, as he's a bit like a volcano at the best of times, and I remember going home and practising all week – *all week* – and then just before Christmas he said, 'I'm a bit happier now.' I knew then I'd got it.

Don Bennett:

We had three months of it nearly, on one stroke, before he was satisfied. I'd never do that again with anybody. After six weeks he was fine, really, but in his own mind he wasn't. Mike's not a quick learner, but he's a good learner. He takes every step gradually and then consolidates. Even up to Test level he did that, and he's always been a very hard worker. But what amused me early on was that he obviously hadn't watched a lot of cricket. I make a policy here of not going back to the Middle Ages and referring to players of the past, but one day it slipped out and I mentioned Denis Compton. And Gatt looked at me quite earnestly and said, ' 'Oo?'

Well, I couldn't sit still, you see, so I never saw a Test match. Even now in the dressing room, I have to be doing something. I can't be sitting round watching cricket all day long!

I must have been pushing fifteen in May 1972 when I was called upon to play my first game for Middlesex 2nd XI. I was still playing for Brondesbury, still involved in schools cricket, playing football for NCR, and for Brent Schools and for Middlesex Schools (at a football festival in Skegness) as a centre-half. My great cricket debut was in a two-day game for Middlesex 2nds *v.* Kent 2nds at Ealing, and all sorts of people had come to watch the Great White Hope, including (Sir) Gubby Allen and a few Middlesex committee men. Word had got round that this prospect was 'the best thing to happen in a long time', etc. I went in at 5 or 6, nervous as hell, and in came Test bowler John Shepherd, who used to swing it away a bit. I played forward, nicked it, and there was a terrible pause. Caught behind by David Nicholls for a golden duck. As I took the long walk back I thought, Well, that's it – you won't get another chance. I can't remember if I cried, but I was desperately disappointed.

It was a Bank Holiday Monday the following year when my luck changed. I was supposed to be playing for Brondesbury 1st XI at Stanmore, and I walked past Ted, who was on the phone, buried in some earnest conversation, and suddenly he started waving and signalling for me to come over (Ted is very flamboyant). He slammed the phone down and said, 'Right – nothing for it – you've got to go to *Hove* immediately – I'll call a cab for you – take this fiver – get your bag – they've been let down – fast as you can!' And so off I trotted. Cab to Victoria Station and on the train: I was going to play for Middlesex 2nd XI *v.* Sussex 2nds at Hove.

Well, I got off at Brighton instead of Hove and had to run all the way to the ground, arriving around lunchtime. I glanced at the scoreboard: 70 for 8. I thought: Blimey – I hope that's not us. It was us. Apparently on my arrival, the opposition coach remarked, 'Sent for a schoolboy, eh? You'll need more than a schoolboy to get you out of this rubbish.' I was sweating like a pig from my exertions and didn't know what I was supposed to do, but they were evidently at lunch.

Don Bennett:

When I found myself a player short, I'd told the secretary, 'You'd better get on the phone to Ted Jackson and get that boy Gatting down here.' Anyway, we're 70 for 8, and we're having lunch, and in those days the old lunches weren't all that: you'd got the choice of a bit of salad or a hot meal. And Gatt sat down, and I don't know whether he thought the salad was hors d'oeuvre, or something, but he had that, and then he had the hot meal, and I said, 'Michael, if you're all right I want you to bat next.'

'Cor – bit high.'

'You go next,' I told him. So he went in number 10, and the bowler saw this young lad coming in and bowled him a short first ball – which Mike whacked for 4, and he ended up getting 79. We finished with 200 instead of about 90, and it was a respectable draw. And that is what I remember most vividly about young Mike Gatting.

That was my first meeting with a guy called Ian Gould, who was to be my room-mate for quite some time. We got on extremely well and helped each other a lot: he was on the Arsenal books as well as being a wicketkeeper–batsman, so we had a bit to talk about. We become known at Middlesex as the Terrible Twins. Speaking of wicketkeepers, Mike Sturt commemorated my Hove innings with a little present: a set of pads. He'd heard that I didn't have any of my own, and went and bought me a pair specially. That was very kind.

That period in 1972 was a very important time for me, because Ted was sort of handing me over to Don and finding it a bit hard to let go, which infuriated Don a bit. And in between, I'd been receiving scholarship coaching from the likes of Khan Mohammad, and playing for England Young Cricketers, whose manager was England and Middlesex cricketer Jack Robertson, maker of 31,914 runs and 331 not out *v.* Worcestershire – which is still the highest post-war score by an Englishman. Jack was a lovely gentleman, and a quiet coach, a bit like Curly. He'd place a lot of emphasis on building an innings, and the finer points, to stimulate your brain about the game.

In 1973 I went with the Young Cricketers to the Cambridge Festival. What made it particularly memorable was not the honour, or the cricket, thrilling though they were, but something else entirely. One night, we were out having a drink with the opposition and I think, despite what my brother says about boozy Brondesbury, that this was the first time I'd *really* had a few too many. Plus they were trying to get me to smoke as well, which nearly caused me to cough my guts up and put me off smoking to this day. Anyway, we all fell out of some college bar around midnight and twirled our way back to our hotel, and there in the road were these two bikes.

A more mature bloke of eighteen and myself were well oiled anyway but we thought we'd have a ride around the block before turning in. No lights, peddling along, boyish prank. But as fate would have it, what should cruise by at the bottom of the road, but a Panda car. So we swivelled our handlebars immediately into an alley, which they saw, and the police were waiting for us at the other end.

'No, they're not our bikes, Officer; we've been borrowing

them, you know.' Titter. (Well, I'd obviously been borrowing mine, because it had no crossbar.)

'Oh, you've been loaned a lady's bike, have you? And no lights on. Right. In you get.'

And we were put in the back of a paddy wagon and taken to the station to be duly cautioned and reprimanded. There were frightening phone calls to mothers and fathers, and I was in dread worrying what Jack Robertson would think, and even worse, what Mum would think, because we certainly hadn't meant any harm and weren't thinking of stealing the bikes. The upshot of it was that we were eventually summoned to appear before a Cambridge magistrate, and my parents had to attend, and I was bound over to keep the peace. It was only a lark, really – I'm all in favour of law and order. So that was Delinquent Gatting brought to book. Fortunately the 1974 Cambridge Festival passed without incident. In fact, Ted says my bowling was a bit useful, so I must have gone on the wagon that year.

I was now coming up to the crossroads, when I was going to have to make the big decision about my career, and choose between cricket and football. Steve had by now been spotted by Arsenal, playing in a London schoolboy trial for Middlesex. He would eventually sign for them. I was playing for Watford South Eastern Counties, and having to do special sprint training. They told me, 'You're a good little player but you're a yard off the pace. We're going to see if we can improve your speed.'

Well, I couldn't believe how hard you had to train, but that was another discipline I had to learn, if I wanted to do it badly enough. I was maybe 16½ by now, and I was looking at all these possibilities, when Middlesex tentatively offered me a contract, but nothing definite. So I'd done my O-levels at John Kelly, and stayed on for the sixth form to maybe retake a couple I'd failed, do my A-levels – and if the worst came to the worst I might be a PE teacher. I was asking everybody what I ought to do, but I think I'd made up my own mind really.

Still, I had another string to my bow. Yes, Frances Edmonds, I was a part-time plumber. Our friend Les Elliott, when he wasn't doing amateur dramatics and operatics, had returned to his erstwhile trade, and when I wasn't coaching at Finchley in the school holidays, I worked for Les.

Les Elliott:

> There was the time he worked with me on a central heating job. I was downstairs finishing up, and he was in the loft laying the fibreglass. Now, when you're putting down fibreglass the last thing you want to do is to open your mouth because of the dust, and I could hear him up there, singing away, and all of a sudden there was a crash. He'd come through the ceiling, hadn't he? Luckily he came through the one room in this maisonette that the couple hadn't decorated, and the tallboy broke his fall or he might have been a tenor. Then there was the time we had to take out one of the sink units in this house. Mike didn't just take it out – he demolished it with a club hammer. And it was the wrong one. Set into it! Then there was the occasion I got my hand stuck on a live pipe, and I was trying to tell him to shut the electricity off.

He'd been putting up this old lamp with a metal clip and you're supposed to clamp it on the rafter but he'd put his hand on the galvanised tank and it had shorted out.

'Are you all right, Les?' I shouted, sticking my head through the loft door. 'Oh I see – I thought you were practising your dancing.' I wasn't much of a plumber's mate, all things considered. So I thought, perhaps I'd better play cricket.

CHAPTER THREE
The County
1973–77

Although I didn't play my first 1st-class game for Middlesex until June 1975 (soon after my eighteenth birthday), I'd already found out the shape of things to come. Three years before, to sharpen me up a bit, Don Bennett had invited me to have an evening net with the pros, who understandably proceeded to take the young hopeful down a peg or two. My abilities and my longing to be the best had carried me along at top speed to this point, and suddenly I came smack up against a professional element who were older, fitter, quicker. It really was an eye-opener. I stood at bay in the nets as the bowlers swung it all over the place, and I couldn't lay a bat on it. I was deeply embarrassed and shocked. I suppose, until now, I'd had it easy. I was so proud to be following in Alan Knott's footsteps by going straight into the England Schools U-19 side, playing against Scotland and Wales, and feeling I was getting somewhere; and I'd grown accustomed, as a youngster, to being with men and playing with men. But playing cricket against the pros was going to be a totally different game. I had to make sure I strengthened up my artillery; I was determined they weren't going to work me out.

In 1973 and 1974 I played mainly for the 2nds, helping them to two of their three consecutive U-25 titles. This was a 40-over competition for 2nd XI players with one capped player in the side and we were lucky: not only did we have the young talent, but everyone worked well as a unit. I also played for ESCA (the English Schools Cricket Association) and I was 12th man for the England U-19s *v.* West Indies U-19s at Lord's.

Don Bennett

I'd told Gubby Allen, who takes a bit of impressing, that this Gatting boy looked promising, and when he was made 12th man Gubby was a bit disappointed because he wanted to see him.

Well, on the morning somebody was unfit and Mike was picked to play, so I rang Gubby and said, 'Are you coming across? Gatting's in the team now.'

We went over and England were batting, and I expected Mike to come in at number 6 or so, as he was 2½ years younger than some of the others. Wayne Daniel – later, of course, a Middlesex colleague – was bowling. Even then, he was an *exceptional* young bowler speedwise, and he removed one opening batsman 3rd or 4th ball. And then who should come in at number 3 but Gatt. I thought, Oh *blimey*. What's going on here? The pitch wasn't very good: it had been relaid and they were testing it out, and the ball was taking off and it was very unpleasant. I reckon Mike got hit a dozen times by Wayne, and I think he was dropped in the slips, but he got 30-odd.

As soon as he was out, Gubby Allen got up from his seat and he said, 'Well, I haven't seen enough to know how good a player he is, but I'll tell you something – he's got a hell of a lot of courage.'

When I was seventeen and a bit, Middlesex offered me a contract. It meant turning down the apprenticeship I'd been offered by Watford FC, which meant that Steve was going to be the only professional footballer in the Gatting family (he was playing cricket in Middlesex 2nds as well). I missed football so much I started playing up front the following year for Hendon Reserves, like Denis Compton (or Denis 'Oo as I would have said in those days). This was to cause certain problems, like the night I turned my ankle right over in a final replay and hobbled past Don Bennett in the middle of a three-day cricket match, with huge strapping up my leg.

Don, who'd played for Spurs and Coventry himself, said,

'If you're ever going to do that again, *don't* do it on the sly. Come and have a word with me first, so we can cover you.' (*Don Bennett*: 'I'd done the same thing myself, but then *I* was getting good money for my football'.)

Round about this time, I went on a couple of trips abroad. One was a long weekend playing cricket in Schiedam, in Holland, when I found myself riding back on a scooter from a late night out. I don't know how I came to be on the scooter, and I don't know how I got off it, but the next morning they stuck me under a cold shower, took me to breakfast and force fed me because we had to play a game. I remember trying to get out like anything, not being able to, and at last being bowled, rushing back to the showers and being violently sick. The other trip was with Frank Russell and the Cricketers' Club of London when I went to Rheindahlen in Germany, and a place called Elmt on the German–Dutch border. We all drove over there in convoy via the Dover–Calais ferry and stayed on an army base, where you could get about thirteen pints of beer for 2s 6d or a gin and tonic for 3d – silly prices compared with off-base. Can't remember much about the cricket, but we went to a naughty nightclub one evening and I saw my first blue movie over there, so you can see I was a man of the world now, a seasoned traveller!

Obviously, more important things were happening as well. My first 1st-class game for Middlesex was on 25 June 1975, and if you consult *Wisden* you'll see me in there, in that first-round Gillette Cup match *v.* Buckinghamshire at Lord's: it says 'Gattin' had a bowling analysis of 2–0–6–0, and that I was caught Poll bowled Jones for 29, having played 'with impressive maturity' – my goodness! I was probably over-awed, if the truth were known, and we got a lot of runs in that match, which is probably why I bowled two overs – because we were winning comfortably. Mike Brearley batted through the innings for his 124 not out and we beat them by 99 runs. I wondered what my new skipper thought of my hustling and bustling.

Mike Brearley:

I suppose he did seem rather bustling in a way that appeared confident for a youngster of sixteen or seventeen, but one of the things I do remember was, when he was about eighteen, I took him to the ground one time in my car for a 1st-team match, and he was sitting next to me and he said something about 'the way young people behave these days', and I was rather amazed by this. Around the dressing room, he was chirpy and liked to be active all the time. He talked quite a bit and he doesn't easily sit still. His voice is quite loud, and there is this knocking of the ball on the bat which he does, no doubt partly to build up his confidence and get the feel of the ball, but more a matter of just doing something; making a bit of noise.

I was quite keen to do the right thing, and at Middlesex they'd always try and help you if they possibly could. But it's like going to a new school: you sit in the corner and keep quiet for a little while, and then you might venture an opinion and make a mess of it and get told off for not doing this or that. You accept that you have to learn; that you have occasionally to keep your mouth shut and listen – because I was always one for putting my foot in it and speaking out of turn. Not meaning to be pushy or anything; just trying to help and contribute when I wasn't yet in a position to do that. One was a bit wary of the other players for a little while. Obviously, because I hadn't watched much cricket (apart from the International Cavaliers on telly) I didn't have boyhood idols as such, but you knew that people like Fred Titmus and John Murray played for England and that you had to mind what you said.

It was very different from what it is now – ' 'Allo, Gatt! How you doing?' 'All right Teddy!' – in my young days, it was no nicknames and fairly formal. So you'd start taking a bit of a chance, and then you'd get cut down to size, and then you'd get up again and keep climbing up the slippery escalator, missing out the greasy steps if you could.

My next 1st-class outing was again at Lord's: this time in a 3-day game *v.* Worcestershire. The match was drawn, and I remember Vanburn Holder caught me on the boundary off Hemsley, and I only got 10. Hemsley was bowling his in-swingers and I felt, after a sticky start, that I was a bit unlucky to get out playing my first attacking stroke but we were going for runs and I suppose I was lucky to be batting, and to have somebody posted at deep square-leg in my honour. I was nervous, but this wasn't my first ever game at Lord's. It was simply playing in a high-expectation county match which I found harrowing. I think I was in for about an hour. It certainly *felt* like an hour.

I played in two other county games that season, and a couple of John Player League matches. In an away game against Notts I ran in quite well in the 1st innings and then mucked it up by playing a bad shot and got caught by Johnson – at square-leg I think it was – off Clive Rice for 18. In the 2nd knock I got off the mark with a boundary and then was bowled by the seamer Stead for 4. I don't remember much about the Middlesex *v.* Gloucester game at Lord's in July, when I made 1 and 0, but the John Player match *v.* Glamorgan at Cardiff was quite interesting because with Brearley I helped to put on 114 for the 2nd wicket, before Glamorgan were skittled out for 76. I made 55, and batting with Brears helped me a lot (I always call Brearley 'Brears'). It was just what I needed to finish off the season decently, after not playing particularly well before, and it gave me the impetus to try harder. I think 1975 had been a goodish season for me in the 2nd XI – I got 145 against Surrey and headed the averages with 911 runs – but we had a fine side in the 2nds, and we could have done better really.

There was *obviously* an enormous jump from school and club cricket to 1st-class cricket. I wasn't used to the sort of chess they were playing, where they pinned you down with defensive field placings and 'dot' balls, that are hard to get away. In club cricket I'd been used to the simple pleasure of hitting the ball hard and going for my shots, because you could expect two or three bad balls an over. There weren't such rich pickings here. It was easy to fall between two stools: you couldn't hit everything for 4, but if you thought in terms of grafting and nudging it for 1s and 2s all the time, you'd miss out on possible boundaries. So you had to learn to look for the loose delivery, meanwhile keeping the scoreboard ticking over. I was all right on the 4s – I loved simply belting the ball – but if somebody bowled it straight I wasn't too good at nudging. I had to study this Clive Radley bloke up the other end, who was a past master at the business, and could dab or deflect practically anything they served him up. If anything, what was most congenial to *me* was the John Player League type game, in that there weren't many close catchers around, so if you nicked it you weren't necessarily going to be caught. This was less claustrophobic for me; I could relax a bit more and go for my shots.

So that was my 1975. Middlesex reached two finals that year and lost both of them: the Gillette Cup to Lancs and the Benson and Hedges to Leicestershire. I don't know what went wrong, though I do remember actually sitting down and watching both games out of concern and camaraderie. I remember Mike Smith trying to catch Clive Lloyd at mid-on in the Gillette, and the ball going straight through his hands, and I think that put the last nail in one of our coffins. John Murray retired that year as well, without seeing the triumphs that were to follow for our county.

In 1976 I packed quite a lot in, because I played half a season for Middlesex, went with Young England to the West Indies, came back for a week, saw Middlesex take the County Championships and then shot off to Canada with D. H. Robins' XI.

I had some funny games for Middlesex that season. I got out in all sorts of ways – clean bowled a good bit – averaging 28.00 with the bat, and 30.90 with the ball (I came 7th in both County lists). My limited-overs batting average was 31.20: perhaps I was still saying to myself, 30 is enough. I think the reason I ended up *playing* in 1976 was that they dropped the

Trinidadian Larry Gomes, because I can remember thinking, If they keep him, I'm never going to get a game. Well, they didn't, so I did!

Four matches stand out in my mind: one was a John Player game against Notts in May, because in that I was run out in rather unusual circumstances. I shouldn't have been given out really because I wasn't attempting a run: I thought the ball had gone under the advertising hoardings for the winning 6, and I was on my way to the pavilion with Norman Featherstone when Stead threw it back in. I made 85 though and I think that gave me a little boost because we won as well, by 6 wickets.

In the 3-day matches I was just beginning to get into the swing of things after a shaky start when I had to leave for the West Indies trip. We'd played Sussex in July and I got my season top score, 94. I was clean-bowled by Waller. If only I could have hit another 6 there, I might have avoided the four-year-long 'he can't get 100' campaign that was to follow (and which was to dog me in my early Test career as well). I took 3 for 15 with my bowling in Sussex's 1st innings, anyway, so that was something. Brears made 106, and we wrapped it up by an innings and 54 runs. Then we went up to Bradford, where Yorkshire beat us by 1 sickening run. An unbelievable match, that. Radley actually came to the wicket with his arm in a sling because he'd broken a finger in the slips, and tried to make the 5 runs we needed for victory, but he was stumped. I think panic may have set in in our 2nd innings because we'd started well but Cope's off-spin did us on what we call in the trade a Bunsen Burner (turner – turning wicket).

My last match was the home game against Leicester, when Middlesex lost by a hurtful 301 runs. That was my first sight of David Gower. He looked like Shaggy in *Scooby Dooby Doo* but he batted brilliantly and I was fascinated watching him hitting the ball so sweetly, and knowing we were about to tour together. I remember bowling at him and going past the outside edge a couple of times, but if you bowled it anywhere near hittable he would get on to you very quickly. He seemed to have rather a lot of time before deciding where he'd place it, and he got his maiden 1st-class century. I didn't make many runs but I had my career-best bowling performance: I took 3 for 9 in my first 6 overs, though I finished with 16–2–44–3, in their 1st innings. Anyway, we lost comfortably. It was the first of many very competitive games with Leicestershire, because there always seems to be a bit of a niggle between their bowlers and ours, and the batsmen have to suffer accordingly.

I didn't play for the rest of the season. Fortunately, the lads (for now they were definitely the lads) kept on winning and had a great run. Of the next 9 matches, they drew 2, won 7 and lost 1.

It was a very exciting summer altogether. Steve was playing well for Arsenal and was in a couple of European matches, though I hardly saw him at all, let alone playing football, because our paths seldom crossed. One person I did see was a lovely young girl called Elaine Mabbott, who lived in a big house near Enfield Cricket Club.

Elaine Gatting (née Mabbott):

> I was at a Friday night dance with some friends, after a Benefit game, and I'd been chatting to Ian Gould, when Mike came over with one of the other cricketers, who seemed a bit flashy, and asked me to dance. I refused. I didn't know who he was or anything about him. He was quite persistent, and in the end a friend of mine sort of pushed me on my way with him, so I didn't have much option. It turned out that he could do most of the *Telegraph* crossword – and he was a Spurs supporter as well, so we had that much in common. I saw him a couple more times, then he was off for about three months playing cricket overseas. As time went by and we got to know each other, we became friends, as much as boyfriend and girlfriend.

I think she'd had her eye on Gouldie rather than me, actually. Anyway, a couple of days after the dance I was invited home for a cup of coffee, and I went round to this posh tree-lined avenue in Enfield in my 'new' old chocolate-coloured Triumph Herald. I had the hood down and the tape deck on, and I was going up and down 'the street where she lived' revving the lovely little 1300 engine, looking for the wretched driveway. Up and down, up and down. Couldn't find it. In the end I had to look for a phone box to ring her up and ask for directions. Talk about embarrassing.

Right, let's go to the West Indies. I was with England Young Cricketers: the tour was organized by the NCA and the manager was G. H. G.Doggart, whose Public Schools side I'd played against at Rugby. All the players were Under-19, and a very good squad we were (all but two were playing 1st-class cricket, I think): Gouldie, 'Shaggy' Gower, Richard Williams, Ashok Patel (with whom I'd been playing since our Wykeham days), David Munden, Paul Allott, Matthew Fosh, Alan Lewis Jones, Paul Downton, Chris Cowdrey the skipper, Ian Wilks of Surrey, Nick Kemp, and myself. There was one guy who bowled fairly well in the first game and then just could not bowl straight. I think they had to take the poor bloke to one side in the finish and get him bowling at a single stump outside the boundary rope while we were playing. Quite incredible.

Now, Cowdrey, Downton and Kemp had all been on a schoolboy Grasshoppers' tour of South Africa, so trouble flared early when they showed their passports, and we weren't allowed to visit Jamaica or Guyana, which was a bit silly. But it was a great unbeaten tour: we won 6 of our 9 matches and drew the rest. I remember one of their fast bowlers, though, was a chap called Malcolm Marshall – about my height only skinny – and he bowled at warp speed for two or three overs before he had to slow down to impulse power. In one of the limited-over games in Barbados we warned Ian Gould not to try and hook Marshall as he was very quick, but Gouldie ignored us, had a go, and Marshall sat him on his bottom. Otherwise we did all right, and we got a lot of runs. Funnily enough, I didn't think I batted particularly well except in the one-day game at St Kitts, when I made 128. But I managed to get 467 runs and top the batting averages, as well as taking the most wickets (30) on the tour.

There was a very happy holiday atmosphere, a bit like a boys' outing really. We were staying at White Sands Hotel right on the beach in Barbados – I've always made a bee-line for it ever since – and as soon as we got there among the palm trees it was straight off with the gear and straight in the sea; fifteen white bodies thrashing and splashing. What surprised us was that the water was so warm – almost tepid.

The West Indians clearly loved their cricket, and ours as well. One day we passed through a village in Grenada and there was a bloke on crutches who'd only got one leg, who discovered we were going down to practise. 'Ah, you're the England schoolboys!' he said. And after we'd left, this bloke apparently hopped all the way down to the ground, arriving just as we were getting back on our coach. It wasn't a short distance, either: he just wanted to watch us practise. So we stayed and entertained him for a little while. In the islands the fans would be up the trees and over the boundaries drinking rum and coke, and they're fairly knowledgeable and waggish, though we couldn't understand the dialect half the time as they'd get a bit carried away.

There was only one on-field incident and that was down at St Kitts. We won the match easily in the end, but their captain was bowling, and seeing Chris Cowdrey the non-striker slightly out of his crease, he didn't let the ball go but turned round and whipped off the bails – I think they call it 'whitechapelling'.

Chris had been batting well and the match was getting a bit tight when they did him. I'm afraid I retaliated in kind when their last two batsmen were in. It wasn't very smart, and I had to apologize to their captain afterwards, but we had warned them twice about backing up too far. Apart from that isolated incident, it was an excellent tour.

We came back from the Windies in September, just in time to see Middlesex clinch the County Championship against

Surrey at the Oval, to give Fred Titmus a sort of retirement present to go with his MBE. I was so pleased, too, because John Murray's old understudy Mike Sturt, who'd played club cricket with me at Brondesbury, had come out of retirement to keep wicket. Fred Titmus got a few Surrey scalps, and so did Alan Jones I remember, and Philippe Edmonds, whose bowling was very different in those days before his back trouble – less flighty.

We had to go to Buckingham Palace to be presented with our little replicas of the trophy, and meet Prince Philip, Patron of the Lord's Taverners. It was very nerve-racking, meeting His Royal Highness, and I was sweating profusely as we walked up the grand staircase. By the time we got to the door of the ceremonial room, my heart was beating so loud my tie was throbbing. I hate wearing ties. The one thing that really stood out about the room was the high ceilings and beautiful paintings.

No sooner had I seen Middlesex triumph, than I was off again, this time to Canada with Derrick Robins' XI. That was a great glimpse of the world, and we were well looked after. We started off playing in Vancouver, and then we took a boat to the lovely island of Victoria and went right across Canada, ending up in Nova Scotia. I liked Canada a lot: it's a huge, clean, friendly place, and flying across the Rockies, when you're nineteen, fairly takes your breath away.

We had a spot of bother in Edmonton, Alberta, because a couple of the lads had been as schoolboys to South Africa. I found all the political demonstrations rather puzzling, because I'm frankly not interested in politics. I knew what they were protesting about, but the boys who'd gone to South Africa were just kids, trying to better their cricket, so what was the harm in that? Anyway, a lot of university people sat down on the pitch, and they were asked nicely to go away, which they declined to do, and the police left them there till lunchtime. When it came time to restart the match, they still wouldn't budge, so the first wave of riot police came quietly out of the bushes and warned the demonstrators that if they didn't leave, they would be removed. Some left peaceably, but some didn't.

So then there was a lot of pulling at coatsleeves and punches aimed at the police, and then the police dogs were summoned to the middle in a show of teeth. The last dozen students were trying fairly hard to obstruct various policemen who heaved them, kicking and screaming, into the waiting paddy-wagon. I think the hard-core protestors were left in there, as well, for about 2½ hours to think things over. It was a hot day, so they must have been baking. They were standing up for what they believed, I suppose, but it was their own fault really. There was another little sit-down protest, or rather lie-down, on the pitch at Ottawa, though when the bowlers sent down a couple of deliveries they thought better of it. But most of the Canadians were very kind to us, and the friends I made I've still got. A very good trip indeed.

Nor was my globetrotting to end there, even. I'd apparently only just missed selection for the England tour to India, but it didn't matter: in January 1977, I went on the first Whitbread Scholarship scheme to Australia, to play cricket for three months for Balmain, which is one of eighteen clubs in the New South Wales Cricket Association's Grade competition. I was not yet twenty, and what I learned about cricket there toughened me up for the rest of my career. It taught me about mental attitude, about the hardness and pride for which the Aussies are famous. Most of them on a cricket pitch will curse and swear and tell you what they think of Pommie bastards playing their game – and that's putting it politely. They're always talking at the batsman, trying to put you off your stroke.

I knew for the first time what it felt like to be put under merciless psychological pressure, and I was able to learn to adapt, in a situation where it didn't *really* matter whether it knocked me down or not. I learned that you don't walk until you see the finger go up (I made the mistake of walking voluntarily once, and got a very sour reception from my skipper). I learned how to bat for a day if I had to, and you often had to. And when I came back, I had a bit of extra steel in my character that wasn't there before. It really was quite a big turning point for me, because although I had been outwardly self-assured, this gave me a bit of real confidence in myself. I really did feel, thanks to Balmain and the Whitbread scheme, that I could do a job of work after that. I was to spend three seasons there between 1977 and 1980.

I count myself very lucky that the family I stayed with out there included a good, quick leg-break bowler who played in the same side as me, and showed me a few tricks of his trade. What with Ted Jackson's bowling at Brondesbury, it was like being given the key to Aladdin's cave, or should I say Abdul Qadir's cave.

I wasn't the only one on this fantastic scholarship: there were three others. Bill Athey came with me to Sydney, and Graham Stevenson went to Melbourne in tandem with a drinking partner, a young chap called Botham. The Sydney pair were better off: we played more cricket, and I got on well with Athey. I don't think 'Both' got much real encouragement down in Melbourne, and I'm sure he was not very keen on being told how to bowl, albeit by expatriate Frank Tyson. In Sydney, Ath and I were under the guidance of a tremendous bloke called Peter Spence, who took us to coaching squads and let us practise with the State team. Bill was billeted over the other side of the harbour at Manley, so he had to come in on the hydrofoil for his work-outs. All *I* had to do was get on a bus – and I was used to that from England.

I missed England. I wasn't homesick when I first got to Australia, but it reached a peak about mid-February when for the first time in my life I suddenly realized I was all on my own on the other side of the planet. It was nice being housed with a family and I liked them a lot, but I missed being surrounded by all the people I loved back home, and I was very lonely. Mind you, when it was time for me to fly back to England I didn't want to leave Balmain either, because I got attached to it. I'm just a softie at heart.

I learnt something else in Australia: how to watch Test

matches. They're quite interesting really, aren't they? I remember going to Sydney to see my first England *v.* Australia game, and sitting there, daydreaming about how lovely it would be to play in a Test. Even more exciting was going to Melbourne Cricket Ground and seeing the Centenary match on 12 March 1977. England lost by exactly the same amount as a hundred years previously – 45 runs – but it didn't matter: I enjoyed it just as much. Derek Randall got 174, having been called back by the keeper Rod Marsh after he'd been given out, caught behind. Marsh said it didn't carry.

I remember being in the hotel room with Derek afterwards: he was drunk as a lord and sleeping on the floor – and who wouldn't be, after getting 174? I remember sitting there watching the highlights on television, and 'Arkle' (as he is universally known) was jumping up and down – he can't keep still at the best of times – and he got his bat out and started waving it around.

I kipped on the floor because we'd all come down specially from Sydney. We helped in the nets; I bowled a bit – I was grateful for any task I could lay my hands on. This was Test cricket! Both was there as well, *and* two hundred former Test cricketers, though I was very young and didn't really recognize the old 'uns. But you could see it was a fabulous occasion, with the MCG full to bursting, and the sun blazing down. What a great game of cricket that was! I wasn't even in it, and I was happy as Larry.

CHAPTER FOUR
New Heights
1977

1977 was a terrific year for England, regaining the Ashes, a great year for Middlesex, and an average year for me: a 33.18 average year to be exact. I'd set myself what I thought was a realistic target of 1000 runs for my first full county season, and I made 1095, but there were no 100s in there and people began to discuss my 'not having made a 1st-class century'. It annoyed me a bit because I was doing my best, and being consistent was surely the important thing: I did hit 14 half-centuries. Also at this stage I was still possibly an innings-belter, rather than an innings-builder. I was learning. I was also learning about the mixed blessings of being selected for England: what it was like to be picked and not play very well (as happened on my first tour) and what it was like to be picked and not play at all (as happened in the Prudential Trophy). It did cross my mind, you know, that this book might be called 'Mike Gatting – the Ups and Downs, and the Ins and Outs'.

We started our campaign in the County Championship with two draws and then were at home to Glamorgan in May. In those days we felt we should beat Glamorgan as they had a fairly inexperienced side and we had this young fast bowler called Wayne Daniel, who would come rushing in and part people's hair, and I don't think the Welsh lads fancied him very much. Mike Selvey was bowling well too, and in their 1st innings Glamorgan really got rolled over, 87 all out. Then we assembled 380 for 6 declared (I made 40 not out), of which the key knock was a magnificent 140 from Mike Smith. 'Smudge' is a very nice man who graduated from slow left-arm spinner to opener, and a very good opener at that.

Glamorgan prolonged the game until lunchtime on the last day, when we won by an innings and 85 runs.

Our next assignment was Notts at Notts, where I came up against their inspiration, all-rounder Clive Rice, once again. They were good, but they struggled against our pace attack: in each innings Wayne Daniel took 5 wickets and 'Selv' took 4. In their first knock, we got Derek Randall out for 0. Arkle was jumping up and down and chuntering to himself as he always does, and Brearley said to Wayne, the bowler, 'Right-O, let him have a bouncer 2nd ball.'

Wayne steamed in, let fly, and Randall hooked it straight down Clive Radley's throat, stationed specially at deep square-leg. But what was more surprising was that Arkle did exactly the same thing in the second innings as well. 'Right-O, 2nd ball, let him have it.' Randall hooks – caught Smith at deep square-leg for the pair. Quite amazing. Brears also got Rice out by using almost a deep fly slip 1st innings and a leg gully in the 2nd, reasoning that Rice, having played a flying back-foot shot and nicked it to the deep fly slip before, would try and hit it the other side. Which is what he did. I was getting free tactical tuition from the England captain.

They put together 200 and then 57, and we trounced them by 254 runs. I was fed up because I thought I was going to get my first 100. It had been a flat, friendly wicket and the sun shone all day but at about 6.10 in the evening the ball quite suddenly started seaming about. I couldn't make this out, but was told, 'Oh, the tide's come in on the Trent.' Rice was bowling, one or two went sideways, and finally he had me lbw for 82. I was very disappointed, but I suppose I was swimming against the Trent.

Our next County match was my first visit to Dartford, against Kent. The ground is fairly small, the wicket was fairly lumpy and bumpy, and Shepherd and Julien did us some damage. We lost by 238 runs. Then we redeemed ourselves against Sussex at the beginning of June, winning by 7 wickets, drew with Hampshire, beat Cambridge University and travelled up to Ilkeston to meet Derby and disaster. Mike Smith was captain while Brearley was away separating the Aussies from the Ashes, and not only did we lose by an innings and 177 runs, but Colin Tunnicliffe – who'd helped reduce us to 21 for 7 and 54 all out 1st innings, *and* 138 in our 2nd – kept hitting our spinners back over their heads for his 82 not out, murdering everybody. I remember facing Mike Hendrick for the first time on this reddish-green wicket. I didn't know much about Hendrick, who would run up and hit the seam, without necessarily knowing himself what it would do. Down came a bouncer, I top-edged a hook and got caught for a duck.

Then came Worcester at Lord's. Brearley was back and made a sheet-anchor 152, and Wayne bowled extremely fast. I think five Worcester players were injured in the attack, four by Wayne and one by Selvey, though Basil D'Oliveira made a soldierly 58, before we eventually put them away by an innings and 10 runs. Against Notts, again at Lord's, I remember getting out first innings to 'Knocker' White – I think I was trying to run it down to third man and the ball stayed up the hill and just hit my off-stump. I should have got stuck in, having weathered the seamers, so I was a bit upset about getting out to the spinner who wasn't even turning it. Anyway, we set Notts 325 in five hours and they came unstuck, so we won comfortably by 123 runs.

Two drawn games followed, against Yorkshire and Essex. We'd tried to make a match of it against Yorks, setting them 282 in 4 hours, which we thought was quite generous, but I remember fielding at short-leg and watching Geoff Boycott blocking it out. He just didn't want to know. Against Essex we had to push it along second innings but we couldn't make the rate, largely because Stuart Turner is a difficult bowler to get away. I got my first real insight into how you play off-spin watching Keith Fletcher in that match handling John Emburey. I talked to Keith Fletcher (the Gnome) about it because I wanted to learn.

The next game, even though it ended in a draw, was memorable: Middlesex *v.* Gloucester at Lord's. First knock we made 343 for 6 declared, Brears having batted the day out for 145. I was put down twice but got 79, and *The Times* correspondent said nice things about me: 'At the age of 20', he wrote, 'Gatting has yet to find out what a difficult game it is . . . no one was especially keen to be in the way of the ball when he whacked it.' Gloucester then collapsed from 48 for 0 to 80 all out. Fielding at short-leg, I studied Philippe Edmonds bowling them out, mostly with arm balls! It was turning a bit, but for some unknown reason Philippe got it to swing. He'd bowl 3 that turned and left them, then he'd bowl an identical delivery that, instead of turning, swung in. More than once he got them so confused, he had them out lbw with the one that went straight on with the arm. And John Emburey, who was equally fascinating to watch, winkled out four up the other end. When Gloucester followed on, they staged a recovery with an opening stand of 155. The final day, Edmonds and Emburey bowled and bowled, and at last they were all out for 337. It was 5.12 pm, and the umpire got mixed up and allowed us 1 over less than we should have had. Despite protests, he was adamant, so we had to slog to try and get 75 in 12 overs and fell short in a last mad dash.

There followed a very similar match against Essex, with our spinners toiling for three days, and our 2nd-innings target again 75 runs. This time we got them with 3 balls to spare. Then it was up to Abbeydale Park, Sheffield to meet Yorkshire on a pitch that was afterwards reported as dangerous by both captains. Wayne put a lot of people in hospital quite unintentionally. At one stage David Bairstow had bruises all over his legs and body, and five or six of them had to be given medical examinations. I managed to get 57 of our 1st-innings 181, and Smith hit a masterful 141 in our 2nd. We won by 157 runs. Then it was on to Leicester. Middlesex have a long-standing superstition that if we beat Leicester we won't win the Championship, and vice versa. Well, we lost to them on a spinner's wicket, though I had a bit of a stand with

Norman Featherstone and got 71, which was in my usual sort of vein.

The County Championship title was eventually to be shared between Middlesex and Kent, and if anything was the linchpin of our success it was a tactical decision by Mike Brearley in the game against Surrey at Lord's in August. Weather having ruined most of the first two days, Surrey were tumbled out in an hour and a half, for 49. I nipped out the last two myself, to give me the odd analysis of 2.5–2–2–2 (in their 2nd innings I got the same two, Richards and Pocock, out again for an even better 1.3–1–1–2, to finish with 4 for 3). Now, in those days you couldn't forfeit an innings, as happens now, so Brearley reasoned that our only chance of victory was to declare after 1 ball, bowl them out again, and then try and knock off the runs in our last innings. So that's what we did, skittling them out for 89 and then chasing 139 in 88 minutes, to win by 9 wickets. Poor old Monte Lynch, nice bloke as well, got a pair before lunch, which was quite a feat.

It wasn't all plain sailing from this point: we faltered against Warwicks and Perryman's swing in the next home game, losing by 34 runs despite a heroic century from Smithy. They'd set us a stiff target, knowing we'd go for it as we were pushing for the title. Then we had a fiasco at Wellingborough against Northants, where Bishan Bedi and Peter Willey rumbled us and we lost by 128 runs. I was out lbw to Willey 1st innings, and second knock I hit Bedi into the road, tried an encore and got caught at long-off. Silly boy! There followed a drawn game against the Australians (I was run out for 0) and a draw against Sussex, but next up was Somerset at Chelmsford. The match had been postponed and moved from Lord's to accommodate the Gillette Cup semi and preserve the pitch for the final (in which we were also involved), and although the match was drawn, the 7 points we gained proved crucial.

In the meantime, our limited overs campaign was going well in every department. In 1977 we were to win the Gillette Cup, reach the quarter-finals of the Benson & Hedges and come an unheard-of 3rd in the John Player League. The highlight for me? Well obviously my first Final at Lord's against Glamorgan in the Gillette. I was unbelievably nervous. We'd had a very tight first-round match with Kent where Wayne Daniel and Mike Selvey scrambled us home with one ball to spare, and we'd got past Warwickshire and Hampshire to reach the semis, where the weather was terrible, Somerset panicked and we'd won by 6 wickets.

But the amazing thing about the final was the huge crowd: I'd never stood up in front of so many people before, let alone played cricket in front of them. I vaguely remember going in, shaking, and getting 15. I never settled, and couldn't get to grips with the situation at all. What I do vividly recall was holding 2 catches in that match. They both happened to be off left-handers, both off Featherstone's bowling and both at long-on. I'd just been bowling myself and I'd got Rodney Ontong out, caught behind, and then Llewellyn, who is well known for hitting out, came in and took a liking to my bowling, spoiling my figures. He actually hit one of the biggest 6s I've seen at Lord's (not off me, fortunately), straight into the commentary box.

Then he tried a repeat performance against Featherstone as I stood at long-on. The ball went up many a mile, and I remember crowds of Taffs shouting, 'Drop it! Drop it!' – Welsh fanatics who'd come up in coaches with their leeks – and I got right under the ball and managed to position myself as it came down out of the blue sky, got my hands up high and finally secured it safely. I had it and everybody was suddenly dancing about. I was *so* relieved. And then when Malcolm Nash came in and hit another sky-er off 'Feathers', and I managed to hold that as well, it was quite some feeling. We were in a bit of trouble batting before Radley, our great Finals man, nudged and niggled 85 to get us home. We won by 5 wickets.

The other limited overs highlight for me was bowling Boycott in the Bensons! It was at Lord's in April and Middlesex won by 12 runs, but the astonishing thing was that I'd come on first change. Boycott had got 7 (he probably batted 10 overs for those), and Rad was fielding at 2nd slip, and somehow, though he didn't play a particularly bad shot, it just carried. It wasn't a bad ball, either, but you can imagine the look on Boyx's face. He was always upset about getting out, so he was pretty sick about getting out to me.

Our last County Championship match was against Lancs at Blackpool, on a 'Bunsen Burner' (a turning wicket), and we needed a victory to stay in the title stakes. The horrible thing was that we were put in by Clive Lloyd and bundled out for 148 (I got 50), 2 runs short of a key batting point. So we now had to bowl them out a bit smartly or the party was over. Fortunately Edmonds spun through them and they were all out for 108, and then we batted a little more adventurously in our storm-interrupted 2nd innings, declaring at 237 for 6, with myself, and the indomitable Radley, getting 60s. Then Lancs came back in and this time it was Emburey's off spin they didn't like, sinking at one stage to 130 for 9.

We were all on tenterhooks thinking they must expire any minute to put us in the trophy cabinet but Jack Simmons stayed in, and stayed in, and it got more and more frustrating with every over. When *finally* they were all out for 186 and we'd won, we had to wait with baited breath for the Kent match result to see if we were to take the Trophy outright or share it. Kent won – so we were joint Champions. Then it was off amid the Blackpool illuminations to celebrate, and as this boy Gatting had never been to Blackpool before, you can imagine he had all the fun of the fair. It was a lovely way to end my first full season with Middlesex.

The England selectors shone their torches on me twice in 1977. The first time had been early in the season. I'd been included in the Prudential Trophy squad for the 3-match series against Australia, and though I didn't get a game, it was a honour to be at that final match at the Oval on my twentieth birthday, watching the Aussies splosh to victory in torrential rain and darkness after we'd beaten them in the first two matches. On the other hand, it wasn't very nice being all keyed up and then not being able to take part, particularly since I was missing my Middlesex games as well.

All this was to change, though, for that winter I was picked to go on the England trip to Pakistan and New Zealand: my first tour! Gower, so very talented, had not been invited, and as it turned out I was to be picked in Karachi ahead of Ian Botham as well. The tour fee was a lot of money in those days, £5000, because Kerry Packer had forced up our market value a bit and Lord's were desperately keen not to lose any more players to his clutches. The Packer effect sent shock-waves down the system: even the County wages increased, because a businessman had shown the administrators how much money could be made if you ran cricket profitably. That was one of the good things to come out of the Packer era (floodlit cricket being another) and I think Lord's got a fairly fearful nudge from behind about what cricketers were worth. Mind you – in the last ten years we haven't really kept pace, so perhaps they need another kick up the bum!

We flew out from Heathrow on 24 November, and after suffering my first real case of culture shock, I made my debut for England in a place that was to figure rather prominently in my career ten years later – Faisalabad. In the drawn match against United Bank, I didn't bat. Boyx made 123 not out in England's 284 for 1 declared, and that was the story of that. But I did bowl a bit, removing one of their openers, Talat Ali. I didn't play in the Peshawar game, or in the 1st Test in Lahore either, but that Test lives on in my memory as a subtle blend of tedium and terror.

The cricket dragged itself painfully to a draw, a feature of which was Mudassar Nazar's century, which took a mere 9 hours and 17 minutes. It was the slowest Test 100 of all time, and quite painful to watch from where I was, up in the commentary box. When he was on 99 the Pakistani crowds injected a bit of excitement into it by sweeping on to the pitch in a frenzy of support, and after a brief bout of brick-throwing and a few running fights, they were driven back by police.

Another much worse riot was to follow, on the third evening, after some political activist had been arrested. When Bhutto's daughter turned up to sit in the big covered stand, the rival faction on the other side started throwing chairs on to the canopy, and when the police waded in, all hell broke loose. There was teargas fired into the 35,000-strong crowd, and the players were rushed off the pitch under a hail of rubbish and seats. Some bricks that had marked the boundary were turfed up and thrown at police, the law made a stand in the middle of the pitch before being forced back, and the wire fencing and gate to the dressing room enclosure came crashing down under the weight of seething Pakistani bodies trying to get in.

It was quite frightening waiting for the police reinforcements to come and rescue us. We'd barricaded ourselves in, putting chairs against the doors as bricks and rubble rained down on the dressing room, smashing the windows. We'd left one window slightly ajar for air and there we stood, with bats in our hands, listening to the crowds chanting and swarming outside. 'It's all right,' they shouted, 'we're not after you. We're after those nasty policemen.' Fortunately, when the cavalry came, they got them in overwhelming quantities.

After we'd won a couple of one-day internationals, the 2nd Test was in Hyderabad, and again I was omitted from the side, but I was doing a bit of commentary with Don Mosey, talking about the cakes and presents that well-wishers had sent the BBC team. Now, we were in the middle of the Sind desert, staying at a blue-painted hotel with bare carpets and a swamp out the back, and I was sharing a room with Graham Roope. Our mozzie fly-screen was busted, and we had a showerish thing in the loo with some buckets. The spray had only cold water, so you had to fetch hot water from the tap, mix it up and pour it over your head. There were no baths, so all the bowlers were really struggling.

One night the drains suddenly blocked up, and we had to paddle through three inches of water to get to the loo and clean our teeth, and there were a lot of cases of back trouble, insect bites, and diarrhoea. The only *good* thing about Hyderabad was that they'd just built a new pavilion, but even that was a bit cramped for dressing room space, so we made Geoff Boycott change in the loo, as he had expressed a desire for his own room.

Anyway, the Test match was going on in this mind-boggling setting, and here I was in the commentary box discussing chocolate cake and other culinary delights with Don Mosey, as Bob Willis was charging in on his famous knees-up run, with the wailing from the minarets and the mosques in the background and the carrion birds floating around up top waiting for somebody to drop dead in the terrific heat. There was one shaded green strip just in front of the pavilion, and the rest of the outfield reminded you of Frankie Laine's song about the burning sands: diabolical, right up to the wicket. So you had a feeling of unreality about the Test match, which drifted to another draw after their skipper Wasim Bari delayed his declaration and let England off the hook: captain Brearley and vice-captain Boycott saw us safely to the close.

A drawn game against the Punjab XI and a one-day international in Lahore, won by Pakistan, and watched by the Prime Minister, James Callaghan, was followed by a Sind XI *v.* England XI match in Karachi, just prior to the final Karachi Test. This is the game that everyone remembers because it was the one in which the famous Stick Insect, Sikander Bakht, the skinniest man you've ever seen, caused a change in the England captaincy. It was the 5th over of the match when it happened. Sikander is by no means lethally fast, but one delivery flew off a length and hit Mike Brearley on the arm. We knew something had broken because we all heard a loud crack. Brears was philosophical – he always is – but you could see he was downcast. This meant that Boycott would be taking over as England skipper – a long-standing ambition.

Now, because I happened to hit 59 in that Sind XI match, I was chosen ahead of Botham for the 3rd Test, and I'm afraid my debut was a bit of a damp squib. Nothing much happened really, apart from a few oranges being thrown on the pitch, and my not getting any runs. There had been some excitement before the match when the Pakistanis had tried to slip a few Packer players into their side, ours having been banned. We'd all stuck our necks out against the BCCP. 'If you do that,' we said, 'we're not playing.'

The Test was drawn by day four really. Captain Boycott condemned the pitch because the bounce was so low, and criticized the Pakistanis for avoiding defeat as though it were a national disaster. Roope, Boyx and Arkle got 50s, and Edmonds took 7 for 66, all in a dreary cause. My only contribution was to take a couple of catches off Philippe's bowling. As for my batting, I got 5 and 6 in the match. After getting off the mark first innings with a 4, I padded up to Abdul Qadir a *long* way forward (it was supposedly his googly – the usual story) and in the 2nd innings I missed a full toss from Iqbal Qasim and was given out again, lbw. I was ever so nervous, and when I got out so cheaply second knock as well, I was very, *very* disappointed and crushed.

I tried to make excuses. I thought I'd been a bit unlucky, with the first decision particularly. But the truth was, I was on the defensive. I was smarting, and terribly upset about failing. I had desperately wanted to avoid doing the wrong thing, and as often happens when you think like that, I'd gone and done it. I was in a negative frame of mind. Dennis Amiss says in *his* autobiography that when he walked out to the middle in a Test match, he felt as though it wasn't him: that in some strange way it was another bloke in his whites. It's true – you do feel like that.

I suppose it's partly because 'England expects' but you so want to do well that you tend to freeze, and negative thoughts filter into your mind about not getting out, when what you *should* be concentrating on is simply doing what you're good at, whether batting or bowling. It sounds simple, but when you're out there in the middle, it takes a while to learn the correct mental procedure: perhaps that's why so many of us fail.

Anyway, we left our draws behind us in Pakistan, and flew

out to New Zealand in January for a new start. A rather jet-lagged game in Auckland was drawn. I batted a long time for 43 not out 2nd innings. I missed having Brears to talk to up the other end (he'd gone home) and my team-mate Clive Radley, who'd flown out to replace him, had his own batting philosophy: 'Get the runs, never mind how.' We had an exciting game in New Plymouth, a lovely ground set in a bowl amid parkland beyond a huge grassy slope. I recall Terry Horne, for Central Districts, trying to get the 1 run they needed for victory and having his leg stump removed by Willis with literally the last ball. I managed 66 and 10.

It was great being in New Zealand after the rigours of Pakistan. In fact, the first thing the lads did on arrival was to go into the restaurant and order dozens and dozens of oysters. Bob Taylor led the charge on the shellfish, and though I didn't like oysters much I found some with bits of bacon on so I was happy, and there were toasted sandwiches, beer, and wine – it was so nice to feel you were back among people who liked the same things you did.

There followed a 3-day game against Canterbury at Christchurch, where we were put in on a green wicket and struggled against the Hadlee brothers. I got out to Dayle 1st innings for 5, and after Willis had bowled us back into contention, I made just 1 run second knock before being stumped. Botham was busy carving an England niche with a great 126 not out and the match was drawn, with Canterbury failing to reach 260 in 210 minutes.

I wasn't picked for the 1st Test at Wellington – I never expected it. I was just sitting in the crowd when England lost their first ever Test match to New Zealand by 72 runs, after having been set to score a mere 137 to win. Boycott, 'the first captain ever to lose to New Zealand', had batted over seven hours for 77, and we were to see, for the first time in this match, what a disgruntled Boycott could be like. It was not pleasant. He was having a bad trot himself, and when the other batsmen failed in Wellington he accused everybody of playing like schoolkids. He didn't shout, but he was brutally blunt. When he got out for 5 against Young New Zealand in Temuka (which we won, thanks to a century from Randall), he turned his gaze on myself and Paul Downton.

We'd teamed up to play golf, and we were looking forward to it, but instead we had to bowl that afternoon at a grim Boycott in the nets. He had us running in, knackered, for nearly two hours, along with an assortment of local school-kids, so it wasn't much practice for him anyway. But it was the only method he knew of glueing his game back together: to practise and practise. This was a side of him we hadn't seen before, though we always knew it was there because he's renowned for his dedication.

In the Christchurch Test I sat it out again and watched Both march us to glory with his maiden Test 100 and his 5 for 73 and 3 for 38, with 3 catches. I was glad like everybody else. I never felt there was anything but friendly rivalry between us. Both thought, perhaps, that he was the better player and should have been picked in Karachi, and that was fine. In those days I was naive with the Press and might possibly have said something that was lifted out of context, because people kept telling me what a lot of animosity there must be between myself and Botham, trying to stir it. Press-men, once they get slightly sold on a subject, tend to stoke the stove. Well the only thing I've had to do with Both over the years is to earn his respect, because he's a great player and great players don't give it away. In my early matches I hadn't done anything to warrant a great amount of respect, though Both and I were alike in some ways. We both had a lot of hustle and bustle. We both desperately wanted to succeed, and we were both contending for a Test place. That's not bitter rivalry – that's healthy competition.

In the 2nd innings of that match, there were a couple of incidents. One was when their bowler Ewen Chatfield suddenly turned and whipped off the bails with non-striker Derek Randall out of his ground, which was regrettable. But there was another Boycott episode too. We were 3 down for 67 and Boyx was on 20-odd, going at his usual pace, when

Botham came to the wicket and we thought, 'If we're going to stand a chance Boyx has got to get out and some hitters have got to get in.' Boyx drove one to mid-on, called for a single, got three paces up the wicket and saw he wasn't going to make it.

'No!' shouted Boycott.

Botham, meanwhile, had begun running, and he'd started, so he'd finish. Past Boyx he galloped, and up the other end. There followed a hue and cry about who should be out.

'Boycott!' chorused the fielders, and a few other voices from the pavilion; 'Boycott must go!' Whereupon he came back in the dressing room, sat in the corner and stuck a towel over his head. Run out, for 26. Meanwhile Both was out there, smashing it about, and when we lost another wicket somebody was elected to ask Boyx for the batting order.

'You've got a vice captain, haven't you,' came the sullen reply. 'So use him.'

We'd wanted to declare that night but Boyx wouldn't hear of it. We had to argue our point very forcefully in the morning and fortunately, despite these difficulties, England managed to pull it off.

Contrary to what Peter Roebuck has written, I wasn't inhibited by Boycott's rule, though it was clearly a different ship from the one Brearley had been skippering. Brearley's authority seemed to flow spontaneously, whereas Boyx was more meticulous: everything had to be planned and polished and itemized out. His captaincy was rather like his batting – he wanted to do it exactly right; to make an impression. He was never very flexible. His favourite saying was, 'With your ability and my brains, we'll make a player out of you, lad,' so even his praise came out a bit backhanded and condescending. I suppose that's fair – you have to learn. Brearley, though, would try to make you feel part of things, as though you'd helped make the decisions. I suppose if a captain is confident in his ability, he can afford to do that, whereas one whose position is under threat tends to be harder, more defensive.

And in between all the bad aspects about Boycott's captaincy, if you picked his brains, you'd get some very good and valuable information out of him. Such as, 'When the new ball comes, lad, don't go at the ball – let it come to you. That way it doesn't pop up to short-leg.' Or, 'When you play a bad shot, don't make excuses. Accept the truth. Admit that you've played a bad shot and resolve that you'll not do it again. You'll be a better player for it.'

I still value those gems from Geoffrey Boycott. I was very defensive myself at the time – and I needed telling, because I was apt to make excuses. If something went wrong, it was never my fault, because I couldn't bear it to be my fault. I was so desperate to do the right thing.

Well, I was picked to play in the last Test in Auckland, and once again I did the wrong thing. The match, and therefore the Series, ended in a draw; Geoff Howarth, proving his place, hit a mighty 100 in each knock; Botham took 5 wickets in an innings again and made a 50. I sat about in pads for about six hours while Rad hit a marvellous 158, and then went in and got the sum total of nought, bowled by Boock. As a matter of interest, Both got the same ball I got, but whereas mine hit my off-stump, Botham's missed his by a whisker and he went on to make 53. So he marched ever onwards and upwards, and I marched back to Middlesex with my tail between my legs.

I didn't play in another Test match for two years. Oh, another joy – I broke my nose. I was fielding at silly mid-off when Geoff Howarth padded one away that flew in my face. I went off the field and they stuck some tweezers up my nose to try and straighten it out a bit, and then I came back on again. So I was left with a slightly bent snozz.

CHAPTER FIVE
New Depths
1978–80

The next two years, 1978–79, were to be a lesson to me. I suppose it had all come too easily. My ambitions had all been realized by the time I was 21. Now, being dropped made me appreciate that just *playing* for England once or twice wasn't enough. I wanted to play well. This period in the Test wilderness at 21, living in a flat in Southgate, probably did me more good as a cricketer than anything else. I had a lot to learn still. I had to make a lot of adjustments to my technique, and cope with the pitfalls, and other worse pitfalls waiting for me on the other side of them.

The year 1978 was Botham's 'Goldenballs' year; the time of his 'Colossus' headlines. Both was lucky; he had natural ability with the bat and with the ball. Being a genuine all-rounder takes so much pressure off you. If you get no runs but you go out and get 5 wickets, there are no vultures circling over you. That makes it so much easier. As a batsman, you've only got one chance. I think, at Test level, that's what helped Both so much more than myself. I had one shot, with the bat. He had bat and ball, and he was a brilliant bowler who could swing it at pace.

At Middlesex, though, I was more of an all-rounder (albeit not to the extent I had been as a schoolboy and colt). That double edge to my sword is what probably helped me at County level. If I was going through a bad patch, at least I was getting some wickets and so I felt useful. You don't get dropped because the captain thinks, 'Well, Gatt's not getting many runs, but we'll play him with the ball.' A sort of insurance policy. I'm convinced that helped me through the lean patches. In 1978 I was 53rd in the 1st-class averages with the bat, scoring 1166 at an average of 33.31. But I was an admittedly somewhat flukey 8th in the bowling averages, with 26 wickets at 15.80 apiece. It kept me ticking over.

In 1978 both Pakistan and New Zealand were here. Bob Willis was labelled a thug for hitting Pakistan nightwatchman Iqbal Qasim in the mouth, and I didn't think that was fair. Fast bowlers in general don't really mean to hit anybody, even though some might say 'We'll knock the Poms' heads off', or things like that. It's just a bit of image-making. They don't genuinely want to hit you on the head, because they know full well it can kill somebody, and I can't think of *any* fast bowler who would be keen on having a dead man at the other end of the pitch. At the same time, helmets were being introduced – pioneered by Brears and Dennis Amiss – I think in response to the West Indian pace attack of the 1970s. As far as I can see, those helmets have been a very good innovation. I don't agree that if batsmen hadn't adopted helmets, bowlers would bowl fewer bouncers – I don't think they'd have behaved any differently at all. And quite apart from offering physical protection, the helmet saves a batsman from being intimidated. This is important. I've always maintained that cricket is a game fought in the mind and not just on the pitch.

I didn't have any part in those Tests – I didn't warrant it – though I played against the Pakistanis at Lord's for MCC in a drawn game (making 13 and 41, I don't remember how) and against the New Zealand tourists too, more of which later. I didn't start off very well with Middlesex, in 1978. In fact, apart from a 61 against Cambridge University, I made just one 50 before July, which is a long time to be without a decent score. And what with Brearley, Radley and Edmonds being absent on Test duty, Middlesex couldn't seem to get cracking, losing to Essex and Warwickshire, and twice to Kent.

Later on, both my County and myself managed to get our respective acts together – Middlesex won 8 of their last 10 games and I made my first two centuries – but by then we'd missed the boat, dropping down to 3rd in the Championship. The late start had nobbled us, really. In the limited overs competitions we went out in the Gillette quarters to Lancashire, lost our Bensons quarter-final to Derby and finished third from bottom in the Sunday League – all in all, a bit chastening after our earlier successes.

My personal 1978 season was intriguing, looking back. In early May, we lost comfortably to Essex at Chelmsford. That's when I got my first, and hopefully my last, pair, stumped Smith bowled East, and caught Smith bowled Lever. The first innings was a bit of a nightmare, actually: it was 6.25 and they had a lot of men around the bat – I wasn't quite sure how to cope with it. So I did what came naturally, which was to go down the wicket and try to whack it. I'd tried it the ball before as well, and this was five minutes before the close of play, if you please. But I thought in my wisdom that I'd try and take the attack to the bowler. So I got stumped, and at 6.27 another batsman had to go in, and to confound it all, even the nightwatchman got out, which meant that in the space of five minutes we'd gone from a reasonable position to 'Nelly bar the door', thanks to young Gatting.

I got a real rocket from Mike Smith. Everyone knew what had happened and when I stumped up the dressing room steps I was greeted by the funereal features of Graham Barlow, which suddenly spluttered and creased up with laughter, setting off the rest of them. Still, Mike Smith was absolutely right and I was absolutely wrong.

In the next game, against Lancs at Lord's, we won by 1 wicket eventually, but it was quite a hairy affair because these new helmets hadn't yet reached our shores and Colin Croft was steaming in. Now, I don't think I'm being unfair when I tell you that Croft is the nastiest bowler I've ever faced in that he has this horrible action, bowling from very wide of the crease. He didn't appear to care whether he hit you or not and I think even his West Indian team-mates thought he was a bit funny. Anyway in he came, sent down a bouncer and cracked my mate Ian Gould on the head. At the beginning of the season we'd been talking about how long it might take to get medical help on the pitch in an emergency, because several batsmen had already been skulled by fiery new pace bowlers.

Well, in Gouldie's case it took nearly five minutes to get a doctor on the pitch – I don't know where our physio was. Ian was shaking and we weren't sure if he was concussed, unconscious or what. He went to hospital that afternoon, and they let him out that night. We found this quite strange as well, as he was wandering around in a daze. It all seemed to be done very shabbily. As for me, I fended off Crofty for an hour and a half amid rain and interruptions, reached 88 and then went back to whack Hogg and got caught at deep gully by Abrahams. I was disgusted with myself. John Emburey hit the winning runs for us – good old Embers.

There was a fairly crucial game against Kent at Canterbury in June, one of the early-season losses which hurt our Championship hopes. It was slightly special to me too because Kent really did me up for a dog's dinner. I'd just negotiated Croft at Lord's, and here I was facing the relatively friendly pace of a guy called Kevin Jarvis, who happened to be a mate of mine, to make matters worse. And I got bounced out by him in *both* innings. He dropped it short, I went for the hook, and got out for 14 and a duck. It was one of those times in my life when I felt I'd been made an idiot of, and I learned a lesson I've never forgotten: even if a bowler isn't lightning fast, you have to be a bit wary – especially early on in an innings.

A couple of weeks later I had another nudge up the rear, in an away match against Worcester. I failed with the bat again, and Gouldie got his maiden 1st-class century – a fine 128. Keith Tomlins, another twenty-year-old, made 94, and the pair of them transformed the match (although rain robbed us in the end), falling just short of a 6th-wicket record partnership for Middlesex, with 209. Now, myself and Ian had come up through the 2nd XI, rooming together and scoring 100s together, and watching these two play so well, knowing my friends were doing more for Middlesex than I'd ever done, really hurt me and made me determined to do better.

Yet another nudge came when I was demoted to number 7 against Essex in July. Brears is a great believer in slipping people down the order when they're not in good nick, and moving them up when they come good. (Later on in the season I was promoted to number 4.) Anyway, this match gave me a bit of a dig because in those days all the Essex lads were comedians, and they kept walking up to the pavilion and craning their necks to see when I was finally coming out to bat – taking the mick, but paying me a sort of compliment as well, I suppose. I managed to get 50 1st innings and also to take the wicket of Mike Denness, clean bowled: I knew he was a candidate for lbw but I think I nipped one through him in the finish. Once again though, the weather intervened and despite a couple of declarations, the match was drawn.

When Middlesex played the New Zealanders, I got out twice bowled Lance Cairns for the sum total of 1, and the tourists stuffed us by an innings and 10 runs on a pitch that warranted official inspection afterwards. Lance is basically an inswing bowler and I played two very poor shots. Crisis point had now been reached. Something clearly had to be done about my batting for me even to make the grade as a County cricketer now, let alone play for England again. This realization was a blow to my confidence and very demoralizing. The only thing that kept me going was that I got a few wickets in that match (3 for 11 at one point). But it was getting me down hearing people say, 'It's all right, Gatt. You're bowling OK, so batting at number 7 is about the right place for you at the moment.'

The next match, against Leicester at Lord's, strengthened their case. We won the toss and put them in, and in their first innings, I took 5 for 59, and they weren't rabbits either because I got both openers, Dudleston and Steele, and followed up with Davison, Birkenshaw and Clift. I bowled for something like 15 overs, and at one stage my figures were 4 for 30, I think, but when I came back on again I wasn't so effective and tarnished my analysis a bit. There were four batting collapses in this low-scoring match (I managed to top-score with 53), but Selv and Wayne sneaked us to victory with the winning runs. That's why we didn't win the Championship, you see: we'd beaten Leicester.

What with people taking the mick and chivvying me up about the disastrous start to my season, I was, imperceptibly, becoming a more disciplined player. As the summer wore on, I was learning by my mistakes to battle a little longer. Being hurt had fired my determination and that in turn helped me to concentrate: the two go hand in hand. I desperately wanted to play for Middlesex and not end up languishing in the 2nd XI, and they must have talked about leaving me out, though they didn't – they gave me a chance.

When you're in a bad trot the dressing room doesn't exactly fall silent when you walk in, or anything, but you do hear whispers, and you do wonder: somebody has been left out of the side, somebody else is lucky to be in it; what on earth is so-and-so doing here? etc. Basically, that's what had happened to me in the England team. You just felt uneasy and out of place, that they had picked you because they had to, not because you were really wanted. That's why, whenever I'm captaining Middlesex or England, I'll go out of my way to make everybody feel at home, because I know what the cold shoulder is like.

It was at this point in the season that Middlesex began firing on all cylinders. Though it was now probably too late, we were rolling. Over went Glamorgan by 176 runs; over went Notts by 111, and five more counties would be trounced before mid-September. On 9 August we met Yorkshire at Lord's. Play began after tea on the second day, in a one-innings contest. Put in, we immediately lost Smithy but Featherstone and myself kept things moving. Feathers was playing well, and I watched him for a long time, nudging his 1s and 2s without giving his wicket away. So I settled for trying to bat all the way through, like I'd done at Balmain, trying to keep the scoreboard ticking over and not doing anything stupid.

I may have hung about for quite a while in the 90s, but once I got to 99 I swept Phil Carrick for 4 – and it was a dream come true. My first 1st-class century. To do it at Lord's as well – that made your eyes water! People had had faith in me during my stumbling season, and it was nice to say 'Thank you – you see, I *can* do it: it's taken me a bit of time, but I've got the idea now.' You felt so different inside. It had all been worth it, the geeing up, the getting cross, the determination, the concentrating harder. It was a tremendous feeling.

Ironically, as happened in my little 100 for Wykeham, I believe they delayed the declaration by a couple of overs so I could get my century. And then Yorks were bundled out in under three hours and we won by 167 runs – so a very good match for Middlesex as well.

We went on to an innings victory over Derby next, despite staging an early batting collapse. *Wisden* makes another nice little comment about me here: 'Then Gatting generated a recovery that swung the match. Poulter, lasting for an hour, and Tomlins gave him excellent support while he displayed some thrilling strokes that brought him 80 in boundaries.' I got 128 before being bowled by a guy called Russell, who was a little dobber, really. He bowled about my pace, though a little better than me; he just ran up and dobbed it on a length and you couldn't get him away.

But there was one shot I played in that innings which I don't think I'll ever forget, I don't know why. Russell bowled me one short of a length just outside off-stump, and I don't even really know how it happened, but I went back and hit it off the back foot over mid-on with a straight bat – which is an extraordinary shot for me. To this day I don't know where it came from. I don't remember the circumstances of the match, or even how we won because I was just so thrilled to get another 100. But I'll never, ever, forget that shot. Suddenly, it all seemed to come together.

After that I had to play against New Zealand for Young

England and I was batting happily in tandem with skipper David Gower, who got a languid century. I like to chat in the middle, but David doesn't; he says, 'Don't worry about me,' and just gets on with his batting – well, flying, really: that's the only way you could describe it. There he was with his long golden hair, caressing the ball without a care in the world, making it look so easy. And there was I, concentrating and studying. I thought I might get my third 100 in a row, you see, and there was a prize, a gallon of port, or something, and I'm very interested in collecting wines so I would have appreciated that very much. But I only got 88 so I didn't win it. Bev Congdon came on, and I clipped this one off my toes very hard, whereupon Richard Hadlee at square-leg dived full length along the ground, catching it one-handed about a foot off the turf. The game ended in a draw but it was interesting because we had a good young side out there.

So that was it really, for 1978. Middlesex made 3rd off a storming finish, and one reason for that, I do remember, was that Wayne Daniel was really hitting his straps that season. He'd come bouncing back recently from the sunny Caribbean and batsmen couldn't handle him. He was unbelievably quick. There was a lovely match in the Bensons against Sussex at Hove, which we won by 8 wickets and in which Stuart Storey had made a comeback. Storey was now their 2nd XI captain and they'd called him back in for a bit of experience. Anyway Wayne was on, running down the hill. He'd got Mendis caught by Featherstone very high at 1st slip, and he'd hit Barclay flush on the forearm and they'd got a leg bye, and in came Storey to face.

Wayne let him have one just short of a length. It flew up, hit his elbow, his chin, and his shoulder, glanced off his glove, and shot in a straight line to cover point 25 yards away, where it was caught by Barlow. Storey stood there, dazed. That was the end of his comeback. But that was our Wayne: quite frightening, yet he's one of the nicest blokes you'll ever meet, and we've been so lucky to have him at Middlesex for ten years. I could tell you lots of lovely stories about his bowling, going back to the bruises he gave me in schoolboy cricket. We always wondered why he didn't play more for the West Indies, but their loss was our gain. He's been a genuine asset to us, our 'Diamond', and it's been a pleasure to play with him.

That winter of 1978–79, I went on another Whitbread Scholarship to Australia, to play my second invaluable season in Grade cricket for Balmain, the other English lads this time being Agnew (Leicester), Larkins (Northants) and Tavaré (Kent). I hadn't been picked, of course, for the tour of Australia in which Brearley led us to a 5-1 triumph and a lone trumpeter sounded the Last Post on Sydney Hill. I'd have given an arm and a leg to have been there – I'd always longed to go on an England tour of Australia. Still, I was out there in Balmain and very grateful for that, getting another toughening-up exercise, another winter of practising and practising, working on my technique and my grip (I'd developed a fault there), another winter of Aussies chattering in the slips, bowlers grumbling and swearing and fielders taking the rise, that made English cricket, by comparison, seem all peace and meditation. How can I ever thank them? Scoring runs over there was helping me sort myself out. I'd also met a coach in New South Wales on my previous visit, who was very much into sports psychology and positive thinking, and when I saw him again, he showed me a copy of a book, *Winning Ways,* by the West Indian former player and radiologist Rudi Webster, on positive thinking in sport, which he'd been telling me about on my last trip. I hadn't taken much notice, to be honest, but having been through a rather self-doubting season in 1978 I said, 'Let's have another look at that book'. He copied some pages for me about the batting side of things, and they seemed to put into words my own innermost feelings as a youngster: the negative thoughts battling against the positive ones; the little negative man in your mind saying, 'You'll never do it!' and another little bloke in a weaker voice saying, 'Yes you can!' So I read on, fascinated. When I eventually became Middlesex captain I went back to those ideas of Rudi Webster, and in fact I used my own version of them to help generate a positive approach in the dressing room.

At the beginning of 1979, though, I had more of a losing approach. In spite of dipping into Webster, and my couple of 100s last season, I was thinking, you know, Gatt, perhaps you're not cut out for this after all. I had a nasty feeling that if I didn't turn the corner shortly, this was going to be my last season at Middlesex. That I wasn't going to make it.

The season itself was a very funny period for me. I started off with the best intentions and in fact managed to make it into the World Cup squad, but as before, I didn't play, and from that point on things started to go rapidly downhill, and it was only in the last few games that I began to play anywhere near my true form. Middlesex, who had had such faith in me, themselves had a very poor season. I can't put my finger on why. We'd lost a few people to Test matches, as we had before, but we still had a fundamentally strong side. In the 3-day game we slumped very badly, finishing 13th, and we were disappointed in the limited overs competitions, reaching the semi-final of the Gillette only to lose by 7 wickets to Somerset after Burgess and Garner had cut us to pieces. Botham rubbed salt in our wounds with the matchwinning 6.

In the Bensons we had a good game with Kent at Canterbury, in which I got my first Gold Award because I managed to get 67 of our winning 178 before this chap Graham Dilley bowled me out. Minor Counties we beat quite easily, the Yorkshire fixture was rained off and we beat Notts on a faster scoring rate (I got 51), ending up meeting Yorkshire in the quarter-finals. There we played very badly on a dangerous wicket. It was my birthday as well, and I didn't get a very good present: 0. Although they struggled to make 108 they beat us by 4 wickets. And as usual in the John Player League, we were still pulling our hair out. We seemed to do comparatively well each year in the longer limited over competitions by playing our two Test spinners Embury and Edmonds. But in the 40-over game it wasn't working. Perhaps we went about batting more hastily, there being less time.

We didn't know what was wrong. Brears used to get quite exasperated about our Sunday record. One year he interviewed individually every member of the team to ask us what we thought could be done. Occasionally he would get very upset over the way one or two batsmen gave their wickets away, and quite rightly got stuck into the culprits. He also had the odd exchange with Philippe Edmonds, but fortunately these flare-ups were few and far between. *Apart* from Sundays, we were a happy ship.

From my point of view, the first thing was the Prudential Cup, which came at the beginning of the season. Once again I was named in the 13, and ended up not having a game at all. I was very keen to pick up where I'd left off with Middlesex in '78, to try and cement a place. But now I found myself for about three weeks rushing around in the nets preparing for the great Prudential appearance that never came, missing important County matches, while I hung fire and watched England lose to the West Indies in the final.

When I got back to Middlesex, the immediate worry for me was that Roland Butcher, who'd taken my place, had started scoring runs. The only bloke struggling a bit was Mike Smith, and he was an opener. It was at the Oval, on 7 July when Brears took me to one side. I was having a net, ready to play Surrey, and I suppose Middlesex were under some sort of obligation to pick me because I'd been selected for the World Cup three weeks before – albeit not playing.

Brearley said, 'Look, Michael, we've got a bit of difficulty here because the only chap not making many runs is Smudge. So here's what I suggest we do: *you'll* have to open. What do you think?'

I was a bit staggered. 'Well, er, yeah, OK,' I said, without really knowing if it was OK. I couldn't say no – I desperately wanted to play: I'd been sitting on my bottom for three weeks as it was.

So it came about that I opened for Middlesex for a few

ABOVE Brondesbury Cricket Club. I'm front row, 2nd from left. Next to me, on my left, is 'The Fuhrer' Martin Edney, and Mike Sturt *(private collection)*

RIGHT My first Middlesex cap. Mike Brearley seems equally pleased *(Patrick Eagar)*

LEFT The wedding arch
(private collection)

RIGHT My family mean so much to me: Elaine, myself, James, Andrew *(Rex)*

ABOVE The disgruntled Geoff Boycott; a side of him we had never seen *(All-Sport)*

ABOVE In Bahawalphur, with a purpose-built groundsman *(All-Sport)*

BELOW An early example of my tendency to go lbw to Qadir *(Patrick Eagar)*

RIGHT My brother Steve: an FA Cup final spot with Brighton to his credit *(private collection)*

LEFT The transition from County 100s to England 100s didn't come easily *(All-Sport)*

RIGHT The 'double double'. Graeme Fowler, my partner in the history books, reaches his 200 in Madras *(All-Sport)*

BELOW Diving in the Middlesex v Somerset Benson & Hedges Cup final at Lord's 1982 *(All-Sport)*

LEFT 'I'd tell him if he was being an absolute idiot.' Philippe Edmonds *(All-Sport)*

LEFT More celebrations. Squirting champagne in Gower's ear after England's Ashes win at the Oval, 1985 *(All-Sport)*

BELOW The reverse sweep. Usually, it has served me well! *(Patrick Eagar)*

matches, replacing Smithy and later replacing Brears on his Test calls. It was all useful experience, showing me how to tighten up my game and giving me a bit more practice against the new ball. But it was also tough going. In four matches I made 26, 2, 33, 22, 39, 12 not out, 23 and 26 not out, and in one of these knocks I got run out by Mike Smith and got very cross because Smudge was beginning to get some runs and I was having to mint all mine. And after that run-out I was told I was going to be 12th man.

It was then, probably, that I reached the lowest point of my career so far. Just a few weeks ago I was the young hopeful, the World Cup selection, and now suddenly here I was, not even required by Middlesex, going to play in a 2nd XI game against South African Schoolboys at the Bank of England ground at Roehampton. It's hard to describe how I felt: deflated, choked, very unhopeful about cricket, very low about myself. But even as I hit rock bottom, I realized there was only one way back up: I'd just have to get my head down and get some runs in the 2nd team, and earn my place all over again. I had a long talk with coach Don Bennett, and he reassured me.

'You know exactly what you have to do, Gatt; you've told me that. Go out and do it. You don't become a bad player overnight, and provided you stick to the basics, you're going to be all right. By the way – I'd like you to captain the Seconds in this match.'

I went in against the South African Schoolboys racked with nerves. *What if I get out cheaply here?* said the negative little voice. *Hold on, hold on,* said the positive voice, *you've played for England, you've been picked for the World Cup, just a while ago – you've got some experience. Try and use it! Yes,* said the other voice, *but supposing I get 0 here* . . . . It was terrible.

Don Bennett:
As a matter of fact the reason I asked Mike to play in that game was that his brother was playing. And I thought it might help if I made Mike captain. I'm a great believer in

letting young captains take charge, as well, and I was quite impressed when Mike had called us all to a little pre-match team talk. That was really the first time it had entered my head that this was captaincy material . . . . Anyway, they went out to bat and Mike and his brother were at 3 and 4, and at lunchtime Steve said to me, 'Could you do something about our captain?'

'How do you mean?'

'Well, he won't stop rabbiting, telling me how to play.' (Steve, you see, was very quiet and methodical.) 'Can't you quieten him down a bit?' he said.

'You're kidding!' I told him. 'It's the first time he's done this for us – he's keen!'

'Phaw!' said Steve. 'Good job we're not both like that.'

And they carried on as before. Of course, Gatt just wanted his brother to do well, but every over he was down the wicket giving Steve another earful of advice.

Fortunately Steve survived – he was a very good little cricketer – and I had a bit of luck and managed to make 100. But that was the first real test of my character. I'll never forget how I felt, or the relief afterwards, finding out that I'd made it back into the 1st XI, albeit opening, albeit moving to number 5, and going up and down like a fiddler's elbow. At least I was playing for Middlesex again.

But 1979 in general proved a very unsatisfactory season and a very, very frightening year for me. On more than one occasion I felt an abyss open up before me: I had a long, long way to go before I could call myself a cricketer, and I wasn't qualified to do anything else, either, job-wise. It was going to be a terrible, hard struggle. My batting was unreliable – I'd got to get out of the habit of weathering the quick bowlers and then getting out when I should have been setting my stall. My last few games were my best ones: I got 93 not out against Somerset at Lord's, and 30-odd against Sussex and Imran's bowling at Hove – where he remarked that I kept hooking his bouncers.

One hit me on the side of the head and went for 4 byes but I kept going.

Imran said, 'Great cricket! That's what the crowd want to see.'

'Thanks,' I said, 'but don't you mind being hit for so many runs?'

'No, not if I get people out.'

He got me out. It was a good ball that nipped back off the seam and clipped the bail, and Imran finished with 4 for 56 and 5 for 50. Against Worcester in the penultimate game of the season, I got 42, and then 56 against Notts. So, a slight glimmer of hope in the end, and I thought, well, the worst must be over. Little did I know then what Tests were in store . . . .

Happily though, having survived the lowest point of my Middlesex career, I found help was just around the corner, in the shape of Balmain CC. Because while England were getting a pounding in the 1979–80 tour of Australia, Balmain was about to relaunch Mike Gatting as a cricketer.

The turning point of my career, looking back, came in September '79. I was invited by Balmain, the Australian club I'd played for on my two Whitbread Scholarships, to go back and spend a full six-month season with them as captain and coach. I went out there, depressed and demoralized by 1979 and thinking perhaps my cricketing days were numbered. And I came back from that very successful, very happy season, a refreshed, confident bloke with a beard, ready to make a lot of runs for somebody. Balmain had made a new Pom of me.

I'd been given the opportunity to take charge of a 1st-Grade side in a competition just as good, if not better than our own 2nd XI system, and also the chance to look after the club itself, with all its various levels. It gave me just the tonic I needed that somebody had so much faith in my ability. I was very lucky to have the support of Peter Spence, the NSW coach, club chairman Fred Bennett, who was on the Australian Cricket Board and later managed tours to England, and

Cliff Winning, patron and secretary. As I was keen to make a few changes at the club, we sat down together and devised a plan to turn Balmain into a winning operation after twelve years in the doldrums. We stuck to that plan, despite scepticism, through the season. We had a reasonable rather than great side, but the atmosphere at the club was good, with all levels mixing socially. I thought it important that we ran the club *as* a club.

It took me nearly a month to get fit for bowling in those conditions. Forget 'Fat Gatt'. You should have seen me thundering along the beaches and cliffs and jumping in the Bondi surf to cool off. It was a lovely place to train, but I also worked and pushed myself harder than I'd ever done in my life. Our first game was against a club called Waverley. Their captain was a tall, blond bloke who looked vaguely familiar. It was Tony Greig. The match was reduced to 90 overs after rain, and after 45 of those we were struggling, 120 for 7. I didn't declare, but batted on to 140 all out. Greggy was annoyed that we'd overshot the halfway mark and they went out and knocked off the runs and beat us. When we walked back in the dressing room, I sat down with my team, whom I'd hardly met, and introduced myself with a debriefing session.

'If we want to do well this season', I told them firmly, 'we've got a lot of work to do. Like it or not, I'm here, and I'm captain, and I shall be working as hard as anybody to get it right.'

I was as good as my word, I think, because I bowled twice as many overs that season as anybody in the club (300 all told), and I managed to get 55 wickets at 19 apiece and 800 runs, averaging 55, as well as doing coaching sessions in schools. Cliff Winning spoke to a reporter at the time and praised me up. He told the newspaperman,

> Gatting has galvanized this club. Here we are, tasting success at every level when we haven't won the Championship for 12 years. He has the players, juniors upwards, eating

out of his hand – they even accept the chore of running four laps of the ground on practice nights!

Balmain made the semis of the Grade competition that season, and we won the Club Championship as well – I also managed to get more points in the *Sydney Morning Herald* competition than anybody else and win myself $500. (There was a points system in which the umpires of each match used to award 3, 2 or 1 point to the players who did well in the match). Those six months were among the happiest of my whole life, and I'll never forget the friends I made or the transformation at the club. It helped me get back on the rails as a cricketer. I was very fit and very busy. I'd bounce across country in my big old Valiant station wagon, from my home base with a nice family called the Richardsons, and later with Peter Spence, just five minutes from the ground.

And so it was that I spent Christmas and New Year Down Under, feeling very glad to see the back of 1979. Now here I was, playing my first match of the 1980s and getting 100, feeling that 1980 looked set to be a much better vintage for me. All the hard work was paying off – it often does – and I think being away from my usual environment helped too, to give me a fresh start. I was really looking forward, in March, to going back and making my mark with Middlesex. On the other hand, I have to tell you that I love Australia, and really enjoyed the life style. I was happy as a sandboy playing cricket and socializing with people, and I get on very well with the Aussies. I could easily go and live there really, but I don't think Elaine would like it.

Ah yes – Elaine. I'd phoned my girlfriend to wish her Merry Christmas, and while I was on the phone, boldly going where no man had gone before, I said, 'And why don't you come out and join me?' So amazingly, she gave up her job and all on her own, just a young girl, she got a flight out to Australia. It sounds funny now, though it was quite disturbing at the time, but when she got off the plane, the first thing she said to me was, 'I want to go home.' It might have been the insecurity of being upside down and far from Enfield, or it might have been the long, lonely flight thinking, What if I don't get on with him? What am I going to do? But she wanted to go back straight away.

'Don't be silly, Elaine', I said, in my most charming, cheerful voice, 'you don't want to go home!'

'Yes, I do!'

'Well, at least give it a couple of days', I pleaded, 'and take it from there.' Thank goodness, the Aussies made her so welcome, and she fitted in so beautifully, that she stayed.

Elaine Gatting:

I decided to join Mike because it was a great opportunity at nineteen to be able to visit Australia, not to mention the fact that I was missing Mike. With hardly any hesitation I gave up my job, gathered up all my savings and booked my flight. It was only when I got to the airport to leave and had to say goodbye to my family that I began to have second thoughts.

Having had a 26-hour flight alone with no idea what was ahead of me I started wondering about the wisdom of my trip. I had been apart from Mike for three months when I saw him waiting for me and I suddenly felt unsure and desperately wanted to go home. Mike persuaded me to stay and I'm very glad I did.

I met some very friendly people who made me feel very welcome and it also saw the start of Mike's beard. If that beard ever goes – I go!

We had a wonderful three months together out there, during which my designer stubble turned into the face-fuzz I have now – well, she liked it, and it was no good having a baby face and captaining a lot of hard-bitten Australians.

While we were out in Balmain, the England touring team were playing a day–night match in Sydney, as part of the Benson and Hedges World Series. I'd been invited to practise with the England lads and it was nice to see them again, though their Ashes Series was in ashes and they were a bit glum. I copped quite a lot of stick for bouncing in and telling them about my club, and how successful my team were – they were Aussies after all! Anyway, with Peter Spence and his wife to be, Honey, I took Elaine to watch the match. Graham Stevenson and David Bairstow were at the wicket and England needed 35 off 6 overs, and I said, 'If there are two blokes who can do it, it's those two out in the middle.' Well they did, and we won by two wickets, and that evening I found I'd won rather a lot of money as well. As we headed back for Balmain in Peter's car, I must have been feeling so elated about things that when we pulled up at the traffic lights I turned to Elaine in the back and said, 'Will you marry me?' She said yes, so we immediately turned the car round and went for a Chinese meal to celebrate.

Elaine Gatting:

To this day I'm convinced that if England had lost, he wouldn't have asked me!

CHAPTER SIX
A Different Bloke
1980

So 1980 was already turning out to be a vast improvement on 1979: good for my cricket and good for me. Those six months with Balmain had set me up: they helped my batting (I would average 41.90 in the coming season). They helped my bowling (though that wasn't to be taken too seriously back in England). And above all, they helped me. The eve of the Middlesex season found me a different bloke from the one who'd played for them up until now.

While I'd been away, there had been some disturbing incidents in cricket. Ian Chappell, Colin Croft and Michael Holding had all been in trouble for openly dissenting with umpires. Colin Croft had knocked one flying, and Holding – normally the most amiable of sportsmen – had kicked down the stumps, which was completely out of character. I thought at the time that it was all rather shocking and surprising. Little did I know what fate had in store for me in Faisalabad. In fact, 1980 was to see me in the role of on-field peacemaker, trying to avert a punch-up between two opposing captains – more of which later. Since overcoming my childhood squabbles I've been a peace-loving person and a respecter of the law, with a very long fuse.

Middlesex had a new addition for 1980, in the shape of a 6 ft 7 in South African strike bowler, Vintcent van der Bijl. With Wayne and Mike Selvey, and new men coming on, we now had a truly formidable pace attack. At the end of the season, having been in contention for all four major titles, we were to be called 'the team of the decade'. Our Schweppes County Championship campaign and our Gillette Cup run were both to end in triumph, and I should tell you about this unusual and historic Middlesex season before getting down to my own renewed career as a Test player, which was happening simultaneously.

After three draws and a one-day thrashing by the West Indies (I made a modest 27 of our 124 all out) we beat Sussex at Lord's by an innings and my batting was coming together: comments were made that I was hitting it with a straight bat. Vintcent, Selv and Wayne knocked them over for 195 and 146 – Wayne always bowls quickly against Sussex. We won again versus Somerset at Taunton despite Botham, who had just been named captain of England, smiting various 6s and running in appallingly fast, especially when Brearley was batting. I managed 81 not out and Gould collected 8 dismissals behind the stumps – a tremendous effort. We crushed Surrey at Lord's with our pace and spin attack, Radley and myself sharing a stand of 248, both of us, oddly enough, finishing with 136. (Well, I would have got more than him but Rad kept nicking the bowling!)

Then in the next match against Yorkshire the pair of us put on 177 in 38 overs, and Rad *again* made 136 not out, as if trying to prove a point. I managed to make another 100 (I was coming in at 5 or 6 these days – a bit more congenial to me than opening). Carrick and Sharp did as much for Yorkshire though, with a 165 stand, Sharpy, a gutsy little chap, getting his maiden 100. The match was drawn.

Another draw followed, against Surrey, despite the heroic Vintcent taking 5 in an innings and despite a fine knock by Brearley. I think this was the one where Philippe Edmonds started hooking Sylvester Clarke into the road, which, as Clarke is fairly lethal, takes some doing. Then there was a win over Essex, a rain-ruined abortion against Warwickshire, and another draw against Northants in which I got run out for 1 by Geoff Cook's throw-in and cursed myself for three days afterwards. Allan Lamb hit a cracking 112 off us, as well.

I wasn't there when we beat Hampshire by 5 wickets, though I heard all about Roland Butcher cutting loose for his 153 not out. Once or twice a season Butch can be relied on to play like the best batsman in the world and take any attack apart. He won us the next (Yorkshire) match as well, hammering 179. We then drew against Kent. This was an interesting period for Middlesex because Brearley had decided that since my wicketkeeping brother Steve had gone off to play full-time football, we needed a new 2nd XI keeper. So he signed the young Paul Downton of Kent.

Unfortunately, Ian Gould, who'd been keeping splendidly and making runs until this happened, suddenly fell apart. It was horrible to watch my mate struggling, perhaps feeling the threat of competition bubbling in the second team, and sadly Ian ended up leaving Middlesex. He'd been my closest friend, and the affair caused a few raised eyebrows in the dressing room because we felt it had all been a bit hard on Gouldie. Still, to be fair to young Paul, he and Brearley made a very good opening partnership and in the Kent match, against his old county, Downton shared 100 stands in both innings.

At Lord's against Essex, Emburey – who gets called 'Knuckle', 'Ernie', 'Embers' – anything but his real name – got his nose smashed to pieces. We had everybody round the bat and Stuart Turner kept popping it up in the air off Wayne, who was bowling at a ferocious pace. In the end Turner had a huge wind up at this particular delivery, and it flew straight for Ernie at short gully, rearranging his features. Wayne took 4 for 11 in 25 deliveries, and we had an innings victory, Mike Selvey and Wayne having bowled us to crucial points in the table.

It was now August. As I've said before, losing to Leicester, Middlesex always think they're going to win the Championship, so you may imagine our optimism when we were trodden underfoot by an innings and 100 runs – our worst defeat for a very long time. We'd batted badly and didn't deserve anything better. We also lost to Gloucester, though I had no part in that, and missed seeing Mike Procter's stirring 134 not out on a rotten wicket. Now, at this point obviously, things were starting to look a bit grim for Middlesex, and we sat down and tried to sort out what was going wrong. If we were going to win the Championship, we had to do better than this. Well, we did – the next two games were the ones that really set our seal on the trophy: the Notts match at Lord's, and the Uxbridge match, against Derby.

The Notts game we owed largely to Graham Barlow and Vintcent – not usually such a dab hand with the bat. Together they put on 152, brick by brick, after we'd tumbled to 86 for 6 against Clive Rice. Emburey, battered nose and all, then wreaked havoc with the Nottinghamshire batting, sweeping them aside for 84 and 183. An innings victory! So now, because Lord's was otherwise engaged with Gillette matters, it was off to Uxbridge, where the wicket is known for early life, if you're prepared to make the effort. Vintcent was prepared. His figures were 5 for 34 and 5 for 25. Derby could only set us a modest 199 target and we got these for the loss of 1 wicket.

We were now firmly on top of the table and prepared to take on any challengers. We went down to Hove and Sussex as high as kites, but unfortunately Kepler Wessels, in one of the most defiant innings I've ever seen, humbled us with a magnificent knock of 254. They'd been made to follow on, and we thought we really were about to clinch the title when he started. It went on and on, all our best bowlers being sent to the front, and eventually it was Gatting who managed to get him caught at point by Emburey. But by then the damage was done and the match was drawn.

So I wasn't to be present when the lads finally *did* clinch the title down at Cardiff, when Brears – *Brears*! – got 124 before lunch, and we declared leaving Glamorgan to stumble after 235 in four hours. We won by 72 runs: it was Vintcent, really, who knocked them over. Understandably, the players had a few jars to celebrate, and poor old Graham Barlow got stopped on the motorway heading back to London. He blew into the bag and got a marginally positive reading, then went to the station and got a negative reading. He'd only had one glass of champagne and half a pint of lager, so they let him go, and he toddled off, thinking, Thank goodness for that. But we'd won. We'd won!

There were quite a few drinks being guzzled after the last match of the season, against Kent at Canterbury. All I can remember about that rather sozzled game was the sight of my captain Brearley, on a turning wicket, knocking a magnificent 104 out of 'Deadly' Derek Underwood. I was too dazed to get many runs myself. It was so nice being in a Champion County dressing room again, and we'd bounced back in considerable style. I agree with Brears that the major factor in our success was Vintcent van der Bijl. He had not only bowled well himself but he had helped and inspired and kidded the other bowlers in the side, talking to youngsters like Simon Hughes and Bill Merry, and being a bit of a card in the bar with his stories about cricket and his native South Africa. He was a team man and a lovable character, and it was a great privilege to play with him. In his own field, which was fast medium, he was the finest I've seen.

That summer, while Middlesex were going from strength to strength, there was a 5-Test-match Series between England and the West Indies, as well as a special Centenary Test at Lord's between England and Australia. I was chosen to make my home Test debut in the 2nd Test against the West Indies. It was a great thrill, but I would be putting my head in the lion's mouth as well. The West Indies were the most fearsome and formidable side in the world, still preening themselves after crushing England in 1976 and, under Clive Lloyd's leadership, turning themselves into a mean machine. They were ruthless, professional, and looking forward to pounding away at us. Our new captain was 'Beefy' Botham. We'd lost the 1st Test at Nottingham, albeit by only 2 wickets. Gower had been dropped, and I was picked to jump in the deep end at Lord's, of all places.

I felt very tense when the match started. It was so bad, that it was hard to get to grips with the situation. Australia had given me confidence, but I still had some growing up to do when it came to Test matches. I'm sure everybody could see how nervous I was walking out to bat, amid the hubbub of a Lord's Test crowd. Lloyd had put us in, and Boycott had gone with just 20 on the board before Gooch hit us out of trouble, but then a collapse began and we needed steadying. I managed to get off the mark, still struggling to control my butterflies; my first run came off Colin Croft and went between the bowler and widish mid-on. I was beginning to settle in, on 18, thinking, well, this isn't too bad really, when Michael Holding came back on. The very first ball he bowled did me for pace. Over went middle and off, and that was the end of my home Test debut innings.

England slithered towards 269, with only Goochie's marvellous 123 standing between us and disaster. We now had a bit of leather-chasing to do. Desmond Haynes sent us scurrying to all parts in a tremendous 184, and Viv Richards hammered 145 as only Viv can, and they piled on 518. The only nice thing I remember was racing round from mid-on to shy down Colin Croft's middle-stump and run him out. Otherwise it was all flogging and fetching. We'd started our second knock looking up at some mountainous task, when the rains came and the match ended in a draw.

The 3rd Test, at Manchester, was dark, damp and dreary. Botham, our captain, was desperately keen for us to do well, and not get into a good position only to collapse in a heap, as happened at Lord's. But we didn't bat at all well 1st innings. I'd begun to get into the swing of things with 33, and then got a snorter from Marshall. It seemed to signal another clatter of England wickets. Rose and I had put on 91 to take us from 35 for 3 to 126 for 4, but we were all out for 150. Which wasn't good. Still, we had the West Indians in quite a lot of trouble at 25 for 3, and 67 for 4, before Lloyd played a captain's innings in front of his home crowd, to ease them to 260. In our 2nd innings, the wicket was a little flatter, and much to my relief I managed to get the first Test 50 of my career.

I can remember one shot vividly to this day. Holding was bowling from the station end and he sent down a good ball just short of off- stump, and I stood up and did something completely uncharacteristic: I hit a drive off the back foot. I had no idea it was coming, but I watched it go, beating cover, and shooting all along the ground for 4. I didn't hit it all that hard, yet it went like a rocket, and I remember Holding walking back to his marker, shaking his head – I'm not sure if it was something I'd done. Anyway, they took the new ball, Marshall and Garner, and I played at a widish one from Joel which held up a bit and was caught at slip for 56. We were going quite well, on 391 for 7, when the rains came again and ruined another Test.

I was feeling quite pleased with myself now, having got a 33 and a 56, and I was wrong; 56 is not a score that captains like, or that batsmen should learn to like, particularly in a Test match. It's not a very good score: it's one that a captain would hope his batsman could use as a basis for a 100. I hadn't gone on and got a 100 with mine, and this was to be my plight for the next three or four years, frustrating my captains and frustrating me. But I *had* taken 90 runs off the fastest and most ferocious attack in the world, so I couldn't help feeling a bit excited, could I?

At the Oval, in the 4th Test, I was doing fine, got to 48 and then I was attempting to pull Colin Croft just before lunch when I got an underneath edge. Sick, sick. I got very cross about that. You get to 48, I said to myself, and then you go *on*! I don't remember much about my second knock, I'm afraid (caught Murray bowled Garner for 15). Gooch hit an inspiring 83 first innings, and we reached 370 and almost had the West Indians following on, but then they fought their way out of it. The match ended in another rain-affected draw, after Peter Willey hit a brilliant undefeated 100 when we were struggling.

The final Test was at Headingley. That was also drawn, though we were on the receiving end of most of it. I do remember getting out to Croftie first knock, for 1. They'd stationed Marshall at very deep leg gully and I'd really whipped this one off my waist, but unfortunately it went straight to Malcolm. Second innings, I was left in no-man's land, by one that nipped back from Holding, and was again out for 1. So it wasn't a very good finish. But at least I could look back and say, well, I've done it – I've played in a Series against the West Indies and as far as I was concerned anyway, it wasn't a flop. I'd got back my confidence after the dismal tour of 1977–78 and the even more dismal depths of 1979. And there was still one Test to play.

The Centenary Test between England and Australia, at Lord's, began at the end of August. I'd cut my teeth against the Aussies in a couple of Prudential Trophy matches – having at last been permitted to play in the Prudential – and though England had won both, I hadn't done anything to shout about, getting 17 not out and 2. Now came the great day, and the great privilege. It was clearly a very, very big occasion, the counterpart of the one I'd seen in Melbourne as a spectator, with lots of old players present, and lots of flashbulbs popping.

The match itself, the showpiece, featured this bowler called Dennis Lillee, who was a bit swift, and another chap called Lennie Pascoe, who was a bit raw but keen to get at us. The Aussies were bristling, fit, and raring to go, and they won the toss and went in. Wood and Hughes produced two very fine centuries, after yours truly had managed to catch Greg Chappell at square-leg off Old for 47 (I remember thinking, I do hope Chappell doesn't make too many). There was one quite amazing shot that Kim Hughes played that made you want to take your sunhat off. Chris Old was the bowler, and Hughes danced down the wicket and hit him high and straight over long-off. It ascended for miles, dropping in the tiling of the commentary box roof. That's as well as I've ever seen anybody hit a cricket ball. A tremendous knock from Mr Hughes. They ended up declaring at 385 for 5 and then England shuddered to 205 in reply (Gatting getting out lbw to Pascoe for 12).

The Aussies went in again, and we'd already had some rain, but now it fairly tipped down, making a sodden mess of the outfield, and the lower half of the square, which was uncovered. Saturday morning, when it stopped, Lord's was awash, though you'd never have thought so, seeing the sun blazing down. As we were in the field, and we didn't fancy planting any rice, we were glad when the umpires decided not to send us squelching out, as it could have been very dangerous. But the crowd saw the sun shining, had a few drinks, and got very hot under their collars.

Eventually, in the afternoon, the situation exploded, and there was a seething mass of MCC members pushing and shoving umpires David Constant and Dickie Bird, and one or two stuffed shirts so forgot themselves as to aim punches at them. It was just diabolical, I thought, for members of perhaps the greatest cricket club of all time to behave like a set of rowdies, and it soured a very special occasion. We thought it ungrateful, considering the cricketers were playing their hearts out.

Eventually, at 3.45, the secretary Jack Bailey announced, 'We will now start!' as if to say, 'or else', and play got underway again, the Aussies declaring at 189 for 4 on Monday evening, which left us to make 370 at about a run a minute. We got off to a shaky start, 43 for 2, but managed to steady to 124 for 3, which left 'Sir' Geoffrey Boycott and me at the crease.

At tea, there were discussions about whether we should go for it, with the more fiery players saying yes, we should, and Boyx saying, 'This is a Test match against Australia. I'm not going out and playing it like a ruddy one-day game.' So Boycott and I jollied along for half an hour after tea, and then I looked at Geoffrey, and Geoffrey looked at me – a bit severely, because he knew what I was like.

'No, lad', he said. 'Get your head down.'

So we put up the shutters; Boycott passed a couple of aggregates, and helped himself to another undefeated Test ton. I got 51 not out. There wasn't a lot I could do – I felt a bit lost in the circumstances, and Boycott's experience led the way.

So the match ended in a draw, and a rather undignified chorus of slow-handclaps. People were disappointed, but there was a lot of pride at stake. I'd enjoyed it. I'd got a taste of playing against these Australians. Whatever Packer had or had not done to interfere, these were fine, hardened, professional cricketers, who expected no quarter and gave none. And I'll never, never forget Kim Hughes whacking Chris Old over the commentary box.

The Schweppes title was not Middlesex's only success of 1980, by a long chalk. We were doing extremely well in three other departments: even in the John Player we'd started by winning our first 6 games, and we won the last 4 on the trot as well – unprecedented Sunday form. Unfortunately we messed it up in the middle, losing 5 consecutive matches in the slump. I'm not sure what happened, or why. There's Middlesex, there's Sunday League, and we never seem to marry the two together. We finished a comparatively disappointing 3rd. I managed probably my best year in the competition, though I still hadn't got a John Player 100.

We had a great run in the Bensons, winning 4 of our 4 preliminaries to qualify for a quarter-final against Sussex at Lord's. I hoped I'd helped a bit towards it, with 83 not out and 95 not out in earlier rounds. Now, this quarter-final was rather extraordinary. We won it eventually by 29 runs, though not before a memorable flare-up on the pitch which was to send shock-waves through English cricket and it was none of Gatting's doing, either.

We went in first, and Imran, who was bowling, couldn't seem to control the ball. Altogether, he bowled 11 wides – and Sussex's extras were to total more than our margin of victory. We managed an unenviable 195 and it needed some very tight bowling from Wayne and Vintcent, Ernie and Philippe, to peg them back; Tony Pigott was batting, it was a nip and tuck, and the situation was getting very tense indeed, with Wayne bowling sharp and short.

Suddenly one delivery reared and whacked Pigott on the arm, and the non-striker Imran, who had himself been warned for bowling too many bouncers at tailenders, intervened, objecting to Wayne's short-pitched stuff. He still continued to object, to umpire van Geloven, and I noticed, out of the corner of my eye, Brearley began to get rather cross. Brears headed for the middle and one somehow sensed there was about to be a spot of bother.

'It's all right for you to bowl bouncers', he called out to the opposing skipper, 'but when we do it to your batsmen, you don't like it!'

Now Imran, not what you'd call a self-effacing sort of bloke, had a bat in his hand and he listened to all this imperiously.

'Don't you talk to me like that', he warned Brearley, and the start of an argument drifted towards the fielders, some of whom went to investigate. It got louder and louder, and when I spotted Brears striding towards Imran, and the Sussex skipper hoist his bat in the air apparently ready to welt his opposite number, I stepped in and tried to break it up – at which point Brears got very annoyed with *me* as well. But I persisted because they were eyeball to eyeball and looked to be on the point of a punch-up. You could imagine the headlines: 'Captains Bundle for Benson Honours – Skippers' Shindig ends in Slaying.'

'Look', I said, 'don't be silly. Leave it. Come on.'

Anyway the drama gradually subsided, Wayne went on bowling, and thank goodness we got them out. I managed to chip in with 3 wickets, which helped to make up for my batting – I'd got out for a song to 'Bomber' Wells – and we cleared the Sussex hurdle into the semis.

There, we met Northants and Sarfraz, on the Test pitch at Lord's. I was pressed into bowling 11 overs and I bowled expensively, getting 3 late wickets. Wayne and Vintcent couldn't peg them and they got off to a flying start, before Emburey pinned them down to 206. We quickly lost Brearley, Radley and Barlow followed by Slack, so the next morning I was left with Vintcent to make 79 off 14 overs. Vintcent hit a couple of 6s to get the rate down, got out, whacking, and the rate went up again. Gouldie and I needed 20 in 3 overs. With 14 deliveries to go, I couldn't stand it, had a rush of blood, and heaved across the line at Sarfraz, getting out for 91. I'd never do that now, but that was the end of our Bensons run.

Our Gillette campaign, though, was unstoppable. We got into the semis after Simon 'Yosser' Hughes and Mike Selvey had bowled exceptionally well against Worcester (I managed 95 not out against Notts in the cause as well). We met Sussex, at Hove – a grudge match, if ever there was one, after the Bensons stir. There was a buzz around the ground as we cobbled together 179, but then Diamond Daniel, always a menace at Hove, bowled one of the quickest bursts I can remember and ripped through them, collecting 6 for 15. With Vintcent's tight control, nipping out the dangerous Imran, we won a low-scoring match (I was top scorer with just 32).

Lord's, the Final. There's always a special, electrifying atmosphere at Lord's Cup finals – the place comes alive with 25,000 people in it – and my nerves started the old jangling again. I enjoy that atmosphere now, but it takes some getting used to because you can almost feel the pressure as a physical force. Put in, Surrey assembled 201, having begun very quietly and then accelerated a bit late. We started even more tentatively, creeping towards tea with Brears still there, having lost Downton and Radley. Brearley and myself managed to add 64 to our 57 for 2, and after tea I felt we simply had to get on with it. Roger Knight and Intikhab Alam had bowled quite tidily and now Robin Jackman returned with his sleeves up. We were 121 for 2, needing just 81 to win the Gillette Cup. It was a bit tense. Jackman came in, I went down the wicket and had an enormous hoick. My off pole flew out of the ground. Brears hit the roof.

Don Bennett:

It looked terrible. When he came off, he was very disappointed, and after about ten minutes of winding down, he came over to me and said, 'Well, come on then. I expected a rocket from you.'

I said, 'You won't get one from me, Gatt. At least you were trying to be positive. Anyway, one's enough – you got the most monumental rocket from the captain – I heard it from here!'

Mike Brearley:

I was probably cross because I thought we had the match, and if he got out, we could easily lose it. He's such a strong player anyway that he doesn't *need* to slog – he can hit the ball with orthodox shots so much harder than most people.

Luckily for Middlesex, Roland Butcher, having played himself in, opened his shoulders, and from being slightly pushed we were suddenly absolutely walking it. He smashed Jackman into the stands and hammered him over deep square-leg, hitting four or five 6s, one of which was the exact shot I'd tried to play, only he connected! He got 50 not out. Man of the Match Brearley got 96 not out and we strolled in by 7 wickets, to become not only County Champions but Gillette Cup winners as well – particularly nice in Gillette's last year of sponsorship. We'd had an amazing season, and we'd nearly pushed over the other two titles as well, having figured in all four in July. Perhaps it's just as well that we *did* lose a couple, or it might have waylaid us somewhere along the line.

In this carnival atmosphere, I got married. I'll let my wife tell you what happened.

Elaine Gatting:

He was playing in the Gillette Cup Final on the Saturday, so we'd decided to set the wedding date for the following Tuesday, 9 September. Had the final been rained off, I don't know what we'd have done – we'd have had to have waited for a free day. Mike was living in his own flat in Southgate then, and we had two best men – Mike's brother Steve at the church, and because Steve had to play a football match, Mike's best friend Ian Gould was to be best man at the reception, which meant that he was over here the day before, pacing up and down the garden in a state of high anxiety trying to prepare his speech. At the ceremony everything went smoothly except for one or two hiccups. I'd turned to jelly halfway up the aisle and had to be dragged to the altar by my brother Mike, and then my husband Mike – which was a bit confusing, what with two best men as well – gave me his right hand instead of his left, and he had the ring on his wrong finger.

So while the Curate was blessing us, my new husband was going *twist, twist, wrench*, trying to get it off, which was fairly embarrassing. But otherwise we sailed through it, out under the archway of raised Middlesex bats and on to the reception. After the meal Mike held my chair out for me, so I could go and look at the presents. Somebody shouted, 'Oh, the cake's coming – sit down again', so I sat, and as Mike hadn't pushed the chair back in, I sat straight on the floor. I wasn't hurt, no, but I nearly wet myself laughing.

But the best was yet to come. Elaine should explain what happened on our honeymoon.

Elaine Gatting:

We went down to St Ives, Cornwall. It was idyllic. A local artist did a portrait of us, and we went horseriding, which I've always loved, and which Mike took to, once they'd found a horse big enough for him, though he had a bit of trouble rising to the trot. On the hotel pitch-and-putt course he taught me to play golf, and I didn't do at all badly (*unlike* the time he taught me to play squash and I ended up hitting him across the legs with the racquet because he was treating me like a four year old). It was all very romantic, and we'd been there just two days when Mike suddenly got a phone call at the hotel. He'd been invited to play cricket in Bristol! He said yes as well. As we had some friends over that way, we went and stayed with them afterwards. The Cornish spell had been broken.

Well, they'd asked me to play in a floodlit exhibition match, England *v.* the West Indies, you see, at Bristol football ground. It was only for one night – I didn't think that was too bad. The fee was about £500 – and I thought, 'Well, that'll pay for the honeymoon, so why not? It's only a night's work – then we can nip off and see David and Liza. In my defence, I was not only being my usual thrifty self, but having to think about business. Elaine's brother and I were about to go into partnership with a schoolmaster, Phil Smith, and open a sports goods shop in Radlett. We reckoned our break-even figure was £20,000 and I looked on the shop as an investment for myself and Elaine. My mother-in-law Jean, who is very astute and the perfect secretary, did all the book-keeping. Our first day of trading, in November, we banked £1000, as well.

Amidst all this excitement, my first home Test matches, Middlesex's historic season, wedding bells and the chink of tills in the shop, I was invited on two tours, the first to Zimbabwe, and the second, with England, to the West Indies. The little Zimbabwe trip was organized by Middlesex, and gave some of the youngsters a chance to shine, like Norman Cowans, Rajesh Maru, Bill Merry and Keith Tomlins. I remember it rather well because it was the last social occasion I was to share with my friend Ian Gould. We'd heard he was off to Sussex, and it was nice to have a little tour with him, and a few drinks and reminiscences. There was a marvellous atmosphere in the side, and because we were in a country where black people had been looked down upon, there was a bit of good-natured leg-pulling of Roland Butcher, Norman Cowans and Wilfy Slack, who took it in the spirit intended and more than once got their own back. It was a friendly, happy tour and we were very well looked after. We got a taste of Africa, and a bit of insight into the recent turmoil of independence, saw a game park or two, played in Harare and

Bulawayo, and were surprised at how dedicated and competitive Zimbabwe cricket is, particularly in the three 3-day games where we were held to a respectable 1-all in the rubber.

No sooner was I home to my new wife, than I was off again, on the England tour of the West Indies. It was to prove a very sad trip, in more ways than one.

CHAPTER SEVEN
Tours and Test Fifties
1981–82

A more serious tour was to follow my Zimbabwe trip: at the beginning of 1981 England were off to the West Indies, and I was in the squad. Botham was captain; we had a few injury problems, which didn't make the selectors' job any easier, but it was thought that there were some rather friendly 'skipper selections' in the team. Anyway, Roland Butcher got aboard in recognition of his sterling knock in the Gillette Cup Final, and Graham Stevenson was another to be given his chance. The tour manager was Alan Smith; his assistant was Test stalwart Kenny Barrington, whom all of us naturally looked up to. It was to be my first tour with Barrington and, sadly, the last.

We left on 15 January and the tour officially opened in Trinidad on the 23rd, where we had a spot of bother winning a four-day game against a Young West Indian XI which happened to have Roger Harper in it. It was a high-scoring game on a rain-affected pitch which later took spin. David Gower got a graceful 187 which was magnificent to watch; Boycott got a couple of 80s and I managed 94, which *seemed* to augur well for me. How little I knew. Two wins followed in the Windward Islands in which I didn't play, and then there was a one-day international at St Vincent, where we seemed to be on a certainty after they were extracted for 127 but then we fell 2 runs short ourselves. Colin Croft was the main destroyer, with 6 for 15, one of those being me. I had no part in the drawn game against Trinidad and Tobago, and looked forward to the 1st Test in Port of Spain. All being well, I might get a few runs.

The 1st Test squad was announced, and it became clear

that not only had we left out a batsman, but that the unwanted batsman was Gatting. I remember more than one person remarking at the time that they thought this slightly odd. England succumbed in the match to Messrs Croft and Co, and were made to follow on; although Boycott then grafted a defiant 70, we lost by an innings and 79 runs. I remember Captain Beefy had said, in a stirring mid-match oration to his troops, '. . . and if we don't save this, heads will roll!' but unfortunately none of them rolled in my direction and I was left out of the 2nd Test squad as well. My thumbs were getting well twiddled. In fact I wasn't to play another 1st-class innings for six weeks.

Whilst we were in Trinidad, something happened that was to dislodge the first stone in an avalanche, with the England team underneath. Bob Willis had broken down and was unable to bowl, and a replacement was sent for, chosen on merit. Robin Jackman arrived to a warm welcome from the lads, and together we innocently made our way over to our next venue, Guyana.

It was then that we realized something was afoot. Only Captain Botham was fully in the know, but we picked up snippets of information along the grapevine, to the effect that poor Jackers, having played and coached in South Africa with black youngsters as well as white, was about to have his visa revoked by the Guyanese government. The scheduled matches against Guyana were abandoned through bad weather as we pressed our tumblers to the hotel walls, trying to find out what was going on in the Jackers Affair.

We all thought that if they weren't going to let Robin play, it was a bit of a farce and we might as well go home. There were meetings and more meetings. Word had apparently come from Lord's that if the situation wasn't resolved fairly quickly, there would be no 2nd Test. Meanwhile we were getting rusty in the rain, and trying to practise in a mozzie-infested gym, in between tending our bites and worrying about what was going to happen to us all.

We arrived at Berbice for our 2nd one-day international.

When we went back and forth to the cricket ground, not for us the usual car or boat trip – no, we were flown out in a couple of army helicopters. You couldn't hear yourself think, let alone discuss match tactics. Jackman having been made 12th man pending further argument, the game got underway. The rumours had attracted a sizable crowd eager to see for themselves the England suspects, and there was an ongoing hubbub.

When I went out to bat I came as close to getting one in the nose as Colin Croft could contrive, but managed to duck my face out of the way as his bouncer rocketed over my shoulder. I'd gone in number 3 for some reason, and we were struggling so I had to get my head down in other ways. I was on 29, having seen off the lightning pacemen, when I got out to the comparatively friendly Larry Gomes. We never really got going, raising just 137 all out. We had a glimmer of hope when Viv Richards went for 3, caught hooking, and they were reduced to 11 for 2, but Gomes and Lloyd saw them home by 6 wickets – a taste of the disaster to come. Then when we got back to the hotel, we had the main course. Robin Jackman was served, by an armed guard, with a deportation order.

The 2nd Test was cancelled. It was now March, and as the rumpus continued, some of us were very much looking forward to going home out of it. We were cricketers. Jackman was a cricketer. If they didn't want him, they didn't want us. 'Come on', we said, 'let's go back to England.' Poor Robin was allowed to play at last in a four-day game in Barbados. I was asked to go in number 3 again.

The Barbados attack was formidable: Sylvester Clarke, Malcolm Marshall, Collis King and Wayne Daniel. It was the first time I'd played against Wayne since our schooldays, but of course I'd seen the damage he could do, at Middlesex. I weathered that particular storm, though, and I was settling in rather nicely when Marshall got his hands on the ball.

I remember telling myself, over and over again, Remember not to try to hook Marshall . . . not to hook Marshall . . .

not to hook Marshall. Whatever you do, don't try hooking Marshall. I was out hooking Marshall for 11, caught down the leg-side. I wasn't positive enough, you see. If you're going to hook, hook, don't talk. So I was as cross as two sticks about that, but in the end, the match petered out in a draw. Emburey took 5 for 92; Jackman, despite all his worries, took 4 for 68, justifying a place in the 3rd Test.

The Bridgetown Test began in a pall of gloom. It wasn't so much that the Jackman row was rumbling: we'd got used to that, and things were more peaceful now, politically, than before the previous Test. No, it was something closer to home. We'd been working very hard in the nets, quite cheerfully as it happens, and Kenny Barrington was running in bowling leg breaks at us. Ken would always help as much as he could, and in spite of all the anxiety he must have suffered in the last weeks, he was his usual keen, competitive self, doing all he could to hone his England lads for the Test. In fielding practice, he was so enthusiastic that he even bruised Graham Gooch's hand trying to whack one past him.

We knew he had a coronary condition, and had been warned by doctors to take things easy, but nothing daunted Ken. Only a little while before this, he had apparently been chatting to Robin Marlar, who says, in a *Wisden* tribute, that Ken was in high spirits, with 'absolute faith in the ability of Botham and Gatting'. That night, on the eve of the Bridgetown Test match, Ken Barrington died of a heart attack. We were all shocked and terribly upset. We had all admired him so much, and each of us felt that we had lost a friend. It was a great shame.

Elaine Gatting:

I was looking forward to joining Mike in the West Indies and travelled with some of the other wives to Barbados. We arrived while the team were playing. I waited in our room for Mike's return. At breakfast the following morning I had first met Ken Barrington and his wife Anne. Ken had made a point of welcoming all the wives, and he certainly had made me feel a part of the tour. Unlike the manager, who did not seem to approve of wives on tour. Tragically a few days after out meeting Ken died suddenly. The whole tour party was shaken and the players totally devastated, with many of them moved to tears. How they ever managed to get through the Test match I will never know. As to the trip itself, I had not realized how little I would see of Mike, even though he was not playing all the time. Much of my time was spent with the other deserted wives.

So the one Test of this unhappy tour for which I was picked got underway with yet another shadow over England. We played, because it was felt that this was what Ken would have wanted. We won the toss and inserted the West Indies, and they were in trouble at 65 for 4, one of those gone being Richards. Then Clive Lloyd came in – and we put him down. He went on to hammer a century out of us, and to make matters worse I think David Bairstow dropped Gomes on 0, before he went on to make 58. So the West Indies were able to mount up 265, and in reply we got the sum total of 122. Even Boyx got 0. I got 2.

They proceeded to rub our noses in it, Viv cutting and carving 182 not out in their 379 for 7 declared. We were staring at a very vast target indeed. Second knock, I was bowled first ball by Holding for no score. He was so quick, his feet hardly touched the ground. We lost by the yawning margin of 298 runs, and it would have been worse than that had it not been for a 50 from Gower and a truly lion-hearted knock from Graham Gooch, none the worse for his injured hand. In fact, he seemed to be saying, as he clobbered them for 116, 'This one's for you, Ken'. It was quite magnificent to see him standing there in the line of the fastest attack in the world, and taking it apart. Poor Roland Butcher, though he fielded quite well, didn't do himself justice on his home island. He must have been terribly disappointed.

So from that steamrollering, we went to the Leeward

Islands, and with no help from me (I got 4 and 0) England won by 5 wickets, and we had a nice little game of golf as well on the island of Montserrat, to cheer us up. I wasn't to play in another Test on that trip. I'd had the stuffing knocked out of me, and it was time to rethink and regroup. We drew the 4th Test in Antigua, Boyx and Willey getting undefeated 100s, Gooch cracking another fine 83, and Viv leading the charge for the West Indies in their 468 for 9 declared in their only innings. The thing I recall most vividly was Colin Croft's bowling, running so wide at the return crease that to the batsmen he was outside the sightscreens. A ferocious force coming out of a black hole. No wonder both Emburey and Stevenson were out to full-tosses. They swore they never saw the bloke.

So finally, we arrived at the Jamaica Test, at Sabina Park. I'd played in the pipe-opener, a drawn four-day game *v.* Jamaica, and managed to get 93 and 42 (a relief after the previous run of 2, 0, 4 and 0). We'd batted very well in a drawn cause, which meant that at least I could lift my head up before we went home. In fact, I did better than that – I had two helpings of steak and kidney pie. The Test itself was drawn, and I was as pleased as every other spectator to see Goochie's mighty 153 and Gower's brilliant 154 not out.

The West Indies eventually rattled us out, but I think what must have shocked them slightly was the sight of this blond bloke called Dilley steaming in as fast as their own bowlers and making them jump about. Sadly, Graham's boots couldn't stand the strain of it, and as he hadn't brought another best pair, he wasn't able to fire himself up in borrowed boots. Still, it was a great game, and a great fightback by England, with Gower and Willey staving off the West Indian attack. And so ended a double helping of the West Indies. Whatever lay in store for me, it had to be easier than this. I took my lessons home with me, and I worked hard, as I always do, to get ready for the summer of '81.

While I'd been away in Zimbabwe and the Windies, Elaine was spending a bit more time with Jean, her mother. We had our own flat in Enfield, but as that was just two miles down the road, it seemed silly for them both to be alone in their respective homes, so Elaine moved back with Jean. It was a lovely big house, with plenty of room for us all. But Elaine and I did at least have two months together in our new abode.

Elaine Gatting:

> The first thing that went into that flat was a wine rack. No furniture, no carpets – just the wine rack. He'll buy wine like women buy clothes. He's a collector. He'll try something new, just to learn about it. Fortunately, he knows a bit about food too, and he's quite a good cook.

My new bride got to sample some of my cooking. I do a lot of barbecues, which date back to my days in Australia where they're always having barbecues, but I like cooking, full stop. When the mood takes me, I'll have a go at anything. Not sauces so much, because I'm not that fiddly a chef, but anything fairly basic and quite fun to make. Like Exploding Bananas. Now, that was an interesting recipe. When my mate Peter Spence was throwing a dinner party once, Elaine and I had a rummage through the cookbook for a nice sweet we could prepare, and we came across 'Banana Flambée', or 'Flaming Bananas', I think it was called. I thought, Right! we'll have some of that.

So I got one of these big baking dishes, and because we were expecting 8 guests, we put about 8 bananas in. The recipe said, 'Cover with brown sugar, a little water, and rum to taste.' So I poured on the Bunderburg rum rather liberally, and bunged the dish in the oven. And of course the oven heated it up and the next thing you heard was *boooom*! and the whole flipping oven front's blown open to reveal these flaming bananas – literally. The rum went everywhere and it was hard work cleaning the oven, I can tell you. The explosion was quite frightening.

During this winter I was playing a bit of football for Hendon Reserves, and in fact training with Steve at the Arsenal for a while. That was hard work, as well.

Steve Gatting:

You used to be sick, actually – pre-season you would do six weeks of very, very strenuous work: cross-countries, circuit training, a lot of 440s, and laps as quickly as you could. I think Mike could have done what we did and I think he could have made a professional footballer, but he'd have had to have watched his weight. He's really the wrong shape for it. And as he got better at cricket, he was told not to play football in case he broke a leg or something. Even now, he'd probably like to play Sunday mornings if he could, but I think he's wised up to the risks in his old age!

Sometimes I get a bit envious of the footballer's life, but I think we cricketers probably enjoy ourselves more. Football is more of a cut-throat game, really.

Meanwhile, I was putting in some hours at the shop in Radlett. It was only half an hour from Lord's, and I didn't intend to be just the name over the shop. Business was booming, and we were building up our range of stockists. And while all this was going on, I was getting in shape for the 1981 Middlesex season. As it turned out, my involvement was to be severely limited by Test calls and appearances in one-day internationals.

Middlesex paid the price of being a fine side, losing several of its key players to England duty for much of the summer. We were also without the services of Vintcent van der Bijl, who had been such an asset the previous season. Instead we had Aussie Jeff Thomson, the legendary 'Tommo', who came into the side as a spearhead bowler, but unfortunately discovered a lump in his intestines midway through the summer and ended up going back to Brisbane with a hernia. He was not at all the stereotype brash, noisy Australian – though he liked a few beers and had an infectious sense of humour.

Basically, he was rather quiet, despite having been quoted as saying that he liked to see batsmen writhing round on the pitch from bouncers! A great bloke. We also took on another bowler to strengthen our spin attack: Dermot Monteith. He looked impressive as well.

For me, the County season had a number of memorable matches and moments, not the least of them being the traditional pipe-opener between the reigning Champions and MCC – always of interest to selectors and a good game of cricket. This particular one ended in a draw, but wasn't without a hint of controversy. Robin Jackman was bowling to me, I went to drive, made no contact, and stood there waiting for the umpire's decision. There was a huge shout for caught behind, as they thought I'd got an inside edge, but as I hadn't felt anything, I didn't think I'd hit it, and neither did the umpire so I stayed.

Jackers shook his head and muttered a few comments, not all of them printable, to the effect that I was a "little cheat". Anyway, I was given not out, so I went on my merry way. It was a bit of a struggle on a wicket quite helpful to the bowlers, but David Gower, obviously keen to win back his Test place, hit a fine century and a 50. I managed to get 101 not out as well, which was a nice start to anybody's summer.

I followed this up with 158 against Yorkshire in Middlesex's first win of the season. Having elected to bat at Headingley and found the ball seaming around, we had to bide our time at first, but then the sun came out and we piled up a big score which kept us in the driving seat. I usually manage to snatch a few runs off the Yorkies.

It rained a lot during the early season, which meant that we had to play the odd game of squash and generally try to amuse ourselves. Then, having missed quite a few County games, I was in the side that met the Australian tourists at Lord's. Although the match was drawn you couldn't easily forget the spectacle of Tommo charging in at his fellow Aussies. He hadn't been picked for this tour, and he vented his feelings by bowling very severely at them, particularly when we set them 266 in 210 minutes. He was really rushing in. Graeme Wood was taken to hospital with a crack on the helmet. Our own batting was held up for inspection because the Australian bowlers decided to test our hooking capabilities: sadly we didn't do very well. I managed 32 and 75 and was grateful for that because there was a Test match coming up and I think this game might well have sealed a place in it for me.

I was absent for some of the sensations of Middlesex's season. The Essex game at Ilford, for example, when we were docked 7 points for fielding an unregistered wicketkeeper, Chilton Taylor. Apparently Chilton was asked by Brearley at one point to go in as nightwatchman. Said Chilton, 'You've got to be joking. Not on your life am I going in.' Which took Brears somewhat by surprise.

But I was there when we beat Notts at Trent Bridge, on a wicket mysteriously transformed to coincide with the arrival of their new acquisition Richard Hadlee. Brears had made a brilliant 100 on it, anyway, and there was an accident when Eddie Hemmings, batting, was hit by Ernie in the mouth. Play was held up for possibly 2 overs, so the umpire, seeing six o'clock about to tick over, recompensed us with an extra one during which we nipped to victory. Which caused a furore in the Notts dressing room, and a terrible schemozzle the next day, with people ringing up Lord's to complain. Notts in fact went on to win the Championship, and we were the only side to beat them at Nottingham in 1981.

Worst of all, though, was missing the drawn game against Worcester at Lord's, which was what you might call action-packed. West Indian Hartley Alleyne, having taken 8 for 43 for Worcester in the 1st innings, had to be carried off after treading on the ball in the second innings, and Wilfred Slack cut loose with a staggering 248 not out, to go with his 181 not out in the previous match.

Against Glamorgan at Lord's, where we steamrollered the Welshmen pretty flat, I managed to get 99 but was out lbw to Nash with the second new ball. I played only three more

County matches. We sunk Leicester by an innings and 62 runs – which meant that, obviously, our chances of winning the Championship were bleak.

Cricketers can be very superstitious, you know. Not me. The only little superstitions I might harbour are negligible. There's the one about my trousers: I used to stick to a winning pair if I could. And of course I like to keep to my changing peg. And I won't sit in the captain's chair at Middlesex because I like to be in my regular seat near the door. Other than that, I don't believe a word of it. But we beat Leicester, and we finished fourth in the County Championship – make of that what you will. And of course, there's a strong feeling that if there's a very tight situation in a match, players who have not been watching shouldn't suddenly poke their heads in and watch, and those who *have* been watching should stay exactly where they are and see it out. Beefy Botham subscribes to that one as well.

In that Leicester match, young Norman Cowans, on his debut, picked up 5 for 58 for us 2nd innings, with a spell of 4 for 17, Leicester having been forced to follow on. Emburey did his usual sterling job and took 10 for 108 in the match; Clive Radley got a nice unbeaten 100, Graham Barlow got an excellent 152 and I contributed a very fine 0.

I redeemed myself in the last two matches, though. Middlesex beat Surrey at Uxbridge (we like that Uxbridge ground), and this was rather astonishing, because Surrey got 411 first knock – and still lost! It was a Middlesex team effort that pulled it off, to which I contributed 169 – one of those knocks when everything seems to go right. There was a fast outfield and I hit 9 6s, 5 off Intikhab's leg-spin and the rest off Percy Pocock's off-spin, if I remember rightly. *Wisden* points out, rather humorously, 'Radley, sensibly, merely watched such carnage'. But then I did a very silly thing and ran myself out off a no ball. It was the highest score of my career.

Fortunately, I managed to do slightly better in the very last match, against Derby. In a 338 stand for the 3rd wicket with my skipper Brears, I hit 186 not out. You'd think I could remember all the details, but alas. I was just enjoying batting. It enabled me to finish 8th in the 1st-class batting averages with 1492 runs at 55.25. Sadly for Middlesex, the rain interfered, and we could only draw the match. But ending up fourth in the table wasn't too bad, considering we'd been halfway down in July.

We didn't do very well at all in the limited-over competitions. The NatWest, formerly the Gillette Cup, saw our demise in the 2nd round to Lancashire, after Paul Downton and Mike Selvey had had a mad fit and run themselves out. In the Bensons, rain totally destroyed any hopes we had, and in the John Player we finished third from bottom, Brearley's hair having gone a whiter shade of grey.

While all this was happening, of course, there was a Test Series going on, and not an ordinary Test Series either. The England *v.* Australia matches of 1981 included two, perhaps even three, of the most remarkable Tests seen in this country in recent years, and I had the privilege to play in them all. I shall never forget them: they gave a new impetus to my career, and I make no apology for recording the Series in some detail.

The Australians were captained by Kim Hughes, Greg Chappell having declined to tour although his brother Trevor was in the squad. Their pace attack consisted of Lillee, Hogg and Alderman – not a trio to be trifled with. The three one-day internationals for the Prudential Trophy allowed the two teams to square up to one another. The 1st, at Lord's, we won by 6 wickets, having put Australia in and had them 4 wickets down at lunch before Allan Border's rousing 73 not out spurred them to 210 for 7. Whereupon Gooch and Boycott got us off to a solid start, I got out lbw for a first-ball duck, Gower restored order and Botham, the captain, clouted his 13 not out, finishing with a couple of huge 6s to put the lid on it.

The 2nd one-day match was at Birmingham, where Australia won a very good game. Put in, they assembled 249, and we fell just 2 runs short of the target. But the story of the day was that I was dropped twice early on, once off Alderman and once off Hogg. We'd had a thunderstorm, when the new Edgbaston covers saved the cricket, and I went on to get 96 and the Man of the Match award on my birthday. We'd wanted 5 an over with 5 wickets in hand, but Botham whacked one straight up in the air and got caught by Hughes, and Willey hit a screamer to deep point, where Wood glued his hands on it. But we were still on course: I was still in, and we needed 10 off the last two overs, and then a boundary off the last over would have seen us home. I hit Lillee's second ball to wide long-off – and I thought it had gone for 4, but Geoff Lawson ran round like a weasel, dived, and caught it 2 ft off the ground.

So that was the end of my 100, and, because Hendrick was caught off the penultimate ball, the end of the match. We nearly did it, but not quite. Still, I was very grateful to have played, at last, an innings for England where my concentration was wound like a watch spring. And it was another reminder that 'catches win matches', too. I might not have played in the 3rd Prudential, or indeed the coming Test, without those two chances early on. Anyway, we went on to the 3rd game, at Headingley, faced a sizable target and sank to our doom, so the Aussies took the Cup 2–1.

The 1st Test was at Trent Bridge, on a lively wicket. Hughes won the toss and put us in, and we struggled to 185. I was on 52 when I was given out lbw to Hogg – I thought it was a bit high. I'd had a torrid time out there because all around me wickets were going down like ninepins, and if I left one alone, all I could hear were 'oohs' and 'aahs' from behind the stumps, interspersed with 'You lucky Pommie!' and 'You spawny sod!' It took me some time to get my 50 because we were in a bit of a state, but the innings gave me the idea that perhaps I'd got the gift of playing in Tests after all.

Then they went in, and there must have been butterflies among the fielders because Downton put down Allan Border, who went on to 63 – I'm afraid that probably cost Paul his place – and there were some other butterfingers as well. The second day, we basically let them off the hook, and they made 179, which should have been more like 125. And that was precisely what we got when we batted again – 125. We kept plugging away, Graham Dilley taking 4 for 24, but there wasn't much of a target for him to bowl at. We lost by 4 wickets. It had all been about dropped catches really.

Both, our skipper, was now under pressure, and questions were raised about his fitness for the job. As fate would have it, in the 2nd Test at Lord's, Beefy collected a pair. The wicket was dry, and turned. Peter Willey got 82 of our first-innings 311, and I hit 59 before getting out lbw to Ray Bright, just before close of play, playing back to one that came on with the arm. At one stage we had them 81 for 4 in reply, but again Border led a recovery, to 345 all out. Then Bright, bowling into the rough, accounted for 3, Lillee collected 3, and we mounted 265 for 8 (I got 16) and declared. We'd set them 232 to make, shortly after lunch on the last day, and they lost 4 wickets before the match ended in a draw.

Botham was upset. He'd suffered a lot of stick, and been offered the captaincy on a piecemeal basis, and now he announced that he wasn't prepared to lead England one match at a time. He resigned. So amid much stir and discussion, we got our Guru back – Mike Brearley returned to captain England again. The atmosphere in the dressing room changed.

Brears, always tactful and sympathetic with his squad, went up to Botham in the nets and said, 'I know how you must feel, Ian. Do you want to play, or would you prefer to rest?'

Both didn't hesitate. 'Of course I want to play. I'm not going to be left out. I'm not going to let them get the better of me.' Both always wanted to give the Aussies a good fight, but now he was champing at the bit.

The Headingley Test wicket looked likely to deteriorate, so Australia, having won the toss, went in. Dyson and Hughes were making hay, and surprisingly, in view of what had preceded the match, Both wasn't bowling very well at all.

Brearley was about to take him off when he said, 'Leave it with me and I'll get you five wickets.' He was a wicket better than his word, finishing with 6 for 95. Australia declared at 401 for 9.

By now, the wicket was quite sporty – we simply hadn't exploited it. Now we were to pay the price. With Lillee exerting all his guile as well as speed, and with Alderman and Lawson keen and quick, we were knocked over for 174 and forced to follow on. Worse was to follow. We sank to 41 for 4 and then slithered even further to 135 for 7, and I hadn't been any help, dismissed for 15 and 1 in the match. At close of play on the Saturday, cushions having been grasped around the ground ready to hurl at the umpires peering in their light meters, the darkest place was the England dressing room. Our spirits were so low, the only consolation we could think of was that this couldn't go on much longer.

On Monday morning we duly arrived with all our kit, ready, we thought, to leave around lunchtime. The bookies were offering 1000–1 on an England victory, and two young punters called Marsh and Lillee thought this was an offer even they couldn't refuse. Only one bloke still harboured funny ideas about the outcome in *our* dressing room. Striding out to bat, Beefy Botham had a peculiar look in his eye. You can never tell what great cricketers are going to do, and you should never write them off until the game is over. With careful support from Dilley, Botham took the Aussie attack by the scruff of the neck and proceeded to thunder and smash his way to 149 not out.

It was one of the most amazing innings any of us will ever see. He had a bit of luck – you needed a bit of luck on this wicket – but everything met the meat of Both's bat, and everything went for miles. When he'd finished with them early on the final morning, England were all out for 356, and Australia, instead of an innings victory, were looking at a small target of 130 to win. It still looked a formality, but somehow the boot seemed to be on the other foot.

We started off badly in their 2nd innings. Willis had been

bowling from the football stand end and was visibly worn out. 'Let me have a go down the wind', he told the skipper. 'I'm an old man now!' And from the Kirkstall Lane end, 'Goose' started roaring in. Sending down an assortment of no balls and snorters, he got amongst the Aussies to finish the match with the best figures of his career, 8 for 43, and reduce them to a parlous 74 for 7. Bob was bowling short and quite fearsomely. I remember thinking, standing at square-leg, thank goodness we're not facing this.

Unfortunately though, Lillee had started to cut and carve, and with Bright up the other end and 35 runs coming in 4 overs, he looked determined to get them the last 18 runs they needed – it was getting very, very tight. Seeing Brears was about to switch the field around, I walked up to him and said, 'Instead of that, why doesn't Bob just try bowling a *length* at Dennis?' An over later Lillee, having faced a few good-length balls and looking decidedly uncomfortable, tried to chip one through mid-wicket, the ball straightened, and I took the catch at mid-on. But it was a near thing because I lost my footing as I went for the catch and only held it as I was about to hit the deck.

Bright was removed by a Willis yorker, and that was it. We'd won by 18 runs. We were back on the road again. We had our Guru back, we had Both ready to bludgeon all and sundry, and Willis bowling like a man with new knees. We'd levelled the Series with a tremendous victory, and we went to Edgbaston keyed up and ready to do business.

In the 4th Test, for the first time, we won the toss and went in, but the wicket did a bit and we weren't able to put our positive ideas into practice. We managed just 189. This was to be a Test in which nobody could reach 50, and I was out for 21, caught by Alderman at 2nd slip, bowled Lillee. Our spirits recovered, though, when we were able to hold them to 258, a lead of just 69 – 44 of those being extras (Willis bowled the amazing number of 28 no balls).

The third day, we batted painfully slowly, grafting for every run. Bright was bowling into the rough and had three of us bowled round our legs – Gooch, Willey and myself (I got 39). So we were able to set them only 151 to win, another feeble target. It says in *Wisden* that our tailenders were 'urged on by the combative Gatting' but I don't remember that. I do remember we were in deep trouble. That evening, Old dismissed Wood, and with two days to play, Australia needed just 142 for victory. Once again we were staring defeat right in the eye. This time, he must surely get us.

The fourth morning, a Sunday, Willis kept us in some sort of contention by getting rid of Dyson and Hughes. But now they were 105 for 4, and Border, unless we could get rid of him very sharply, was going to see them home in style. They only needed 46. Suddenly, Embers had him: the ball lifted, glanced off Border's gloves and I took the catch at short-leg, out for 40.

The mood in the field was now quite amazing. Willey was loosening up, when Brearley changed his mind and called in Botham. And with Emburey bowling tight and turning screws at the other end, Ian Botham ran in and produced this spell of 3 for none. He had Bright lbw, he got Martin Kent bowled off the inside edge, and he bowled Marsh with the perfect yorker. Then Lillee edged one to Taylor, the wicketkeeper, who caught it, juggled with it, and caught it again just off the ground.

Finally, with Botham having rushed in and yorked Terry Alderman, it was all over. We'd won another Test from nowhere by 29 runs, inside four days. It was unbelievable that England should have won at Headingley, having set such a small target, but now we'd done it again. All credit to Botham, we were now two up going into the 5th Test, in which Alan Knott was recalled.

Again, we began badly. The pitch at Old Trafford was greenish, and at the close, England tumbled in the murk to 175 for 9. Next day we would have been in a worse mess had it not been for Paul Allott's 52 not out, finishing with 231. Lillee had bowled me a slow bouncer to get rid of me for 32. I managed to get right round it and paddle it to Border at

2nd slip, so the great bowler had given me another lesson. We hadn't exactly covered ourselves in glory, but then Willis and Botham, ably assisted by Allott, had Australia in a worse mess, all out for 130 to give us a lead of 101.

The third day, though, we seemed to have thrown it all away again with our batting, struggling on 104 for 5. Tavaré had reached another 50, the 3rd-slowest of all time. Then in came Beefy, and he started smashing it around for another ferocious 100. Couldn't do anything wrong. He was hooking Lillee off his nose for 4s and 6s. With gutsy support from Knott and Emburey, Both got us up to 404, setting the Aussies 506 to win. We had them 24 for 2, but then Kim Hughes and Graham Yallop set into us (Yallop hitting a fine century), and they looked set to stave it off. All we could do was to keep chipping away, Willis producing lethal bursts as he had done in their 1st innings. The last day was ticking past, though. Border (123 not out at the finish) and Marsh were still going strong when Willis came back into the attack to remove first Marsh and then Bright.

Time was running out for us. We took the second new ball and Alderman went, lbw to Botham. Now all that stood between us and victory was young Mike Whitney, the left-arm quickie who'd played only six 1st-class games in his life. With just half an hour to go before the close, Willis bowled one short, Whitney prodded forward and I saw it come towards me and gratefully took the catch at short-leg. Up went the ball, up went England. We'd won, we'd won! Victory by 103 runs. The Ashes retained by 3 to 1 for the Series, with only the Oval Test to come.

Those three wins had been quite thrilling to play in: memorable to watch, historic to record. I'll never forget how we felt afterwards, and to this day I can't remember having been involved in three more tense, exciting matches in my career. It was all quite phenomenal, and for one man to have taken such a commanding role in all three reflected on Ian Botham better than any praise. But he had lifted our spirits, and laid waste with the bat whatever they threw at him.

From being 0–1 down, we had been transformed, and the atmosphere in the dressing room had changed completely, because of him – and because of Bob Willis, for it would all have been very different without Bob. Coming back from his third knee operation, when people had really written him off, he had bowled his heart out and been at times truly terrifying to watch.

And so it was that we rolled into the 6th Test match at the Oval, hoping greedily that we might win that one as well. Graham Gooch, who hadn't had a very good Series, had been dropped, which brought in Wayne Larkins, and Gower lost his place to Paul Parker. It was a very good batting wicket, and Australia mounted 352 first innings, Border having led them with a fine undefeated century. Botham got a 'sixfer' (6 wickets in an innings) and Willis removed the other 4. England in reply started strongly (we were 246 for 3), to which Boycott contributed his 21st Test ton, and I added 53.

I was concentrating very hard on not playing at a wide one and building on my 50 like you're supposed to do, but I got out to a fairly straight ball from Lillee that just hit off-stump. They had taken the new ball and I thought Dennis would swing it. But that was bad thinking – I should have concentrated simply on watching the ball. When I got back into the pavilion, a lot of people seemed to follow and we were all out for just 314 – a great shame really. Second dig, we had them struggling at 41 for 3, but then Border and Dirk Wellham, who survived an easy chance off Willis, got them back in the boat and they declared at 344 for 9, setting us to make 383 in a day. We lost Boyx first ball and Tavaré shortly after, but then Wayne Larkins and myself got stuck in and we put on 70 before Wayne was caught at 2nd slip by Alderman off Lillee.

I did much the same sort of thing, out for 56. Still, I'd made a couple more 50s in the match, and it was quite a good delivery from Mr Lillee. We'd felt that we might get somewhere near the target runs, but sadly Lillee and Alderman got amongst us. It took a heroic 70 not out from Alan Knott to save us from further ado – the match ended in a draw. We'd still won the Ashes 3–1. So while the Aussies went home, we went wild.

I was picked on the strength of my efforts that summer to go on yet another tour: this time it was the England trip to India and Sri Lanka. I've never actually asked Brearley why he declined the job of tour captain: probably his new career in the world of psychoanalysis kept him a bit busy in the winter months, although he has a great affection for India and has since married an Indian lady. Anyway, the job of skippering us went to Keith Fletcher, the Gnome of Essex, and vice-captain was Bob Willis. Our pace attack consisted of Bob himself, Botham, Allott, Dilley and Lever, and Geoff Cook was picked as a possible third spinner, with Emburey and Underwood.

Boycott came with us too, but he was to fly home early amid some acrimony on the eve of a rebel tour of South Africa, saying he was mentally and physically fatigued. India was evidently not his cup of tea: in Nagpur, where we stayed two or three to a room, and had some very treacherous curries served to us in tents, Boyx somehow contrived to have Dundee cake flown out to him specially, and he always seemed to have his own supply of tuck. He was very fond of his honey and ginseng, and he might share the odd bit of chocolate with you if you didn't run him out, but otherwise he kept his food to himself. The rest of us ended up living on fried egg and chips in Nagpur – it wasn't a very nice place to stay.

Much more popular with the lads was the West Zone of Baroda, where the Maharaja had a lovely spread, with a cricket pitch and a pond full of crocodiles. We didn't know if this was to improve the determination of the cricket team, but we watched, fascinated, as a little man fed the crocs with huge chunks of meat out of a bucket. There was a lot of splashing and churning as the crocs ripped this meat to shreds and asked for seconds, and when this little waiter turned round, we noticed one of his hands was missing. We naturally assumed that a crocodile must have eaten it off, but no, it turned out that he'd lost it in the war.

The first one-day international, at Ahmedabad, was in November. My hotel room had rather unusual air-conditioning – a hole in the wall with a piece of gauze netting over it. But apart from that, the hotel was quite nice and clean, for which we were grateful. The match was won by England on a slow, low wicket, and in the end it was up to Both and myself to get the winning runs, 15 at 5 an over. You had to be patient because of the wicket, so we agreed between us, no hurry, no problem, we'll make 5 an over. Fine. Whereupon Both smashed them all in one go.

I wasn't selected for the disastrous 1st Test in Bombay. India won by 138 runs after some very controversial umpiring decisions in the 1st innings (one in particular prompting Keith Fletcher to knock his bails off in disgust), which really destroyed us. We'd had discussions before the match about the possibility of such a thing happening, and unfortunately our worst fears were confirmed. There were very large crowds jumping up and down which put everyone under pressure, no-one more so than the umpires.

I found myself picked for the 2nd Test on the strength of a 71 in the drawn game against South Zone, but perhaps too because Fletcher thought we might need an extra batsman to offset any 'unlucky' decisions we might encounter. We played on a very flat wicket at Bangalore, nothing particularly untoward happened, and once we'd amassed 400 first dig (Gatting coming in at number 8 to make 29), Gavaskar replied for 11 hours with his 172 and there was never much chance of a result.

The second one-day international at Jullundur was on a very shiny wicket which reminded me of the West Indies. One expected to make a few on that, and I managed 71 not out in our modest 161 for 7. In our defence we'd been held up by the morning mist and the fact that they bowled 36 overs instead of the allotted 50. They reached their target with only 4 wickets down, thanks to 88 not out from their Man of the

Match Vengsarkar, who played far too well for us. So they went into the 3rd Test in very good heart.

The wicket in New Delhi was flat, and the match was pretty deadly as well, with Boycott (105) and Tavaré (149) grinding away at their chosen speed. I ended up being sent in at number 7, and Fletcher urged me to jolly it along. I had a slog and was bowled by Madan Lal for 5 in our huge 476 for 9 declared. India were in a bit of trouble at 3 down for 89, but then Viswanath came in and played magnificently well for a century which seemed to inspire everyone else in their dressing room. They eventually overhauled our 1st-innings total, and the match ended in a boring draw.

The 4th Test, in Calcutta, had the only wicket that really did anything: it swung. We actually had a glimpse of victory, when we set India to score 306 in just over a day, but fog kept drifting in from a nearby river, and though some considered that you could still see quite adequately, the umpires declined to come out of the pavilion. A few of us thought this so stupid that we sat around on the pitch. India were saved at least 70 minutes' batting time, and once again there was no result. One reason for the string of draws (if you'll pardon the expression) was that the bottom had fallen out of their over rate. They managed an abysmal 13 an hour, and most of that time they had spinners on! Mind you, our over rate wasn't much better.

We went on to Jamshedpur where, in yet another drawn game, against East Zone, I managed to get 127. It was my first 100 for England – after a wait of 4 years which included 3 tours and 17 Tests. (Paul Allott bowled extremely well, taking 5 for 77 in their 1st innings.) It was quite enjoyable, batting in the Zonal matches and coming in, as I did here, at number 3, which gave me a major role in the innings. In the Tests, I'm afraid I had not so much a role as a walk-on part, so I couldn't really contribute.

Perhaps my best chance came in the 5th Test, in Madras, where I was as high as number 6, but this proved a very frustrating occasion for me. Having won the toss, we'd decided to stick them in on what was usually a bouncy wicket, but then we proceeded to put down both Vengsarkar *and* Viswanath. I think we might even have dropped them twice. Unfortunately Tavaré was responsible for two of these chances, and Vishy went on to a pulverizing 222. He was accompanied for quite some time by Yashpal Sharma, who made a quite unbelievable 140 of his own. India totted up 481 for 4 declared. In reply, we accumulated rather a lot ourselves, Goochie being our most splendid contributor with 127 in our 328.

On day four, it started to turn, and at last, after watching all these other prodigious knocks, in I went. No sooner was I there, than I got one from Doshi that turned, hit my pad and went up to Viswanath at slip. Now, Vishy didn't appeal himself, but everyone round the bat went into contortions. So, having come in at my highest slot in the Test order since I'd been in India, I was given out caught at slip by a rueful Vishy for 0, and as I trudged away, he apologized. I was very, very cross, and remember going into the dressing room and quite uncharacteristically throwing my bat at my case and jumping up and down. The match ended in another draw.

Botham got stuck into Central Zone in a drawn game at Indore. He and I had been playing badminton in the evenings to cheer ourselves up, and in this match we had a stand of 137. I was content to keep giving Both the strike as he battered what was thought to be the fastest 100 ever seen – 122 in 55 minutes, including a drinks interval. After he'd gone, I had a little go at the spinners myself and ended up with 111. Then in the deciding one-day international at Cuttack, India beat us by 5 wickets. Fletcher hit a fine 69, and we seemed to be in sight of the flag until that man Gavaskar got in and took us for 71.

The 6th and final Test finished in another soul-numbing draw, the feature of which was a box of balls. We had to face about six new ones altogether, because Kapil Dev felt that they weren't swinging sufficiently, and Both had smashed one out of shape. So he had the whole box out there in the finish. We'd lost the Series 1–0 by virtue of having been beaten in the highly controversial 1st Test, and we were particularly upset and disappointed because of the manner in which that sole result had been obtained. It was small consolation to me to know that I'd had no part in the match, because I always care very much what happens to England, whether I'm playing or not.

We were staying in a hotel in Kanpur as the Indian tour drifted to a close, and we were greatly pleased at the sight of our wives coming out to join us. I remember four or five of us going shopping one day because the ladies had wanted to look at some shoes, and immediately people started following us. By the time we reached the market about half a mile away, there were huge, surging crowds and the shopkeeper had to tell us all to get out before the throng wrecked his premises. I suppose we'd collected about 400 people, all pointing and whispering, 'Oh look, look! That is Sahib Gooch, do you see? Oh look, and it is very wonderful because that is Sahib Gatting! Look, look!'

Elaine Gatting:

Accompanied by Helen Dilley and Helen Allott I arrived in Kanpur not knowing what to expect but not expecting what we found. Cricket being important to Indians we knew we'd be well looked after but I for one did not realize the extremes they would go to. The hotel had actually had a new wing built to accommodate the England party. Mike and I were lucky enough to be given one of the new rooms and as the two Helens and myself arrived before the team, we asked to have our rooms changed to the new wing so we could all be together. Unfortunately we were unaware of the fact that senior players should have first choice of rooms and we were duly reprimanded that first night. I unloaded my bag of requested goodies – paté, long-life cheese, and family-size jars of Branston pickle! The lads took the mickey out of me but it is funny how the goodies soon disappeared to the team room to be shared out! Our first escapade on to the streets of Kanpur along with the Dilleys and Allotts quickly turned into a scramble for the hotel. Shortly after leaving the hotel we had three armed guards behind us and before long they had been joined by an ever-increasing crowd of onlookers. We ventured into a shoeshop and when we were ready to leave we found the exit totally blocked by the crowd, such was their fascination. We then got a horse and buggy back to the hotel.

But once again I saw little of Mike during the tour of India and Sri Lanka, with only a few days spent together. So I learnt that tours were not glorified holidays and as we had to pay my way totally, I began to feel it was not worth the expense. Shortly after our return we decided to start a family and I have not toured since and nor would I. I would rather we saved our money and, when Mike has the time, spend it on family holidays together.

From India, we popped over, if that is the right expression, to the very contrasting Sri Lanka. We stayed in Kandy, half-way up a mountain, which impressed us all, especially the ladies. We went up and down the coast to Colombo and saw the sights, but unfortunately there was no place either for myself or Graham Dilley in the Inaugural Test, so we spent quite a lot of time together as helpless spectators. England at one point lost 7 wickets in collecting 8 runs, and Bob Willis stood in the dressing room lambasting everybody.

'What's going on!' he raged, letting rip. 'We don't want to lose to this lot!' It was very shaming, and seemed to do the trick because we ended up winning by 7 wickets.

So that was the tour of 1981–82. I'd managed to get some 100s in the Zonal matches in India, which gave me a little bit of confidence, though I hadn't seen much service in Tests. Never mind: I was looking forward to 1982, and playing for England at home again.

CHAPTER EIGHT
County Ups and Country Downs
1982

In retrospect, the Indian tour had been one big let-down for me. I felt like the England outsider again, someone you post at short-leg for want of anything better to do with him, someone to send in down the order for a late slog. I had so little chance of a decent Test innings I couldn't do myself justice. No matter what I tried, nothing came off. The cricket was a lot of old draws; it was boring. I was disappointed. It had been a very hard trip altogether for poor Gatt.

What a relief to get back to Middlesex in 1982 and be part of a team again. There was a sort of legacy from the Indian trip in that all the time there had been a lot of secretive to-ing and fro-ing because Boycott was trying to set up a side to go to South Africa and there was a buzz of discussion about whether people should go, and why shouldn't they, and so on. In the end I think the money attracted quite a few players, though to be fair they were also curious and simply wanted to know what it would be like to play over there.

I had turned it down. I felt that in the present climate, with Pakistan and Indian teams due this summer and a little matter of the World Cup later on, the Board would have to ban the South African tourists from playing for England, and I wasn't at all surprised when they all got three-year suspensions. I wanted to play for England – even though I wasn't playing particularly well for England at the moment. For other reasons I hadn't played for Packer either (the main one was that I wasn't good enough), and I'd been at a meeting sometime before this at which I seconded a proposal by Bob Taylor demanding a ban on playing against Packerites appearing in the Pakistan side.

I am aware of many positive things to have come out of Packer's enterprise, but keeping your England place wasn't one of them. I didn't join the rebel tour of South Africa, and neither did Botham or David Gower. But one of the players who did go, under Gooch's captaincy in the spring, was Middlesex vice-captain John Emburey. This meant two things; first that John was banned from England and gave us his invaluable services all season at Middlesex; and secondly he lost his County vice-captaincy – that was passed down to me. It led to my actually captaining Middlesex for one match in 1982, down at Swansea. I'll tell you about that later, because it was quite a game.

This was to be Mike Brearley's last season with Middlesex; he left cricket in September to concentrate on other things, and Middlesex played very, very well and gave him a rousing send-off. We started off on Brears' fortieth birthday against Cambridge University, which happened to be his *alma mater*, and where Stephen Henderson became the first bloke to make 200 against Middlesex in a university game – and he did it in a minute under 4 hours as well. They declared at 380 for 6, we declared 149 behind, and then they set us to make 292 to win in 3½ hours – and we won quite easily. I managed to get 164 not out second knock, and we went out that evening with Steve Henderson and had a few beers.

We hadn't had much to eat and the drinking went on late into the night, so we rounded off with coffee but I was worried about my car being parked up the road on a double yellow line so I thought I'd better move it or I might get nicked. Unfortunately the police saw me and I got nicked anyway. They thought perhaps I was trying to steal my own car so I was breathalysed and lost my licence. This was Cambridge, where I was arrested as a lad for joy-riding on a girl's bike!

A battle with Essex followed which the rain tried to ruin, but by means of declarations and forfeitures we turned it into a very good game of cricket – all credit to Brears and Fletcher for being such enterprising skippers. Middlesex were set 348 and I think Fletcher thought that a fair old target but we were going great guns when I got out for 90, still 128 short. The advantage had apparently swung tantalizingly towards Essex, but John Emburey batted magnificently well, which was to be a feature of this season, and Neil Williams, on his debut, hooked a 6 off Norbert Phillip and the winning boundary off Lever to see us home by 2 wickets. No point in having boring draws!

Embers got a very fine 100 not out in our 9-wicket victory over Northants at Lord's: his batting really did look rather polished these days, and Brears struck 165 as well. I got out cheaply to Jim Griffiths, a sort of swing bowler who seemed to put the mockers on Middlesex and always got amongst us, even on a slow track. Still, two consecutive wins for us at Lord's couldn't be bad.

Our next game belonged to Wilfred Slack, who pulverized Oxford University for 203 not out to bring us a thumping victory by an innings and 107 runs. I was down at Lord's playing in a drawn game versus the Indians for MCC, in which "Arkle" Randall welcomed himself back on the scene with 130 not out and I didn't do a lot.

Then there was a funny old match against Sussex at Lord's. It was seaming about and Imran was rushing in and Nick Kemp was a bit apprehensive because we were relying on him second knock and there were a lot of giggles in the dressing room as he wandered out into Immy's onslaught, perhaps never to be seen again. But he did us proud, did Kempy, and Edmonds and Embers wrapped it up for us. Philippe took 8 for 80 – and I took a few catches at short-leg. We won by 68 runs – so we won our first three Championship games at Lord's.

Against Derby we were asked for a mammoth 348 in 247 minutes. We had been hoping they'd set us a fairly sensible target but they kept batting and batting, and I think in the end we tried to give them some runs to get rid of them. Middlesex went after it, as we usually do, but rain interfered and in the end we only managed a draw.

I holed out when we were very close. I was having a go at Steve Oldham, though Embers and Phil Edmonds had given me fine support in my 140. I remember one of the shots that *Wisden* says I 'blazed off', though. It was one of those strange unexpected ones which rocket off my bat occasionally without my knowing what hit them. People actually come up afterwards and say 'How on earth did you manage to hit it there?' I really couldn't tell you. I find it quite phenomenal myself.

This particular UFO came about when Dallas Moir, a left-arm spinner, was trying to fire it into the blockhole and all of a sudden I found myself somehow punching this 6 into the Pavilion. People couldn't believe how it got in there off a low full toss, almost a yorker.

I can remember feeling very disappointed when rain robbed us of 2 overs, because we nearly got that mammoth target: and I think we were a bit annoyed with Peter Kirsten, the opposition skipper, for making us go after it and play silly shots in the end, which almost gave them a freak victory. That would have been a travesty, I think. Opposition captains deliberately set Middlesex impossible targets knowing full well we will try and climb every mountain, especially when we are on top of the table as we were here. We ended up just 8 short but I don't think any other side would have gone after them.

Anyway I had a happy match against Kent on a club wicket with a little bit of bounce in it, at Tunbridge Wells. I found myself hitting all these 6s over long-off or long-on against 'Deadly' Derek Underwood, and they sailed into the rhododendron bushes round the ground. It was quite a quick 100 that I got, and I can still see these mauve-coloured rhododendrons, and 'Deadly' standing there with his little fists clenched at his sides, saying, 'If I hadn't have flipping well bowled at you in the nets in India, you wouldn't have been able to do that!' It was probably the first time I'd ever felt at home against Underwood's bowling. It was a great, happy match, in which Wayne and Philippe did Kent some harm,

Rad got a ton, and we disabled them by an innings and 72 runs.

I remember going to a Benefit there one evening, and getting well soused with Graham Dilley who like me was keen to get back into the swing of things after the Indian tour. We drank about a vat of port between us, and have been firm friends ever since. In the match, I recall sticking a mitt out and catching something to dismiss Derek Aslett off Wayne Daniel; I got a bit carried away, telling people I'd caught it despite being legless the previous night, and I received a bit of a telling-off from Brears.

He said, 'I don't care how many drinks you had, but if you'd dropped it I'd have given you a rocket. Don't be bloody silly!' So I learned a lesson there, which was – 'If you've had a few, keep quiet and don't tell the captain.'

We were still top of the table. The team was playing exceptionally well and I was enjoying myself more than I'd ever done in my life because I was in good order and I felt really proud and happy to be part of it all. Our confidence just seemed to flow together. We could rely on one another. If one person missed out on runs or wickets, someone else would pitch in. We were rolling, and Edmonds and Emburey were spinning. So we went to Swansea on a high, to meet the Welshmen, and I happened to be made Middlesex captain for the first time because Mrs Brears was having a baby and Mike had gone down to London to be with her, and Philippe Edmonds was also absent on Test duty.

Glamorgan having won the toss and batted, Embers suggested I have a bowl. We ended up bowling them out for 191 and I took 5 for 34, including the wicket of Javed Miandad with the help of a great catch by Radley in the gully. I wasn't even bowling in boots, as it was a lovely hot day and I didn't think I'd be needed. So I got my first 'fivefer' in flats! We got off to a poor start in our 1st innings but then Butch got a magnificent 122 and the two of us managed to add 195 together. I was going stupid, tried one too many after tea on the second day, and was out for 81. We finished on 352.

Then we all watched in amazement as Wayne Daniel came as close as I've ever seen anyone come to takings 10 wickets in an innings. It was a superhuman effort, in two tremendous spells, and he was only denied by Rodney Ontong being run out from cover. Wayne finished with 9 for 61. So then Graham Barlow and Wilf Slack knocked off the runs we needed and we won by 10 wickets. But that was Wayne at the Mumbles. He just kept on wanting to bowl.

With victory number 7 salted away, we had a drawn game against Yorkshire, and having bowled all winter at Boycott in the nets in India – sometimes reluctantly – I got him out here. It was magnificent! There were 13 lbws in that match; the umpires were giving everybody out. Wayne got a 'sixfer' and even Boyx got a wicket somewhere. There was another rained-off draw against Lancs at Lord's mid-June, which was memorable for me.

Lancashire had put together 280 with a powerful 93 from Lloyd, and then Colin Croft went to work on us, and we were fighting for our lives at 24 for 3 when Butcher and I went to the wicket. We were on and off for bad light and rain, and a bit surprised by the pace and bounce, and we were hit once or twice initially. It reminded us of the time Croft hit Ian Gould on the head.

Butch and I had a chat in the middle, and then Butch went back and suddenly the pair of us were cutting and carving and ducking and weaving, and we added 178 in 35 overs – and half of those were overs bowled by Paul Allott who was not going for very many up the other end. We were offered bad light at one stage but decided to stay out and keep whacking it. There were very few people in the crowd but those who were there really enjoyed it.

It was one of the most exhilarating bits of cricket I can ever remember, because the adrenalin was flowing and I was really pumped up. You could see the whites of Colin Croft's eyes popping out on the old stalks every time he disappeared over the boundary, as if he couldn't believe what was going on. Butch finished up with 82, and I was on 133 not out when rain ruined a good match.

While I was on the march with Middlesex, India were here for a Test series, and by the end of June, so were the Pakistanis. Middlesex played Pakistan in a rain-affected draw, but we were struggling, to put it mildly, against a very determined Imran. Anyway we put that behind us and went to the Oval where it was Middlesex *v.* Surrey *v.* the weather and three declarations and frantic chases couldn't force a result – but I managed to get 192, my highest score to date.

I was out with 1 over to go on the second evening, trying to pull Sylvester Clarke and not quite getting hold of it, caught at mid-wicket. One shot sticks in my mind. Sylvester, having bowled very sharp and short, actually pitched one up, and I went back and across without knowing how, and I let the bat go through and seemed to time it just right, and it went over his head and bounced once on its way to the boundary.

I also remember bowling in that match at Monte Lynch, who liked going back and across as well. I normally bowl away-swingers – or try to – but I thought I'd bowl him an in-swinger and Monte was out, plumb as you like. It was nearly as nice as getting the 192, but not quite. I was *so* pleased to be having such a good season with the bat. Every time I went to the wicket I really did feel that if I played straight I was going to get some runs. I just couldn't wait to get out there!

Then we had to play Leicester on 7 July and we were lucky enough to lose to them by 6 wickets – our first defeat of the season. It augured very well indeed for our Championship hopes, but the truth was that Brian Davison had stood up and struck us all over Uxbridge. We were doing rather well in the other competitions, having had only one defeat – our Bensons quarter-final against Lancashire on 16 June. We weren't to lose a match in the Sunday League until 18 July. Next, we played Notts back-to-back, at Nottingham and Lord's, and twice we won by an innings. The first game Brearley batted exceptionally well for 135, and I managed to keep him company in a stand of 164, getting 96. The slow left-arm spinner Bore came on and bowled little in-swingers as well to try to confuse us – and, to my disappointment, he got me out lbw. I got 3 wickets for 15 in the 2nd innings – but I don't remember that! All our blokes chipped in: Norman Cowans took 3 and Slacky took 1 as well. The second match we beat them by an even greater margin though I was absent by that time, on Test duty, and my replacement, Keith Tomlins, got his maiden 100, which was great work from Tommo.

I missed quite a few of Middlesex's games now because I was picked to play against Pakistan for England on the strength of my County form. But I was in a few intriguing matches on the home stretch. At Southend in a drawn County game, Paul Downton was struggling so much with a hamstring injury that he forgot he had a runner, hopped up the other end, and was given out for being out of his ground. We beat Somerset by an innings at Weston-super-Mare on a very dodgy wicket with the ball rearing off a length – fortunately for us Joel Garner was injured and unable to bowl on it.

Against Yorkshire, in another drawn game, Butcher and I had another whack – we seemed to spark each other off this season. Butch, having come fresh from his 173 against Gloucester, was obviously in very good order himself, and he played a mighty knock up the other end, and whether they bowled short or pitched it up, it didn't make a lot of difference. We put on 237 in the twilight (we didn't mind the light) and I managed to get 141 before being stumped off Carrick. But Butch kept on going and kept on hooking, and in the end he was very unlucky to be run out on 197 – but a very good knock indeed, before the rain came down and saved the Yorkies.

I missed a match against Surrey, in which Brearley's gambling tactics managed to fabricate a win out of nothing and Fred Titmus bowled, and I missed a loss to Sussex at Hove by 3 wickets. But I was there for the last two crucial games of the season when we were chasing points.

We met Hampshire at Uxbridge where we had two seamers

and three spinners (in Edmonds, Emburey and Dermot Monteith) and Philippe took 6 for 48 in their 1st innings. Despite the presence of Malcolm Marshall, myself and Brears got 50s second innings, and we beat them in a low-scoring game by 106 runs, which meant that we went down to Worcester needing just 4 points for the Schweppes County Championship.

Now, the thing I remember about *this* game was that Philippe Edmonds had been given a bat by Duncan Fearnley. He'd been to the factory and come back with this unfinished piece of wood, and he played as never before seen, hitting the bowlers back over their heads, when we'd been in a spot of trouble replying to their 168. Both Philippe and Butch clouted 90s, I managed 61, and we compiled 382 and then it was just a question of trying to wiggle them all out.

By the time I was called upon to bowl, taking 4 for 43, we'd already done it – we'd secured our 4 points and we were County Champions again, but we needed to bat again to make 50 to win the match, and fittingly, in his last game as captain of Middlesex, Brearley hit the winning runs. Whatever was passing through his mind as he left the field that misty evening, he couldn't have asked for a better send-off.

In the limited-overs competitions we were always in contention until the closing stages. In our Bensons group we won four out of four preliminaries including our Somerset fixture, thanks to Neil Williams' bowling, but then lost to our bogey side, Lancs, in the quarter-final, having made only 139 (Rad got 66 of those). In the NatWest we were keen to get our revenge at Lord's in the second round, and beat Lancashire by 2 runs, with Colin Croft trying to hit 3 off the last ball and not managing it.

We played very well against Gloucester, and managed to squeak past them, stumping Chris Broad trying to make the winning runs, but then in the semi-final, fiery Sylvester Clarke did us, and we lost by a long way. I remember nicking the ball onto my thigh pad and getting caught at short-leg off Sylvester for 6.

But in the John Player we were fairly roaring along, 6

points clear by the end of June, and unfortunately we ended up losing a couple on the trot. We lost to Sussex, the eventual League Champions, in a crunch game at the end of August. But still, we managed to win something for Brears in the shape of the County title, and we finished second in the John Player, so we were all very chuffed and happy.

Brears had been a great captain. Rodney Hogg said, 'I think he's got a degree in people,' and I think that was a very apt tribute. Brears was a very respected man, both on and off the field, and it was very sad to see him go.

The Pakistan Series wasn't particularly memorable for me, to be honest, although we won the two one-day internationals – the 1st by 7 wickets and the 2nd by 73 runs at Manchester. I got 76 up there and was Man of the Match, which was nice. I remember Both and I taking it out on the little left-arm spinner Iqbal Qasim and we put on 84 in 11 overs. We totalled 295 for eight, and they were never going to get them. So I was actually quite confident going into the 1st Test match at Birmingham. And what did I do? Got out twice to a bloke called Tahir Naqqash for the sum total of 22 runs.

The first time I think I dragged one on, and the second time I played at a wide one. I was very, very cross with myself. Why did I always do this for *England*? If I were playing for Middlesex and nicked one, it wouldn't carry, or I'd have a bit of luck, but in a Test you could guarantee I'd do something rotten and have no luck whatsoever. Perhaps it was nerves; perhaps it was because I didn't feel a part of the team. In all events I didn't play very well. England won without me, by 113 runs.

The 2nd Test was at Lord's and this time Pakistan turned us over by 10 wickets thanks to Mohsin Khan's tremendous 200. I managed to get 32 not out in our 1st innings and got us to within 2 of avoiding the follow-on, after they had declared at 428 for 8, but Qadir took 4 for 39 and 2nd knock Mudassar could do no wrong and wiped out 6 of us for 32. Destroyed us totally, despite solid knocks from Tavaré and Botham. Mudassar bowled me something I would normally despatch for 4, which I managed to nick to the keeper, Wasim Bari, for 7. What a fiasco.

So off we went to the 3rd and final Test at Leeds. Willis was back in charge after injury, Gower having captained the 2nd Test, and it's probably true to say that Willis wasn't one of my greatest fans and advocates. It was a very trying period for me, because I was thinking to myself, when am I ever going to get a good knock for England? Why can't I get that little bit of luck? Why can't I be in the frame of mind I'm in at Middlesex, where I can go out to bat confident that if I play straight I won't get out? Still I just had to keep plugging away, but it was very unsettling, and so frustrating.

The only good thing about the 3rd Test, from my point of view, was that we won by 3 wickets. I had been moved up the order to No. 3, gone in, got settled, and then got out to Imran for 25, lbw, and I did it twice! I'd become so paranoid by now that I'd developed a fault, moving my foot across slightly without meaning to. Total frustration had set in. I do remember catching their last man out: it was the Stick Insect Sikander Bakht, off Marks, and there was a bit of an uproar because they didn't think he'd hit it. I watched the replays afterwards and I was inclined to agree.

At the end of that Series, though we did manage to win it 2-1, people were doubting me. I could hear the whispers. 'What *is* Gatting doing playing for England?' Or a bit more sympathetically, 'That Gatting can do it for Middlesex – why can't he do it for England? Is it because he freezes? What's the matter with the bloke?' I think what I needed, more than anything, was just a little bit of luck.

I was after all in the best frame of mind that I would probably ever be in, playing at the top of my game for a champion team; for the second consecutive year I was the highest-ranking English batsman in the national averages. I was getting regular 100s for Middlesex, which gave me the feeling I might make a top-line County player – though you could never afford to get above yourself and the main thing is consistency, because that's what earns the respect of your fellow-professionals.

So now I would be setting myself stiffer targets, averaging 50-plus if I could, because I'd done it in 1982, averaging 58.96, with 1651 runs. And what had given me a special boost that season was reaching 1000 runs before anybody else. That meant a great deal to me because it's not easily done these days, with all the one-day stuff. I'd even managed to get the fastest televised Sunday 50 at one point, down at Weston-super-Mare, which was nice because I was beginning to wonder if the television cameras were affecting my batting. Poor old Vic Marks copped the brunt of it, and they gave me a very nice little run chart to keep.

So I'd had, by any standards, a fair old season. And I was hugely disappointed, when they announced the team to go to Australia, that I wasn't in it. I suppose this was because I hadn't played well against Pakistan. I think the fact that Willis was captain might have had something to do with it as well. They were taking Geoff Cook, Graeme Fowler and Chris Tavaré, Derek Randall and obviously Botham and Allan Lamb. Gouldie was reserve wicketkeeper and Norman Cowans won a berth for his fine bowling for us at Middlesex. He'd come up to me at Worcester and told me the marvellous news, and I was thrilled for him.

But I think one of the worst moments of my life was when, in that last Championship game, I was in the slips next to Brearley, and the tannoy gave out all the England names without me among them. I'd had a kind of gut feeling that I might not get in, but when the public announcement came like that, and I was left out, I felt sick inside. Brears talked me through it – he was a very good psychologist and guessed what I must be feeling. I'd been to Australia three times and successfully captained an Australian side, and if I had one dream, it was playing in a Test in Australia, and getting a lot of runs like "Arkle" did that night I fell asleep on his floor.

Listening to that tannoy announcement was so awful that when I was England captain, I tried to let the guys know beforehand whether they're picked or not. They're all spread out over the countryside, and you've only got 40 minutes at lunch and 20 minutes at the tea interval, so it's very difficult. But I think one should make the effort really. Because when I heard those names broadcast, for about half an hour I was sick to my stomach. It really hurt.

So I ended up staying at home that winter, tending the sports shop. Business was brisk and I was putting in a lot of hours and playing a bit of football at weekends. Steve had transferred to Brighton and Hove Albion, and his career was going well. The biggest thing in *my* life at the moment, apart from the shop, was that Elaine was going to have a baby, and I wanted to be with her for the birth.

Elaine Gatting:

When Mike wasn't picked to go to Australia he was hurt. Ever since he first went to Balmain he'd always talked about going out there and getting a 100 for England. Everybody kept telling him that he had never scored his Test 100, which seemed to be the magic figure. Anyway I was expecting a baby (Andrew) and we went to a party and Mike complained of a stomach ache. In the middle of the night after we'd got back to the flat, his pain got so bad that we called the doctor out and he diagnosed gallstones. They wanted Mike to go into hospital. He couldn't lie down, and for two nights he slept upright in a chair, but they gave him some treatment which settled him down a bit, though we were still very worried about him.

The next Saturday, off he went to watch football. I was getting ready to go to my brother's party that evening, and when Mike came home *I* started complaining of a stomach ache. My pain got very severe as well, and in my case it turned out to be acute appendicitis. So there was Mike recovering from his gallstones, and here was I being rushed into hospital for an emergency appendectomy at five months pregnant.

So the two of us were ill. Poor Elaine was the more worrying because she was pregnant, though I have to say that even getting hit on the nose by Malcolm Marshall didn't hurt like those gallstones – it was the most painful thing I'd ever experienced, and I was violently sick after I'd been given the medicine, and the doctor had to come back and give me another lot. So it wasn't our week, what with Elaine going to have her appendix out, and we were very worried that we might actually lose the baby, though I thought – better to lose the baby than lose Elaine.

I think in the end it was all very difficult medical decision, but they simply had to go ahead and operate. Then of course her stitches were trying to keep her tummy together, and the baby was trying to expand it; she was really in an awful lot of pain.

It was not long after this, when, on the Friday before Christmas, I got a phone call, to say that Derek Randall had been injured, and the management in Australia wanted me to go out and join them on stand-by. What was I to do? 'Can I phone you back in an hour?' I heard myself saying, and put the phone down and rang Elaine, who was recuperating at her mother's.

Elaine Gatting:

> My instant reaction was to burst into tears. They wanted him to fly out on Christmas Eve. Mike didn't know what to do, and in the end my brother phoned me up and said, 'We've got a very upset man here.'

I think I'd already made up my own mind, really. I wasn't going to go. It was a painful, confusing, emotional decision. I was going to stay with Elaine and be with her when the baby came. So they asked Trevor Jesty, who had been put on stand-by in my place due to my illness. In my view I should never have been asked, as Trevor was the player on stand-by for the tour. Nobody made a great fuss over it, apart from a local newspaper. I wouldn't have done myself justice in any case: I wasn't fit and I hadn't been practising, as I was trying to get the shop off the ground.

We moved back with Elaine's mum, into the big house, because we knew it would be much nicer for the kiddy than living in a flat with no garden, and very often, while I was off playing cricket, no dad either. Elaine's mum, Jean, was still doing all the book-keeping for the shop, and because she was helping me more and more with all my correspondence, too, her husband having been a cricket club secretary, Jean sort of 'joined the staff', and became my secretary as well. It certainly helped me a lot to have her dealing with complicated enquiries so efficiently.

I was having a busy time of it as well, because in November, while I was coaching at the Finchley Indoor School and playing for Park Street Football Club in a local Hertfordshire league, I was appointed captain of Middlesex, succeeding Mike Brearley. I'd learned a lot, playing under Brears, but he had unique gifts as a captain, and there wasn't any point trying to emulate him. What I was hoping to do was to maintain the excellent team spirit in the side and make the most of our rich resources. I told reporters after the appointment that, if I made tactical mistakes, at least they would be bold ones.

'You can't win Championships,' I said, 'unless you're prepared to lose a few games on the way.'

CHAPTER NINE
The Captaincy Business
1983

It was quite a funny feeling being made captain of Middlesex. Fortunately, not being away on tour, I had three months to get used to the idea instead of being hurled in at the deep end. I could do some ground work, talk to people, and sort out in my own mind what needed to be done. Ambitions go up step by step, but I'd always wanted to captain a County side. Not that I wouldn't have gone on in my happy way playing for Middlesex and giving 110 per cent for Middlesex like I'd always done without being captain; but once you're established in a side, the next thing is that you want to try and help other people.

I was aware that a lot of discussion had gone on about Brearley's rightful successor. Earlier of course most of us thought that John Emburey would be the natural choice, but when John had blotted his copybook over the South Africa business, not informing the Committee properly about his plans, I think in the end I'd become captain by default. Having a chat with Embers about it was going to be a bit of a hurdle, but I went and talked to him anyway.

I said, 'Look, Ernie, I know you should have been captain, but at least you're still going to be vice-captain, and we've got to try and make the most of it. We've still got a very good team, and we can still win things.'

John took it very well, but I don't think Phil Edmonds was exactly thrilled skinny. Even when they originally picked John, he was of the opinion that he should have been captain, and he was a bit upset. And then when John came under scrutiny over South Africa, he thought that his chance had come, and when I was picked that upset him a bit more. He suspected, too, that the reason he hadn't been chosen was that Brearley probably hadn't recommended him.

It was a big step, taking over from someone like Brears, and I remember having a brief chat with him about what I should and shouldn't do. There would obviously be people watching my decisions now and comparing them with what Brearley would have done because he was such a great skipper and an astute tactician. I'd listened to him thinking aloud – 'Let's try this; we'll tinker around here, they're not expecting that.' And he would also blame himself if his hunches hadn't come off. When you're captain, you do tend to blame yourself.

Elaine Gatting:

Even before Mike was captain, it had always been his fault if they lost. There are times when he comes home cross that they didn't win – not bad-tempered exactly, but saying, 'We should have won that' – and it's always because of some shortcoming of *his*. He might have scored 95 or 195, and they might all have got ducks, but it's still never anybody else's fault that they didn't win; only his fault.

Mike Brearley:

He does have natural gifts for the job: I don't think he was a wonderfully astute tactician but he's no-one's fool, and he is willing to think about things, and modify. He's a straightforward person; he's hardworking, he's enthusiastic, he's conscientious, he's keen, he's willing to practise, he thinks other people should practise, he's willing to listen, he's got ideas – and all these things would immediately be evident as captain of a cricket team.

Now, I haven't really been close enough to know how much he's learnt; I know he has learnt to deal with difficult people, and to deal with criticism. I thought that he had learned to be more tactful – but then he went to Pakistan. I remember in his first year at Middlesex he was a bit unpopular with the groundstaff because he complained about them not getting the field dry on time, and about the pitches that didn't suit him. I think that he later realized that it wasn't as simple as he'd thought, and I think he's learnt to be less bull-at-a-gateish about things.

When I talked to Brears that day about the skipper job, what he said basically was 'It's yours now, not mine. I've finished. But if you ever get a real problem, just phone me.' I appreciated that. I realized that I had, like Ol' Blue Eyes, to 'do it my way'. I couldn't do it Brears' way – because I wasn't Mike Brearley. My biggest hurdle was going to be earning people's respect and trying to communicate with team members without jarring their feelings; explaining sensitive things like loss of form, and selection, assessing their reactions, and seeing how they were going to take my leadership – because I was going to be totally different from Brears. I thought all in all the best thing to do would be to try and just be myself. I should do the things that felt right to me, and at the same time, try and get people involved.

I had more reasons for celebration at the start of 1983. Our first child was born on 21 January by Caesarean section, a bouncing boy weighing 8 lb 5 oz.

Elaine Gatting:

It was five o'clock in the morning when I first went into labour with Andrew. I woke Mike up and told him and he promptly turned over. It hadn't registered. Eventually, at half past seven, I got up and had a cup of tea. The pains were getting progressively worse. Finally at about nine, I said to Mike, 'I've *got* to go into hospital,' and he said, 'Well, you can't have it now. I've got to do coaching at the cricket school!'

Andrew turned out to be a sleepless baby, and I'd usually be the one to get up and attend to him. Mike would do it occasionally, but very often he wasn't here, because he'd be off playing cricket, and when he *was* here, there were times, particularly in the middle of the night, when Andrew wouldn't allow his father near him – he'd scream.

Like father, like son, I suppose, because I was always awake, screaming and yelling when I was a baby. Anyway, Andrew has grown up into a very clever little boy now, working on his word processor at the age of four – he could probably have done this book for me really.

In May 1983 Brighton and my brother Steve got to the FA Cup Final against Manchester United. I didn't think they'd done the best by Steve at Arsenal; players were brought in from outside and he had never really had the chance to establish himself, but now he seemed to have settled down very well with Brighton and though they weren't a fashionable club at the time, at least they'd given him a chance. Steve had nearly made it to Wembley when Arsenal had played in the 1979 Final.

Now Brighton had got past Sheffield Wednesday, with Steve in the back four, and they'd made it on to the hallowed turf. Of course, superstitious as I was about watching my brother's matches and not wanting to put the mockers on him, I *had* to go to Wembley. It was rather amazing. I suppose if Steve were to wander with me into the middle of a Cup Final at Lord's he might feel as I did that day. I'd been to Wembley a few times, but never round the back, or in the dressing rooms, or out on to the sacred turf itself. I'd always been just one face in the crowd of 40 or 50,000.

The Cup Final crowd was quite a sight from the middle. I've played in front of big crowds at Lord's, where they're almost on top of you, but here it was like a huge bowl of humanity, and the noise was phenomenal. Down on the pitch, Steve was wandering about much as I would do at Lord's without any sign of nerves at all. Whereas I was in a *terrible* state, and I wasn't even playing! In fact, I wasn't sure how I was going to survive the next ninety minutes.

Steve Gatting:

> He's always been nervous watching me play football, and when I see him play cricket *I* get very uptight, willing him to do well. That's why I don't really watch him that much. Every time I'm there, he never seems to get any runs! So I keep out of the way now and watch it on telly. But before the Wembley Cup Final, they interviewed the two of us out on the pitch, and afterwards he told me I didn't seem nervous at all. Whereas he was shaking like a leaf, especially during the game. I suppose it's less nerve-racking actually to be in the action.

Sitting up in the stands as a member of the crowd, you sometimes say to yourself, Crikey – if I couldn't do better than that I'd give up, don't you? Everybody does it, and it's the same with cricket. If I play a bad shot they all think, Christ, if I couldn't play a better shot than that, I'd shoot myself. It always looks so easy from the stands. But it was a funny feeling watching Steve. Fortunately, in that first Final, he had a great game and he really played well, so I walked out of the stadium all excited and ten feet tall, and Brighton should really have won it and carried away the Cup that day: I'd have been *so* happy for Steve. But unfortunately they had to have a replay, and by this time the Middlesex season had started. I'll tell you what happened when we come to that. Certainly 1983 was turning out to be a great year.

In 1983, too, I was made one of *Wisden's* Cricketers of the Year – that can only ever happen to you once, and it was very nice to be appreciated. I wasn't picked for the early Test matches against New Zealand. I was becoming either a last resort or a troubleshooter for the England selectors. When all else had failed, they would eventually 'send for Gatts'! But I was picked for the Prudential World Cup squad, and that was of paramount importance to the start of my cricket season. Even having been made Middlesex captain, I was still very, very keen to do well for England.

The World Cup took up the best part of three weeks in

June. It was an eight-team, 60-overs-a-side competition. We began at the Oval, against New Zealand, where we got off to a reasonable start, 117 for 3, and myself and Allan Lamb made 115 in 16 overs. Lamb's 102 was a brilliant knock. Towards the end we were running ridiculous 2s to people at long-on – it was a great feeling, rushing up and down the wicket, and trying to help Lamby get on with it, and smashing a few myself. England ended up with 322 for 6, far too many for New Zealand, and we'd won our first game.

Then we had to play Sri Lanka, at Taunton. David Gower batted magnificently well for 130, and I got run out for 7. I'd played a stroke to backward square-leg, gone for a second run, and ended up halfway down the wicket, seeing David hadn't moved at all. Shaggy kept whacking it into the new stand, though, and in the end Sri Lanka were looking at 334, which they didn't get.

Then we played Pakistan at Lord's, and I remember Bob Willis racing in and knocking over two batsmen in a fine opening spell, and they struggled to 193 for 8. I didn't have to bat that game because Graeme Fowler opened and got a very good 78 not out, Gower got 48, and Lamby knocked them off, so we won by 8 wickets. After which we had to play New Zealand at Birmingham. David had another fine knock, but I didn't, our tail didn't wag, and we lost by 2 wickets. We did, however, beat the Pakistanis at Manchester. Graeme Fowler, on his own stomping ground, put on 115 for the 1st wicket with Chris Tavaré, I got in at the death and got 14 not out and Lamby and David got some runs, so we managed to win that comfortably and then we rolled over Sri Lanka at Leeds, to qualify for the semi-finals.

The wicket at Manchester for England *v.* India, was one of the slowest and lowest we'd played on. We got off to a fairly good start, having won the toss and decided to bat, but then we got tied down by their slow bowlers. Amarnath caused particular problems, and there were a couple of run outs and a bit of dawdling. Lamby and myself got into a tangle after he swept one round the corner, I shouted for a single, and the bloke at short fine-leg scored a direct hit at Allan's end. I got bowled for 18 by one that nipped back from Amarnath, and we were going very badly until Graham Dilley lifted us to a goodish 213 all out. Then Bob Willis and the speed merchants ran in, to no avail, as India batted us to death by 6 wickets.

The Final was a phenomenal win by India over the West Indies – a classic case of underdogs playing well in a one-day match, struggling to a modest total and then fretting the West Indies out. My own performance in the World Cup, I thought, was reasonable though the biggest disappointment obviously was the semi-final where I ran Allan Lamb out and didn't play very well. We shouldn't really have lost to India, but I think the Manchester wicket suited them better than us; had we played at Leeds, or the Oval, I think it would have been a different story.

Getting back to Middlesex, we had a very wet start to the season but the side really ran itself, and it was great to have Ernie there all the time I was in the Prudential (he had been banned from the England side). He had the respect of all the players, and he did a great job. The fact that I was away probably helped settle him down because it meant that he was doing the captaining, which is what, probably, he should have been doing in the first place.

After two rain-affected draws, and two completely abandoned matches, we soundly thrashed Glamorgan at Lord's. Slacky and Rad piled up some runs; I got 94, caught and bowled – I still hadn't got 100 against Glamorgan – and Wayne sent Javed Miandad down a real snorter which was caught off the glove just past his nose.

On the second day of the match against Glamorgan (26 May) we had them in a perilous state, and we could have played the extra half an hour, but I had got tickets for myself, one of the other players and the umpires Bird and White for the FA Cup Final Replay at Wembley, featuring my remarkable brother. We'd ordered two cabs for 7 o'clock to zoom to the stadium for the 7.45 kick-off, and as the cabs were outside the Grace Gates, I didn't enforce the follow-on.

The Middlesex lads said, 'Yes, Skip, and if it rains tomorrow we're going to kill you' – because obviously we might have knocked 3 or 4 wickets over that evening.

I said, 'Won't rain tomorrow, lads! Be all right. I've just got to go and see Steve.'

So the four ticket-holders jumped in these cabs which fought their way through the traffic as far as Wembley station, and then Dickie Bird and myself and the other two were puffing and panting up Wembley Way with about five minutes to go before kick-off. We got there in time to hear a massive cheer go up, and we struggled to our seats – which weren't as good as I'd been led to believe but weren't too bad – and away they went.

Unfortunately from my brother's point of view, Steve Foster had come back into the side. Brother Steve is basically a very good left-footed player, and Gary Stevens and he had kept tabs on Whiteside and Stapleton last time, and they played them out of the game. But because Foster had come back into the middle of the Brighton defence, they'd dropped one of the full-backs and moved Steve to right-back, and I'm afraid he was in the wrong place.

In the end, United won 4–0. It was a shame because things didn't seem to go Brighton's way and it was a bit one-sided. I was *so* sorry because, having been in a Cup Final with Middlesex at Lord's and won, I knew what that felt like and I wanted so much for Steve to do the same thing in his sport.

Not so long after that, he had a very serious pelvic injury, and then Brighton went down to the 2nd Division, and just sort of faded away. I really felt Steve could have done a little better with all his talent than he has. He was simply in the wrong place at the wrong time. Still, not that many footballers *get* to a Cup Final, so he's got that feather in his cap and there are still three or four more years left for him, so things might change. I hope they do, for Steve's sake.

So then it was back to Middlesex, a little sadder, a little

wiser. We beat Glamorgan comfortably by an innings and 79 runs, so no harm done there. Then we drew against Sussex at Lord's, because the weather messed it up (I got a century and a duck), and then at Dartford in the Kent match the wicket helped both seamers and spinners. Bob Woolmer got smashed on the toe early on, and hung around for the rest of the match, hobbling to a very good 118. What with that and a very annoying, improvised 92 from Knotty, I just didn't know where to put the fielders.

In the 2nd innings, though, I would almost like to suggest we out-thought them a bit, setting up a fairly complex trap to catch Knott out sweeping. Edmonds and Emburey twirled them out for 87, and we knocked off a small target to win by 4 wickets. Butcher had chipped in with one of his season's specials but poor Wilfy Slack did something peculiar lifting his back foot while playing a forward defensive to Underwood, and got stumped in both innings.

They then won 5 games on the trot while I was in the Prudential – they didn't miss me, what with Butch and Slacky making pigs of themselves and the spinners doing great deeds. At Chesterfield, when I came back, we put Derby in and they managed 151 on quite a good, bouncy wicket. I chipped in with a couple of wickets and 4 catches, and then I remember Nelly (Neil) Williams getting us a very good unbeaten 50, I got 49, and we were 90 in front on 1st innings, before Embers and Edmonds had them on their knees.

Once again the Middlesex Juggernaut, as we like to call it, was rolling. Next match though, at Birmingham, it went into reverse – against Warwickshire. Graham Barlow, at the ground, had decided that he was unfit, so I had to fly Richard Ellis there, as an opener, but he didn't arrive until we were deep in trouble. It taught me a captaincy lesson – *always* cover for people even if they seem OK, because if one opener is suddenly unfit and the other is struggling you're going to be made to look a fool. The spinners didn't bowl particularly well either, so the whole match was a bit of a fiasco and we lost by 167 runs. What particularly annoyed me, apart from the wicket, which was very dry, was that I looked up from my stance at the wicket and saw Norman Gifford delivering the ball when I wasn't ready, and I was caught bat and pad on the off-side, which made me furious. So rather a harsh experience for the fledgling skipper.

Things could only get better, and at Lord's, in a drawn game against New Zealand, they did; I won the toss, we went in, and with the help of some dropped catches I reached 216. It was the first double-century of my career, and all the nicer for being at Lord's and against the Tourists. When I was on 34, I went down the wicket to John Bracewell and offered a very simple stumping chance, but when I missed the ball, so did the wicketkeeper, and I managed to scramble back. The only thing that marred the innings for me slightly was that their attack, without Richard Hadlee, was slightly friendly.

We were well up in the Championship Table after the Juggernaut had crushed Gloucester at Bristol, Simon Hughes having taken 6 for 32 in their 2nd innings, when we came to our voodoo game against Leicester at Lord's, which we had to lose if we were to win the County title. And what did we do, silly boys? We went and won it by 180 runs. But there was a far worse tragedy. Poor Roland Butcher, having gone for the hook, was hit full in the face by a steeply rising ball from the West Indian paceman Ferris. Butch was carried off to hospital with multiple fractures of the left cheekbone. It was a horrible sight. This type of fracture is particularly terrible because the eye sinks down, and it puts out the whole facial alignment. He wasn't wearing a helmet. As I've said already in this book, I'm very much in favour of helmets.

We played Warwickshire at Lord's next, and I was *so* cross about Norman Gifford's behaviour in the previous encounter, I was determined we were going to settle their hash here. They'd made such a mockery of us, that I got stuck into the lads before we started, and told them that it was up to us to give them the whipping they should have had at Birmingham. With the result that everybody went out and played exceptionally well. David Smith got 103 of their 1st-innings

253. John got 4 wickets, Wayne, Neil and myself all chipped in with 2, and then Bob Willis being away in the Test match, we got off to a very good start – 168 for the 1st wicket, thanks to Wilf and Graham Barlow, and then I went in, bent on destruction, and smashed Gifford all over the place for 116, towards our 385 for 8 declared. Second innings, after a solid beginning, they declined to 210, and Rad and I finished up knocking off the winning runs of the 81 we needed. That win may not sound much to you, but it gave me a sort of glowing feeling inside. This team I'd inherited had a lot of professional pride, and if you wound them up as I had done they were going to spring.

We had a fairly amazing game against Essex next, at Chelmsford, where the crowd got very uptight indeed. The wicket was as green as a lawn; we were inserted, and got bowled out for 83 by their seamers, Pringle, Lever and Foster. Graham Barlow, like the boy on the burning deck, carried his bat for 40-odd, thank God – I had never seen an innings like that before. Then Essex went in, went for their shots, took a few chances as we should have done and ended up with 289 – 206 runs on. Which meant that we were well in it. We had an awkward period to bat out before the close on the second day, but Graham Barlow stayed around for 330 minutes for 132, I batted through till lunch on the last day for 160 and Embers got a career-best 133, and we ended up *not* declaring and getting 634 for 7.

Why hadn't I set Essex a target? Well we didn't pull well clear of them until about an hour-and-a-half after lunch, and it didn't seem sensible to make a token declaration they could reach either, because we'd battled so hard to save the game. And then they put on their joke bowlers to make us look silly, but by tea-time you don't really set targets anyway. So we didn't. Why should we? There wasn't any point in giving them the game.

I'm afraid our prodigious batting wasn't well received. Fletcher got really cross; all the Essex blokes got cross, the crowd were booing and shoving me on the pavilion steps, and unfortunately it all got very nasty. Reporters were hovering, television cameras were nosing into things, angry quotes were given to press persons, and for about two years afterwards, whenever I went out to bat there, Essex supporters would queue to shout abuse at me, and boo me off the field when I'd finished.

The lads went down to play Northants without myself, Edmonds, Cowans or Butch there to help and they had a rain-wrecked game up at Manchester against Lancs, in which Mike Brearley came back to steady the middle order. There were a lot of low scores in that match, and in the distance we could hear the rumble of the Essex legions marching towards the top of the table. We had led from 7 June to 23 August and the loss that probably hurt us *most* was the Somerset game, at Lord's, on 20 August. From here, sometimes with and sometimes without me, Middlesex had one win, one loss and three draws before the finish, but looking back, Somerset was the cruncher, and the reason we finished second in the Championship to Essex.

It was an unbelievable game of cricket. We put Somerset in and they got 249. In reply I managed 105 and Embers got 60-odd, which made up the guts of our reply: 242. Then the ground got flooded. There were huge thunderclaps, and even the Long Room was under water. But perhaps mindful of a previous shindig when rain had stopped play at Lord's, the umpires called a resumption and within two hours, with the ball literally turning square, from 72 for 1 Somerset were all out for 119. Phil Edmonds grabbed 5 for 19; Emburey took 4 and Somerset faced some unplayable balls. So we were set 127 in 145 minutes and then, after the loss of 40 minutes to rain, 112 in 80 minutes – or 20 minutes and 20 overs.

I remember turning a ball from Joel Garner off my hip which plopped in the mud and went straight into Nigel Popplewell's hands while I was out of my crease, and that was the end of me, for 0; 3 down for 16. We played some dreadful shots, got a bit behind the clock, and lost by 33 runs. All credit to their little left-arm spinner, Booth, but it was a great shame for Middlesex. We'd lost our first place to Essex, and if we'd won, we would have gone 20 points clear.

So that was it really. Essex were up at Colchester, winning their games quite comfortably, and we were twice at Lord's, playing on the flattest wicket of all time, and having to gamble on declarations. That, plus an infuriating wash-out at Notts, put paid to us, although right up to the last ball, I was telling them, 'We've got to get that Championship, lads – we've got to hang on, it's not over yet!' It was. We came second.

So the highlight of my first Middlesex season as captain wasn't the Championship. But 1983 wasn't totally disappointing. We had a fantastic run in something else and this meant clashing heads with our 1983 rivals, Essex, as well.

In the John Player League, I'm afraid it was back to square one – we finished 8th and didn't do ourselves justice with some pretty mediocre performances. But the Benson and Hedges was a different matter. In our Group we started off winning two and having two 'no results' in the preliminaries. We beat Surrey at the Oval on a faster scoring rate after they'd batted quite strangely, plodding along at 3 an over in reply to our 5 an over. I made sure we got our stipulated 20 overs in as well, so that it constituted a game. Then we cruised home versus Kent at Canterbury thanks to Rad's top-scoring 88 not out.

The rain was coming down relentlessly by this time, and for the quarter-final against Gloucester, at Bristol, it poured and poured for three days. In the end, very reluctantly, we had to toss a coin – and I felt very sorry for their skipper David Graveney when I called heads and won, because it was a very bad ruling and an absolute disgrace for it to be decided in this way. It annoyed me very much. The rules in those days were so vague that we considered playing a game of darts, snooker or skittles to settle the issue. Looking out of the window I even suggested scuba-diving.

So on we trundled to the semi-final, where our opponents were Lancashire, who often caused us a few problems. We annihilated them. You should have seen the glint in the eyes of Norman Cowans and Wayne Daniel when they got a look at the wicket – fairly quick and with a bit of grass on it. Clive Lloyd wasn't there to rescue them either, because he had a groin strain, and they were shot out for the lowest-ever semi-final score of 90. I managed 2 for 8 in 7 overs, but I think they'd already been frightened to death by this time, and despite agonizing stops for gloom and rain, Rad knocked off the winning runs in the evening.

Which meant that we met the Men of Essex for the trophy on 23 July at Lord's. The 1983 Benson and Hedges Final has been much talked about, much written about, but I'm sure you'll want to hear about it just the same. It was very special for me, because it was my first Lord's Final as captain. What can I say? It's one of the most memorable matches I've ever played in for Middlesex – and it started badly because we lost 50 minutes for weather, and then I lost the toss. I do remember them taking a long time to decide what they would do if they won the toss: I certainly would have had no hesitation in putting Essex in. They put us in.

Until about midday, the ball moved about quite considerably, but when the sun began to appear the wicket flattened out a bit. I was on 22 and feeling fairly safe with Rad playing well up the other end, when he clipped one off his legs and said '3'. On the second, I thought Neil Foster had flipped the ball back, and was going to have to pick it up and toss it in. But he had it in his hand. Turning round with a great throw, he beat my despairing dive and in that moment, we went from doing nicely to deep trouble. Thank goodness, Rad played a magnificent knock of 89 not out, but we'd gone askew and finished up with 196 for 8 off our 55 overs.

The sun came out, the roller came out, and the wicket looked a totally different colour. Now, Graham Gooch was in fearsome form, and he and Brian Hardie began to show us how it was done – and I think the pressure must have got to Norman Cowans because he didn't bowl his opening overs very well. Gooch began to distribute his boundaries to well-wishers, and now we were really in quite a disastrous state.

Tea was taken at 6.20. They were looking down on us from the heights of 113 for 1, Gooch having got out caught behind for 46, trying to drive one from Neil Williams.

'We mustn't give up,' I said, but Essex still had 35 overs left to get 84, which is what you might call a cakewalk. 'We mustn't give up.' McEwan had had his tea when he got out to a diving catch by Cowans, off Edmonds, for 34. Now if only we could get Fletcher, we *still* had a small chance. Their lower-order batting was a bit suspect. Philippe was bowling with a silly mid-off, and a short-leg – unheard of in Bensons Finals, especially with a tight target – and our prayers were answered when the Gnome, on 3, offered a bat-pad catch and Rad snapped it up: 135 for 3, still with Hardie in.

A lot of our supporters had by now given up the ghost and drifted home. It was nearly 7.30 and it was getting dark. I put the seamers on. Neil Williams looked at Keith Pont and bowled him a bouncer. It struck him on the helmet, and he dropped his bat on the stumps. Out, hit wicket; 151 for 4. Then Norman Cowans bowled a quite magnificent spell, and Hardie, who after a rapid start was now poodling along, was caught at the wicket, but then Pringle and Turner took the score to 185 for 5, with 4 overs left.

The light was now really bad. Wayne Daniel removed Pringle, and then Cowans was bowling at Stuart Turner, and I had sent the 12th man, John Carr, back from mid-on to a deepish mid-on about halfway back to the boundary because Turner was dangerous and I suspected he would try and whack Cowans. Well, he took a wind-up and actually hit it quite well, but Carr took a magnificent catch over his right shoulder, running back. 187 for 7. Now we had the two Easts at the wicket, David and Ray – who's a bit of a joker. They only needed 10 runs, so he could afford to laugh. David nicked one for 4. I moved Radley in fairly close because Ray was very good at just touching the ball and running. He did this to Wayne and took a couple of little shimmies up the wicket, but the ball had dropped off his pad and gone straight to Radley who ran him out. So in came John Lever. 191 for

8; 6 required. They played out the over, and the remaining East came up to Norman Cowans' end, who was still snorting ready for his last over. Cowans bowled, and East absolutely heaved this one towards me at mid-wicket.

It was fairly dark and I could just about see this red object before it hit my hands and went straight up in the air at quite an alarming rate behind me and I managed to twist round, dive – and grab it. It would definitely have gone for 4 otherwise. It was at that moment, when I managed to cling on to that ball, that I knew we'd win.

I threw it up many a mile and Middlesex seemed to light up in the darkness. One more to go. Norman Cowans ran in, bowled a magnificent delivery, and poor old Neil Foster looked at it in dismay, and was out for 0, all gone for 192. It was a fairy tale – we'd won by 4 runs. Obviously Clive Radley – how does he do it? – got Man of the Match. I ran off the pitch as though we'd just scored the winning goal in a Wembley Cup Final. Arms in the air, pads in the air, players in the air.

But then when I got in the dressing room, I sat down, completely drained and disbelieving. I couldn't take it in that we'd done it. Everybody was thronging round saying, 'Well done Skip, well done,' in the victory hubbub, and in the middle there was a sort of a silence. I felt emotionally, mentally, physically spent. All the tension and excitement that we'd felt out there on the field was gone. We'd won, and it was nice, but it wasn't real. It was a strange feeling. Perhaps you only *really* feel like winners while you're winning.

Obviously, as the evening went on, it sank in a bit more, but you couldn't help looking at the Essex lads and wondering. They must have felt so, so bad, and it must have been an ordeal for Keith Fletcher. He could have called them off for bad light, but he had felt they should keep going while they had a chance, for the sake of all their supporters. It was a tremendous gesture. Whereas most of *our* supporters had cleared off.

In the coming weeks many of them were to come up to me

and say, 'Well, I thought you'd lost.' *I* thought that was a great shame for Middlesex; we'd never really had a great amount of support yet many of them had gone home, and left us to die on our own. Those who stayed behind, our hard-core supporters, saw a great, great match: I can replay every ball of it in my mind like a video. It's still there – implanted. You never forget.

The following month, we were to see the reverse side of the victory celebrations, because we met Somerset at Lord's in the semi-final of the NatWest Trophy, and we lost. We'd come via Cambridgeshire and Derby and beaten Northants in the quarter-finals. The wicket was reasonable. Somerset won the toss and stuck us in, and we all chipped in towards 222 for 9, which wasn't bad; Tomlins and Slack getting 50s. Then they lost 3 quick wickets, Norman Cowans bowling exceptionally well, and then Wayne took an astonishing one-handed catch behind him to dismiss Viv Richards off Neil Williams for just 23. They sank to 52 for 5, chasing 223.

Botham edged a couple, trying to have a slog, but then he got his eye in and began causing us grief. Between some strong hitting, he assembled one of the most responsible knocks I've ever seen him play, with good support from Nigel Popplewell and Vic Marks. I had to put John Emburey on at what was, for him, the wrong end, because Phil Edmonds was on at his normal end. Neither of the spinners could penetrate, and Botham wasn't worried, so I felt I should put Wilfy Slack on. He bowled quite tidily and removed Marks, but all the time Botham was knocking them off, and from 52 for 5, where we were winning quite comfortably, we slithered farther and farther behind and Popplewell was put down in the gully. They reached our total after their 60 overs, and because they had lost only 8 wickets, they were awarded the match.

I knew now how Keith Fletcher felt that day in July. It was a crushing blow. When we had had them 52 for 5 we'd been jumping up and down convinced we were going to do it. Now it was gone. The Bloke Upstairs evidently thought, That

Gatting wondered what the losers felt like at Lord's. Well, I'll give him a taste of it. The only consolation was that this was the semi-final rather than the final, or it might have hurt even more. Of course Both was Man of the Match for his very fine knock. There was nothing we could do about it in the end.

I actually played in two Test matches as well, late in the season. I'd been in and out of England like a French ferry, and I knew, that of all my last chances, this was probably the last last chance. I was going to have to pull something out of my kitbag here. So Lord's, 11 August, the 3rd Cornhill Test, England *v.* New Zealand, was a special day for me. We were all square in the four-match Series at one-all, having lost at Headingley; the England captain was R. G. D. Willis. Graham Dilley was unfit and so was Phil Edmonds, who'd done something to his back in the car park. He was replaced at the last minute by Nick Cook, the Leicestershire left-arm spinner.

England were fielding two other debutants as well: Chris Smith of Hampshire and 'Fozzie' Foster of Essex. Geoff Howarth won the toss and stuck us in. We'd lost poor Kippy Smith, close to tears, lbw to Hadlee for a golden duck in his 1st Test match but Tavaré was well anchored, and Gower, after a couple of let-offs, was playing some splendid strokes. Both of them reached their 50s after lunch, and David was on his way to an elegant century, when I came in.

Lovely day; good wicket, and after a tentative start, I settled in and found myself playing as well as I'd ever done in a Test match. At last, for once, everything was going right; I was Middlesex captain, I was on my home ground, and I was enjoying myself. David went, lbw to Martin Crowe, and Both was out cheaply, lbw to Cairns, but I just seemed to go sailing on . . . .

Wisden:

> . . . off-driving handsomely with a full follow-through and savagely despatching anything short to the boundary. His 50, off 73 balls, included nine 4s . . . .

They took the new ball, but it didn't do much. I think Richard Hadlee was bowling from the Pavilion end; he likes the Nursery end better with its more uneven bounce. So having got my 50 I was able to do what you're supposed to do, and carry on. At the close I was on 74, my highest England score to date, and England were 279 for 5. Now I know for a fact that if we'd had an extra hour to bat that night, I would have gone on and got my elusive first Test 100 in August 1983.

As it was, next morning, Lance Cairns and the fatal Hadlee had switched ends. I got to 81, having negotiated his first couple of overs and then, there being no short-leg or anything, when Hadlee bowled me a short ball, I saw it early and went for the pull. Well, it bounced on the legendary ridge (which isn't supposed to exist) and blow me if I didn't get a thickish top-edge, caught by Wright at mid-wicket. True, I'd probably played an impetuous shot too early, because when you re-open an innings, you should behave as though you have 0. You should be sensible.

I'll never forget that shot. It was a sad thing for me, because I'd got so near and yet so far. It's a long walk back to the pavilion, when you're thinking, if only I'd played that back down the wicket to him. If only I hadn't played a silly shot so early. I had thrown away an ideal opportunity and I'd never hear the last of it now from the 'No Test 100' brigade.

Anyway, England clocked up a respectable 326 and New Zealand at the close had slipped from 147 for 3 to 176 for 6, having been prised out by Cook. Botham cleared up the tail very quickly on Saturday morning, and he then led their bowlers a merry dance in our 2nd innings as well, top-scoring with 61 out of 211. I didn't make much of a contribution, getting an inside edge I think, bowled by the slow left-armer Gray for 15, but the main thing was that our seamers then rattled them out and we went 2–1 up in the Series, winning by 127 runs.

We got in a mess straight away in the 4th Test at Trent Bridge, losing Tavaré in the second over, caught at slip by Cairns off the bowling of Snedden, and it took a determined

72 from Shaggy Gower to stabilize us, in between being hit on the nut by Richard Hadlee. Once we were on our feet, Both and Randall laid into the rather wayward New Zealand attack and we ended up with a sizable haul which really set us up for the match. I got out cheaply lbw to Bracewell trying to make a clean sweep, but we finished up with 420, and after that we never looked back. Thanks to a fine bit of spinning from Nick Cook, with 5 wickets in their 1st innings, 9 in the match, they crumbled for just 207.

Willis didn't enforce the follow-on but decided to load a few more rocks on their chests. Second innings, Allan Lamb led the way with a fine 137 not out, as we collected another 297 to set them 511 in eleven hours which they were never going to manage. I was caught out behind off Lance Cairns, to give me 14 and 11 in the match, though I did manage a couple of catches, one of these being at short mid-wicket to help get rid of Coney off Cook. But I think the most amazing moment came when Kippy Smith, a native South African, came on for a bowl, and took 2 for 31! It was England's match all the way, by 165 runs, and we took the series 3–1.

What share I had in the celebrations is difficult to say. My own performance in the two final Tests had been very uneven. I didn't have the confidence of the senior players, so I didn't have much confidence in myself. I didn't feel people were behind me, like they were at Middlesex. I was still going it alone. The selectors might look at the national averages, supposedly crying out for any English batsman near the top, and they might notice I was the highest qualified Englishman again (for the second year) but they still managed to avoid picking me until last. I suppose captain Willis had as much to do with that as anybody.

My Test form was still in question: it wasn't that I had a phobia about playing for England. It was simply that playing for England was like playing for any other team, and you had to feel a part before you could do your best. Yes, there was a bit more pressure, and that was a factor, but at Middlesex it had been so different. They had made me feel welcome and wanted as part of the side, and simple people like myself tend to respond to that. Playing for England was very nice and I had found a few friends here and there, but I didn't feel accepted or settled. So when you went out in the middle you wondered what was being said ('Gatting's been picked again – teh!') and it built up in your imagination until people seemed to be whispering in corners. At Middlesex it was a joy to be playing. At the annual MCC dinner at Lord's, the Archbishop of Canterbury stood up and said cricket was 'a game to be played, not a battle to be won'. I wish people would remember that in this day and age.

There were a couple of little whistle-stop tours right at the end of 1983, when I had four days in Kuwait as part of an XI picked by former Surrey batsman Dudley Owen-Thomas, and also an incredible trip sponsored by Air New Zealand *in* New Zealand. They flew us 26,000 miles there and back for one 50-over match against the New Zealanders. It was an International XI including Derek Underwood and Norman Cowans, and we had a great time in Rotorua, where I got my golf handicap down to 9, and caught an 8½ lb trout on my debut as a freshwater fisherman. Mackerel is my usual catch, but having fished in Australasia, I've decided there are bigger and better things in the water. In Rotorua, 'Deadly', had caught the first fish, about 3 lb, and I hooked the next three, one of which they cooked in a big steam oven for us after the match with herbs and honey. It was beautiful. But the main tour of that winter was obviously the England trip to Pakistan, Fiji and New Zealand.

I'd been selected to go on what turned out to be one of the unhappiest tours of recent years – at least it began very unhappily. Injury-ridden and ill, we became the first England side to be beaten in a Test Series by New Zealand and Pakistan, and we were accused in the Press of smoking pot in New Zealand and going to pot in general – although a later TCCB enquiry cleared the players of any 'drugs in sport' allegations. So it wasn't a very successful trip on paper – I think mainly because a lot of pressure was loaded on us from outside, particularly by the media. There were also a lot of internal squabbles and there was a very peculiar itinerary.

We went out bright-eyed and bushy-tailed, with a lot of good intentions, stopping off first in Fiji, where it was very, very hot but I managed to open my account with a 142 against a Fijian Cricket Association President's XI, on 2 January 1984; which was nice because we won by 198 runs. The next game against them, though, we nearly managed to lose, having struggled to 146 for 9 on a good batting wicket, and in the end a few of our bowlers had to resort to full run-ups as they were getting very close to our target, and we stopped them just 18 runs short.

So on we went to New Zealand, where I managed a couple of 50s against Auckland, though a century would have been even nicer. The match petered out in a draw as we weren't able to set them a target. The same thing happened at Palmerston North, against Central Districts, though I didn't play in that one. Our first and only win of the tour against the District sides came at Hamilton, where we beat Northern Districts by 77 runs. I didn't play particularly well in that match but Kippy Smith and Randall both got very good unbeaten centuries.

Then we came to the 1st Test match in Wellington, where New Zealand won the toss and went in. Both produced one of his 'fivefers' and Willis got 3, passing Trueman's old Test wicket record of 307 when I caught Cairns off him at slip. They managed just 219. In response England, relying on Botham and Randall for most of them, put on 463. I got 19 and was given out lbw to Cairns, and to this day I still don't think I was out. Well, from that position, we should really have won, and when we had them 165 for 4, it looked as though we might run through them, but we didn't and Jeremy Coney and Martin Crowe led a formidable recovery to 537 all out. Effectively, the match was already on its way to a boring draw, and the more it went on the iller I felt: I'd come down with a bit of a fever. I had actually gone to bed in the New Zealand 2nd innings, but the lads got me up because the bowlers were struggling and it was felt I might be needed to turn my arm over. I was needed.

My first Test wicket turned out to be a good one: century-making Martin Crowe. It was the end of a very trying over, I can tell you. My first ball had been a wide, my second was close to being a wide, the third one went down the leg-side and the fourth one was about right: it swung a bit, he pushed forward, and nicked it to Botham in the slips. Didn't do us any good though, because we couldn't get Mr Coney out. He was the spanner in our works.

The 2nd Test at the beginning of February was quite amazing. The Christchurch pitch was extremely suspect and we ended up calling Tony Pigott into the side from a Shell Trophy game in Wellington, because Dilley was unfit. Our attack consisted of Willis, Botham, Pigott and Cowans. New Zealand, having won the toss, went in and we thought we were doing quite well when they were reduced to 87 for 4, but then unfortunately we started to bowl a lot of rubbish.

I think Tony Pigott, poor devil, was very nervous, having postponed his wedding for the honour of his first Test match, and we couldn't exploit a very helpful wicket. Bob Willis was to let rip afterwards at us all, condemning the England bowling as some of the worst he'd ever seen (I only bowled 2 overs, thank goodness). Richard Hadlee stood up and smashed everything for 99 and all of the Kiwis chipped in towards their 307. Whereupon we proceeded to cover ourselves with further shame by getting out for 82, following on, and getting out again for 93.

It was one of the most depressing dressing rooms I've ever been in. Any hustling and bustling from Gatting would definitely have been out of order. The Kiwis bowled well and caught everything. In our 1st innings I managed to score 19 not out. Ran out of partners. In the 2nd innings I was caught at slip by Hadlee off the spinner Boock, for 0. It wasn't a particularly reckless shot – I was just nonplussed like everybody else.

It's a horrible feeling to see your side falling apart at the seams: you can't describe it to anybody. Everything had gone right for New Zealand, and if they nicked it, it went for 4. Nothing went right for us: if we nicked it somebody laid his hands on the catch. But you couldn't say the England players weren't trying, as some people did. We were trying our best, and we desperately wanted to win. The fact was, the opposition batted and bowled better than we did and if that happens in a Test match, you tend to lose.

When it was over, of course, we were roundly condemned and the sharks were circling in the water, especially for the more peripheral members of the squad, like me. The 3rd Test was at Auckland. We knew it was going to be a very flat wicket, though I wasn't to see much of it: I was left out. They played Kippy Smith and Vic Marks, and they played Neil Foster in the pace attack. And what happened was that New Zealand batted for nearly two days, amassing 496 for 9 declared. Kippy Smith, Randall and Botham replied in kind with 439, and that was that, really. It was a very boring draw and the New Zealanders were satisfied, because they'd beaten England for the first time in a Test Series.

The New Zealand leg of the tour finished with three one-day internationals. I was going in at number 6 and I scored the magnificent sum of 0, 0 not out, and 4. We won the 1st by 54 runs at Christchurch; we won the second in Wellington by 6 wickets (Vic Marks took 5 for 20 and Kippy Smith knocked up a very patient 70) but then in Auckland we got a bit of a hiding, Martin Crowe and Geoff Howarth clobbering the bowling in their 210 for 3 and we lost that by 7 wickets.

So off we went, having covered ourselves in something other than glory, to Pakistan, for the last leg of this unpleasant tour. And it was in Pakistan where the paper talk began, about 'pot' and parties. We tried not to take too much notice of the publicity. It really seemed to be directed at one person – Both – and although it must have put him under a bit of added pressure it didn't seem to worry him unduly.

We played the 1st Test in Karachi and we didn't have a great deal of luck there either. Captain Willis publicly announced, before the Test began, that time was running out for me if I was ever going to establish myself as an England middle-order batsman. And then, amazingly, he asked me to open the innings.

I had batted at most positions by now, from number 8 upwards, so you learn not to let your eyes pop out on stalks, but this was a rather strange affair. Willis came into the room and said in his usual forthright monotone, 'Gatt, I'd like you to open the batting. Will you do it?'

'Open the batting?' I queried carefully, in case I had made a mistake.

'Yes.'

'Why?'

'Foxy's got injured, and you're the only other bloke who can do it.'

So I said, 'Oh! OK I'll do it.'

And with that Willis strode out of the room. Whether he was trying to make me or break me, I don't know.

So that's how it came about that I opened the batting for England with Kippy Smith in Karachi. We put on 41 for the 1st wicket before Kippy got out, caught Wasim Raja bowled Sarfraz for 28. I carried on for a little while with David Gower before I went back to play one from Tauseef that turned and trickled on to the stumps, which was annoying. I was out for 26. There were some interesting decisions over the wickets of Both, Bob Taylor, and Nick Cook, after we'd slogged to 154 for 5, and we ended up all out for 182. In reply they sank to 138 for 6 – in a worse state than we'd been – worried out mostly by Nick Cook, but then their tail wagged a bit, and Abdul Qadir hit 40 to push them to 277.

Anyway, I opened up again with Smith, and I was given out lbw to Sarfraz, and in my view it was the worst umpiring decision I'd ever had. Saf had said, 'How's that! – that's my in-swinger,' sort of thing, and up went the finger. I was a long way forward outside the off-stump, and I've seen pictures to prove it. So we had hardly got in when we were 2 down for 21. David and Allan Lamb staged a slight recovery but then the Man with the Golden Gun went to work, with Tauseef and Wasim, and we were whittled away for 159. We didn't have much of a chance, so we thought. They only wanted 65.

But then Nick Cook spat on his fingers and got an amazing 5 wickets for 18 runs which really put them under pressure, at 38 for 5 and 40 for 6, still needing 25 runs. We got Abdul out, but their wicketkeeper Anil Dalpat struck a few blows and they got home, though not without a panic. So they won their first victory over England in 13 home Tests by 3 wickets.

The 1st one-day international, at Lahore, I was back down to number 7 and Graeme Fowler opened with Tavaré. Fowler hit 43. We never got anywhere near enough, and we lost comfortably on the eve of the Faisalabad Test. For this one we stayed at the Cheno Club, an astonishing little place, rather like a Bournemouth guest house, but without the mod cons. If you've ever stayed in a Butlin's chalet, that's how big the rooms were. We had a little Team lounge which was a bit like a cupboard, and we ended up eating our own food to be on the safe side.

It wasn't the greatest accommodation for a Test match. Graham Dilley was having trouble with an injured leg; he really did seem to be in great pain and difficulty – and on the morning of the match our captain, Bob Willis, withdrew with food poisoning. What with Botham having gone home with a bad knee, as well as Norman Cowans unfit with a groin strain, we were struggling before we had started. It left poor David Gower in charge of an attack that was very dodgy indeed. Dilley was obviously unfit but he played.

We lost the toss and Pakistan took first dig. Yet somehow we had them 70 for 3, and we were thinking how useful this was when Salim Malik came in and scored his maiden Test 100, and Wasim Raja helped himself to a century as well. I had had a little bowl and nipped out the opposition captain Zaheer Abbas lbw – a bit of a rarity because it's not often that Pakistan skippers are given out at home lbw, least of all when they've only got 68. Anyhow, they declared at 449 for 8, poor old Graham Dilley having bowled extremely well without much luck, and with his leg getting steadily worse.

So in we went. Kippy and I put on 127 for the first wicket before he was out, bowled by Sarfraz, for 66. I got caught at backward short-leg off Tauseef for 75 to one that turned and bounced a bit on the very flat wicket. The two of us were supposed to hang around for a few because Graeme Fowler was sick in bed, and David Gower was at death's door as well. So it was quite a surprise when Arkle went in and hit 65; David, on his last legs, hit a magnificent 152; and Graeme, nearly done for, made 57. Vic Marks got a tremendous 83, sweeping and cutting Qadir mightily, and we ended up 546 for 8 declared.

Abdul finished with calloused fingers and 1 for 124, and we even had them in a spot of trouble before the match ended in another draw. A very good and honourable draw it was too, considering we looked like something out of the *Night of the Zombies*. At the end of it, a specialist looked at Graham Dilley's leg and immediately sent him home.

The 3rd and final Test in Lahore was drawn as well. We'd been inserted by Pakistan, and I was out plumb lbw to Sarfraz. It nipped back and kept low, no complaints about that. Graeme Fowler, having done well down the middle order, and being a bit superstitious, asked to stay where he was, and he and Vic Marks were the backbone of our 241. But then we bowled quite well and if it hadn't been for Sarfraz, who added 90 to their account, they might not have got near our score, let alone 343. At one stage, when they were 181 for 8, we thought we were going to grab a lead. Instead of that, Saf and Zaheer pounded away, and we ended up 100 adrift.

So then England went in and we lost Fowler (who had decided to open) and then Kippy in a run out and it was left to myself and Gower to get us out of the mud of 38 for 2. We were going along quite nicely and we'd managed to clear our arrears, when unfortunately there was a mix-up between us and I ended up being run out for 53. Then we lost 2 more quick wickets, Derek Randall for the second time in the match wandering back to the pavilion in disbelief over the umpire's decision. But Vic Marks gave Gower the support he needed and David played a beautiful knock of 173 not out.

I think it was with a bit of persuasion from me that Shaggy then decided to declare, on 344 for 9, setting them 243 to win. They put on 173 for the 1st wicket and looked set to walk it with Mohsin Khan and Shoaib Mohammad helping themselves on all sides, when Norman Cowans came on and bowled a vicious burst. Mohsin was caught at mid-on by Kippy for 104, and then I caught Shoaib, again off Cowans, for 80.

Suddenly it was all happening. Qasim Omar, run out for a duck, Salim Malik, caught by me off Norman, Wasim Raja lbw to Norman, and then a little tactical manoeuvre here; I went back 20 or 30 yards because I knew Zaheer normally flicks it up to square-leg. He'd come out with a runner: I believe he had pulled a hamstring, and his glasses glinted in the sun as he chipped one off Norman straight down my throat. From 173 for 1 they'd collapsed to 199 for 6. Sadly, we couldn't prise out the last four, so the match ended in a draw – but an honourable draw again for England, and we went on to win the 2nd one-day international in Karachi, by 6 wickets – I managed to strangle three to finish with 8–1–32–3, and score 38 not out towards our final flourish.

So we left Pakistan on a winning note and David Gower had given a good account of himself as captain. It showed that there was still a bit of fight left in the England camp despite illness, injury and adversity and despite Bob Willis and Botham going home early. Poor Graham Dilley got back to the UK to find that he had a crushed vertebra in his neck and had to have a huge operation. He had said that one side of him had gone numb and he couldn't feel anything in his left leg after the Faisalabad Test.

I think it was a great effort by all concerned that the England lads managed to pull themselves out of trouble in the end, and salvage some pride. You couldn't help noticing that when Bob Willis had gone home, and David was in charge, things were different. The atmosphere seemed to change – at least that's how it felt to me. It gave me a little encouragement and though I didn't have a Test 100 to show for it, I was feeling I could cope with the pressure a little better. I was playing a little more like the Middlesex Gatting and felt happier inside. I didn't mind being shoved up and down the order, though I'd rather be up than down, and although we lost the 1st Test and therefore the Series to Pakistan, I enjoyed it much more than the New Zealand matches.

Pakistan wasn't a loss as far as I was concerned. It was more of a gain. We came home having played very well in the 2nd and 3rd Tests, and that was a credit to the skill and determination of the England players. It meant a lot to me that I'd been part of that recovery. Even when we copped a bit of stick from the Press for having bowled our overs too slowly in the 1st Test I didn't think any less of our fightback. I'm sure Pakistan, in the same position, would have bowled as few. The England recovery was a great effort, and a very good reflection on English cricket.

CHAPTER TEN

Not Doing It For England

1984

'Why can't you do it for England?'

I was sick of that question. People were always asking me and it annoyed me because I still believed I was good enough. On the winter tour I had set out my stall to establish an England place and get the magic 3 figures, but it had gone wrong, just like every other tour, and of course I worried about it. The lads had taken the mickey when I was chosen to open in Karachi, because now I had batted everywhere from 1 to 8 for England and captain Willis had called it 'my last chance'. 'Why can't he get a Test 100?' people moaned. When Elaine went into the local shops they would ask *her* why I hadn't got a Test 100. 'What's the matter with him? What are you doing to him?' they would say.

What was it about a 100 that was so special anyway? Why was it so different from 99? That it was different in some symbolic way was obvious. Cricket writers didn't produce articles saying 'So-and-so got six 99s this season – what a wonderful fellow he is!' All the articles, the books, and the statisticians went on about Test 100s. *Not* 81, which is what I'd got at Lord's last season. *Not* County 100s – I'd got plenty of those. It seemed you had to cross the dividing line in Test matches. It was a cut-off point on the gauge, like the line between 49 and 50, between 4 wickets in an innings and 5. It meant something different to people.

What I wanted wasn't just one 100 anyway. It was a string of them, because that was a sign of maturity, ability, consistency, determination, all sorts of things. People like David Gower and Ian Botham, because they were so talented, found it easier than somebody like myself. It's probably true that a lot of the time I used to get myself out.

Well, 1984. After the Pakistan/New Zealand Series I didn't think I would be required in the Tests, so my total concentration was on Middlesex. We didn't have a great start to our season either, although we did manage our usual fairly efficient drubbing of Glamorgan at Lord's, before things started to go radically wrong. Rad had got his usual 100, and I was trying to start the season right by progressing smoothly from 50 to 100 when I drilled one to mid-wicket and Mike Selvey, now captain of Glamorgan, took a very good shin-high catch. So I missed out. But we bowled them out twice for humble amounts and won that by 10 wickets.

After that, Middlesex seemed, for some reason, to go a bit flat. We'd got in some batting practice against Oxford University, with me going in down the order, but at Lord's against Northants we got caught on a damp square and my 71 was needed to shore up our 2nd innings. Fortunately Northants didn't fare much better and the weather put us all out of our misery.

The rain reduced our Sussex match to a one-innings affair as well, which we narrowly lost after setting them a paltry 178. I missed the next couple of games at Dartford and Derby because I was picked for the Texaco Trophy matches. While I was away though, the lads lost against Kent, and rain ruined their Derby encounter, so things weren't going very well for Middlesex, and in the Texaco they didn't go particularly well for me.

I can tell you very quickly what happened there. The first international, at Manchester, was quite unbelievable because we had the West Indies 102 for 7 and struggling desperately, and then Viv Richards murdered us for 189 not out and we ended up vainly chasing 273. It's a shame, because if we could really have rolled them over, it might have given us a glimmer of hope for the summer. As for me, I came in number 3, and was out for 0, lbw to Joel Garner. In the 2nd Trophy match at Notts, though, we only had to chase 180, so we hit back there to go all-square in the Series. I came in at number 6 and was bowled by Garner for 6. And then in the decider at Lord's, for which I was dropped, we got a good hiding and lost by 7 wickets, so that was the end of that.

It wasn't that I hadn't tried my best; I'd had the old bowling machine, at Lord's, peppering me with 70 mph–plus deliveries for 45 minutes non-stop, and I've never been frightened of fast bowling. So I went and had a chat with Gubby Allen (now Sir George) and he felt that there was something not quite right with my batting. He came and looked at me in the indoor nets at Lord's for 20 minutes, and it turned out, basically, that I wasn't bringing the bat down straight, and I promised him that I'd go down to Bath with Middlesex and play as straight as a die.

So off I went to the Somerset match, determined to keep my word to Gubby Allen. I had to try and help Middlesex pull themselves out of that sinking feeling. I won the toss and we batted first, and we were 1 down for 88 when I joined Wilfy Slack. I began fairly slowly and I wasn't all that fluent, but I was going to bat all day. That's what I had set my sights on. I was going to be there at lunchtime and I was going to keep batting. Botham bowled a fair bit but then went off injured (he had cut his hand on Friday night and needed five stitches) and Middlesex ended up batting till close of play, when I declared. We were 473 for 7 and I got 258.

It was the highest score of my career and included eight 6s and 32 4s, and it proved to me that I could concentrate for five or six hours a day if I had to. Certainly, if I were to get back in the Test reckoning, I had to do something unusual. Somerset replied with 516 of their own, Popplewell and Crowe got 100s and Brian Rose got 97, and they batted for a day-and-three-quarters. Both, their captain, wasn't taking any further part in the match, and I couldn't get a declaration out of Vic Marks, so the match ended in a very boring draw. We had a Sunday game in the middle of it though, and we beat them in that by 1 wicket.

The 1st Test went off without me (I thought it would) and

anyway I had my hands full with Middlesex here, in a very, very annoying game against Surrey at Lord's, which we shouldn't have lost but did. Surrey set us to make 302 in a day on a goodish wicket. We started off well but the middle order played some unbelievably bad shots against Andy Needham (remember Andy Needham? He was the colt Don Bennett had liked the look of better than me) and got caught all over the place, and we just threw the game away and gave the old enemy 16 points.

Tails between legs, we met Warwickshire, who were lurking about at the bottom of the Championship table, and we played very badly *again* at Lord's. Totals of 139 and 94 were all we could muster in our innings. Admittedly the wicket wasn't very good; it was seaming sideways and bouncers came in low. But we were comprehensively beaten in any case. Then things went from bad to diabolical. We went to the Oval and we lost to Surrey by an innings and 154 runs. We weren't beaten: we were annihilated. On a quickish wicket we could only manage 155 first innings. Monte Lynch got his second 100 against us in as many matches in their handsome 399, and then we went in again and were shot out by Sylvester Clarke and company for 90. Sylvester was steaming in on the second evening, despite being warned for bouncers, and there were only about 20 overs to go, and we were 43 for 3, and 48 for 4 – and I remember thinking, This is stupid!

It was at this point that I think we finally decided that some changes had to be made, because our batting was in a complete shambles. In the last two 2nd innings we'd been bundled out for 94 and 90. We decided to go with our youngsters for the next couple of games, and for Glamorgan at Swansea we left out both Roland Butcher and Graham Barlow. The match, which I missed, petered out in a draw but Middlesex batted solidly, Phil Edmonds leading the way with 142 in our 438 for 9 declared (Rodney Ontong hit 204 not out for the Taffies). They had an honourable draw on a club wicket at Liverpool against Lancs, and so getting a couple of new faces in seemed to have done the trick. Our batting line-up at the moment was: Slack, Ellis, Hughes, Cook, Tomlins and Rad, with Ernie, Philippe and Neil Williams all capable of runs. Things seemed to be brightening up.

What was I doing meanwhile? I was at Lord's playing in the 2nd Test against the West Indies! I was just about to leave the Oval for the Swansea trip, having made all these painful captaincy decisions, when I got the distress flare saying Martyn Moxon had pulled out of the England line-up with a cracked rib. It was an SOS from England, but it was also a lifeline for me, because I'd had a lot of last chances already. England had been squashed senseless under the weight of the West Indies' 606 total at Birmingham, and then bludgeoned to death by an innings and 180 runs.

Once again it was a case of all else having failed and 'sending for Gatts!' Well, for a Test Series against the West Indies what you need more than anything else is a settled side, and England certainly didn't have that in the summer of 1984. A couple of people were seriously injured. Andy Lloyd was smashed on the head by Malcolm Marshall, and spent several days in hospital; Paul Terry had a broken arm, and there were a number of others, myself included, who were in and out for the odd Test match. So it was perhaps no wonder that the West Indies treated England to a 'blackwash' that summer, winning 5 out of 5. It was a very, very hard attack to face, with four of them coming at you all the time. And apart from Allan Lamb, who stood up and smashed them with abandon, it was a Series for England to forget.

And what can I say about my two innings? It's common knowledge what happened to me. Nerves had taken me over. I was lbw offering no stroke to Marshall for 1, and out lbw to Marshall again, padding up, for 29. I was trying so hard, and I remember walking back to the pavilion after my second knock, having padded up once again to Marshall, brokenhearted, thinking, well, that really is the end of me. I know what the papers are going to say. There were all sorts of cutting comments from critics, saying I was one of those County performers who freeze in Test matches, and that I was a spent force. There were some nasty jokes going round about me – for example the one about putting my bat stickers on upside down so as not to shame the manufacturers. And Peter May, then chairman of the England selectors, was known to be of the opinion that Gatting had had his lot.

'Why couldn't I do it for England?' the cry went up again. Possibly in Test innings I was doing something different; possibly I subtly changed the way I played. I wasn't relaxed enough. I talked to Mike Brearley about it, because Brears had had a similar problem about transferring County form to Test matches. Boycott has written somewhere that Brears was never a Test bastman; that he was a Test captain and that was it, and I had watched Brears batting in Test matches and *I* knew that he wasn't playing up to his real ability because I had seen him make so many big innings for Middlesex. Whether he had too much on his mind or was humming the wrong quartet to himself, I don't know.

As I say, cricket is very much a game fought in the brain, not just on the pitch. People watching cricket can't see the pressures involved, so they can't understand what it's like. They can see a bad trot, and so they criticize – that always happens, and of course it makes matters worse. I think, if Brears hadn't had the respect of the players as he did, and been such an excellent captain, he wouldn't have lasted purely on his Test batting record. It wasn't disastrous, but it wasn't particularly good either.

Mike Brearley:

I think it happens at every level, but the higher you get, the more public it becomes, and if success is eluding you at Test level, everyone knows and you're exposed to criticism more. I had several conversations with Mike, and one of the things I can remember saying was, after he kept getting out lbw without offering a stroke to Malcolm Marshall, that what he had in mind was Malcolm Marshall's ability to swing the ball away, so he didn't want to play at balls that he could possibly leave.

Now, if he had been playing in a County match against Marshall, I suggested, he'd know exactly the same facts about him; but he would never do what he did in a Test match. So there was something different that happened to him in a Test, even though it was an identical delivery. And what had happened was that he had started to think negatively, or defensively. He had started to exaggerate the powers of the opposition. In a County match he would have been uncomplicated about them.

I told him that if he could possibly do it, he might try to remember that Malcolm Marshall, although he is a very fine bowler, is a very fine bowler in county cricket too, when Mike scored hundreds of runs against him and his like, and that Mike should think just as positively in a Test match; because he is the sort of batsman who needs to go out and look to get on top of the bowling; and I mentioned what Gubby Allen had once told me, that it usually takes at least seven playings and missings outside the off-stump before you get an edge, and not all the edges are caught. Whereas if you miss a straight ball by not playing a shot at it, then you're out just about every time.

So I suggested a more uncomplicated attitude, and I told him that although he was of course a much better player than me, we had this in common: that *I* didn't play as well, either, against the same bowlers in Test cricket as I did in County cricket.

I certainly was getting out a lot lbw. Getting hit on the pads of course doesn't matter if the ball is going down the leg-side. It's something that often happens if the ball doesn't bounce very high and there's no real importance attached to it. But some critics noted that I had got into the habit of moving my foot early and across the stumps, which cramped my swing, and that's a fair comment, though it didn't happen every time. But the movement of the foot *was* the reason I kept getting out to in-swing bowlers – I kept putting the foot across too far, so that when the ball swung in, I was struggling to get the bat to it. Sometimes, against straight deliveries, the old foot would go across automatically as well: and that's something I had to work on, to stop myself doing it.

I went back to my county on 7 July, not even daring to think about Test cricket for a while. I had a job to do at Middlesex and that was to get them back to where they belonged, at the top of the table, and get my own form back while I was at it. I just had to go out there and get some runs. Our next game was at Uxbridge against Worcester. It was going to turn a bit so I slipped them in first and we managed a lead of 56 on 1st innings with a respectable 377, though we had been 358 for 4, with myself and Wilfy getting centuries. We got back at them again, and knocked a couple over on the second evening, but then we had trouble prising out Patel and in the end I had a go myself and got him caught and bowled for 82. We managed to get rid of them for 211. So we had 156 to get in not much time, and Rad and Butch knocked off the winning runs. We had been having a little team talk about trying to drag ourselves back up the table, and this was our first victory since 1 May.

Unfortunately, we only managed a draw, though a good one, against Gloucester, Colin Metson, Simon Hughes and Neil Williams rescuing us from a very sorry state of affairs, and Colin narrowly missing his maiden 100. Even then, this man Shepherd got them within a few runs of beating us, and the crowd loved it. We lost a whole day to rain against Boycott and the Yorkies at Lord's but then bowled them out exceptionally cheaply and I remember getting barracked by drunken blokes in one of the boxes, who wanted us to declare well before 303 for 8. I don't know whether they were Yorkshire supporters or not but they were well plastered. I managed to get 131 not out. Then we had a feeling we could bowl them out, and once Boycott was gone, and the stubborn Neil Hartley, we succeeded. Another good win for Middlesex.

Slowly we were sneaking up the table. We rumbled over Northants by 7 wickets, and this was probably the closest I'd ever come to getting a 100 in each innings. There was nothing in it on first knock, though we were 17 for 2 before Rad and I managed to put on 207 for the 3rd wicket (I got 146) and Embers provided a final flourish of 54. In their 2nd innings, Edmonds was our main striker and we worried them out for 190, to leave us wanting about 200, and Slacky and myself knocked off most of them. I didn't miss my twin tons by much, with 91 not out, but more important, I was happy and proud to be part of another Middlesex win.

We were getting more and more hopeful of a storming finish, now, in the Championship – it would be tremendous if we could do that from such a lowly beginning. Hampshire at Lord's gave us more encouragement. To be fair, without Marshall and Greenidge, who were playing for the West Indies, they were a depleted side, but we thrashed them soundly anyway by 9 wickets on a flattish strip. We'd started off very badly, 3 down for 23, replying to Hampshire's 350 for 6 declared, and it took a couple of nightwatchmen and 116 from Butch to rally us to 291, before Hughes and Daniel skittled them out very cheaply, Tim Tremlett having sadly been called away by a death in his family, and Middlesex strolled home for the loss of just one wicket. I managed to get the fastest 100 of the summer thus far (in 85 minutes) and won a holiday for myself and Elaine in Jerez, for my 128 not out. I thought it was going to rain, and no, I didn't think it would earn me an England recall.

It was our resurgence in the Championship, I am sure, that helped us play well in the NatWest Trophy, as I'll explain later. But in the Championship itself, we now came to what I considered to be a couple of really crucial games: against Essex, and against Notts. I thought that if the lads could go out and beat these two, we had a very good chance of winning the Championship again – which is what every County skipper dreams about.

Well, we set Essex a very pleasant target at Lord's because we thought they were going to have to struggle. We had played well in our first innings; Rad and myself putting on 142 (I got another 100) and we declared at 329 for 9. But

Essex had struck back with 364 for 7 declared, and then tried their damnedest to bowl us out. It was very hard going; we lost regular wickets and threw away a few, but fought it out to 245, setting them 211 off 33 overs. And then we watched in horror, as Graham Gooch hit ball one for 6 over deep gully and proceeded to hammer 105 not out. If we could have got Graham out, we'd have been OK, but we couldn't. So that was that by 4 wickets. It gave us a bit of a jolt.

Still we were in fairly good spirits for crunch game number two, at Lord's versus Notts in the middle of August. It seemed to me we were producing pitches at Lord's to suit the opposition, which is why Mike Brearley mentioned my getting a bit cross with the groundstaff. Middlesex would have preferred a flat wicket that was going to turn. Well, we didn't get it. We were stuck in on a greenish affair, which bounced a bit as well, so home or away, Hadlee found a pitch to suit his style. He and Saxelby duly dismissed us for 152, but when they went in, we started off exceptionally well and had them in real trouble at 17 for 4.

Then out to the wicket came this Mr Hadlee again, this time with his pads on, and what happened next was quite unbelievable. We dropped a dolly off him when he was on 50 (Norman Cowans being the culprit off the bowling of Edmonds) and then he just went on and on. Finished up with 210 not out, of their 344, having played shots all round the ground. It was upsetting. The ball was still seaming, and the wicket was still bouncing; we just couldn't seem to find the edge of his bat.

And then what did we do? We succumbed to Kevin Cooper (a career-best 8 for 44) and lost by an innings and 43 runs. I knew then that our Championship challenge was over for another year. And it was – despite a marvellous win set up by Edmonds at Bournemouth against Hants, on a real Bunsen Burner, *and* a comfortable win against Sussex at Hove, the title fight was settled between Essex and Notts. If either of them faltered, of course, we would have been handily placed, but we ended up coming 3rd. A good fightback though. In our last game of the season against Kent I had a bit of a flourish. My previous 'fastest 100' had been overtaken earlier on the last day by Allan Lamb, with an 83-minute ton for Northants against Worcester. So I had a whack here and got 100 not out in 79 minutes. Didn't mean much but it was fun.

I'm afraid we finished bottom of the Group this year in the Benson and Hedges competition, in complete contrast to 1983 when we carried all before us. As a matter of fact I still have a souvenir of that happy victory because in 1984 we got our dog, a big black German Shepherd, to keep everybody company, and we named him 'Benson' in honour of Middlesex's triumph. The reason we got him was because the family's other little doggie, Mitzi, died after getting a tumour in her ear which spread to her brain, and althought Mitzi had belonged to Elaine's mum Jean, we all loved her.

Steve Gatting:

She was a bad-tempered little dog, Mitzi, but she was very close to that family, and if you came visiting she would growl and bark just like a good watchdog. But Mike could always handle dogs and if he shouted they'd go under the chair.

Elaine Gatting:

Mitzi was a Sealyham – Mum had always had Sealyhams – and she was a real character, and although we had had her for some years when Mike came into the family, Mitzi became 'his' dog, because he'd always wanted one as a child and had never been allowed to have one. Mitzi was only six or seven when she got this tumour and had to be put down. Mike was absolutely heartbroken. He sat in his chair and cried and cried and he wouldn't speak to anyone. He blamed us because she had to be put to sleep and he refused to go to the vet's with her for the dirty deed.

Well, that's how we came to acquire Benson. As for his namesake competition, we certainly didn't win it in 1984.

The climax in 1984, for Middlesex, came in another limited-overs competition. As often happens, we started out looking as though we must definitely win the John Player this year. We were top of the table in July, then we plummeted to 5th. For me there were a couple of bright spots: I got my first Sunday 100 – in fact I got two, against Surrey and Leicester. That was nice, because I'd had a fairly lean time in John Player cricket, I don't know why.

But in the NatWest, we were doing much much better, beating Northumberland after making heavy weather of it, and squeaking past Notts by 5 runs (thank goodness for our spinners), to get into the quarter-finals against Lancashire. Well, we trounced them. Graham Barlow, back from being rested, hit a magnificent 158, the highest knock by an English-born cricketer in this competition. It set up a victory for us by 171 runs. That match was also the first sighting of a bloke called Patrick Patterson: he bowled quite sharply, and the West Indies were to turn him loose on England with terrible consequences. So, all credit to Graham Barlow. Nobody else got any runs, and all credit to Diamond Daniel, too, for steaming in on our account. We were in the semis.

We got another home draw – Northants at Lord's, and I put them in having won the toss, because they're an easier side to beat if you get their batting out of the way first. Our bowlers kept them under control, Wayne seeing off three of them, and I remember catching Allan Lamb, who might have caused ructions, at mid-off off Edmonds. Lamby came down the wicket and drilled one really flat and hard towards me, but I managed to get hold of it, and they ended up with 226 for 6, which we really didn't have any problems getting, to put us in the Final.

And what a final it turned out to be against Kent! I lost the toss and having decided to bat, they got off to a fairly ponderous start. Norman Cowans bowled his 9 overs straight off at a cost of 24, Wayne was keeping them busy, and just before lunch I asked Slacky to bowl a couple and he got the valuable wicket of Neil Taylor; and then their other opener, Benson, was stumped off Emburey, so from the comfort of 96 for 0, they were suddenly 2 down for 98, perhaps upsetting their lunch.

Unfortunately, Chris Cowdrey came out and hit a blistering 58 next, and they put together 232 for 6. Well, we got off to a quiet start ourselves – they were bowling exceptionally well, particularly Jarvis and Ellison. We'd stumbled along a bit until the 4th wicket went down at 124, when our finals man Rad, and Paul Downton, got together and put on 87. All of a sudden for some reason, Downton had a whack at Jarvis and got caught at long-off by Cowdrey, which was very uncharacteristic of Paul, and then Rad was also out, caught by Tavaré off Ellison.

But fortunately two old heads then got together in Emburey and Edmonds and saw us through to the last ball of the match, which Emburey picked up in the twilight and turned to the square-leg boundary for 4. We'd scraped home by 4 wickets. Clive Radley got his customary Man of the Match for holding us all together. It was a wonderful win for Middlesex which had coincided with our resurgence in the Championship after such a dismal start.

Meanwhile, back at the Gatting household, something was stirring in the mind of young Andrew of that name, now 18 months old, and into everything. We had a birdcage on top of the chest of drawers in the lounge, near the window, so birdie could enjoy a delightful view of the garden. Now, you have to bear in mind here that Andrew's dad fell out of an upstairs window at the age of three, trying to get out on a little ledge to have a look round, and that this was fairly typical Gatting behaviour. Anyway, Andrew had observed this bird from a distance and decided it was vital to his research to have a closer inspection. So he climbed up the side of the chest of drawers and pulled the bird, the cage, the chest of drawers and the whole lot over on top of himself.

Elaine Gatting:

It was about 7 o'clock in the evening, and I rang Lord's to be put through to speak to Mike. Andrew had injured his face and was going to have to go to hospital. I asked for the dressing room, and I was told that I couldn't speak to Mike; that he was on the field, and that I'd have to wait until he came *off* the field. I said that it was an emergency. They wouldn't even take a message. So I waited, and as soon as Mike heard what had happened he rang, and we took Andrew to the hospital. Our little boy had some X-rays because it was thought he might have fractured his jaw, but thank goodness he was all right.

People don't realize the price you pay, as a cricketer, in terms of your family life. I've hardly seen my kids growing up. I've always been away, or out playing cricket until after their bedtime. While I had been on tour the previous winter, Elaine had made a video of Andrew taking his first steps, and it was only recently that I could bear to sit down and look at it. I told Elaine vehemently that I'd missed it, and didn't want to see the film. It was too painful for me. They're only little kids once, and nothing can ever compensate you for missing your own kiddies' childhoods. Andrew used to bring his little mates in to watch television and if the cricket came on, he would point at me on the screen and say, 'That's Mike Gatting' – not 'my Dad' – or 'We have Mike Gatting in our house sometimes'. Nowadays, he doesn't even do that; he just turns the cricket off, because he misses me so much, it upsets him. 'You!' he shouts at the white-flannelled figure on the television, 'You should be *here* with me!'

Elaine Gatting:

Recently, while Mike was away on the long winter tour, Andrew came home from nursery school, and apparently he had been naughty, which is unusual for him because he's normally very studious and well behaved. He came home and ran up the stairs, and when I went in his room he was on his bed, sobbing. I said, 'You've been a naughty boy today, Andrew – what's the matter?' and he said, 'My heart is breaking, because my daddy's gone away.' Sometimes he says to me, 'Why can't you go, and my daddy stay here?'

I think that says it all really.

CHAPTER ELEVEN
Doing It for England
1984–85

I was as amazed as everybody else, after my summer Test debacle, when I was selected to go on the tour of India in the winter of 1984–85. Bob Willis had finished his Test career, and David Gower was now England's skipper. I had played as well as I knew how for Middlesex all summer, and I had finished top of the first-class averages with 2257 runs at an average of 68.39, with eight 100s, but I wasn't thinking of England and I never expected England to be thinking of me.

It was David's doing. Evidently he had not only insisted I be on this tour, but insisted that I be his vice-captain as well. No one could have asked for a better boost to his flagging confidence than that, and it was to alter my whole outlook as a cricketer. You see, apart from those first few Tests when Brears had been in charge, it was the first time in the whole of my England career that I had ever felt somebody genuinely wanted me in the team. Until then, I'd always thought I was tagging along under sufferance, as a last resort. They had picked a fairly young side, and as Both had decided he wasn't going to tour, there was going to be a fair amount of responsibility on the senior players – and my goodness, I suppose, having been nominated vice-captain, I now had to think of myself as one of those, along with David, and Allan Lamb. We would have to do the bulk of the batting, though as it turned out, people like Tim Robinson and Graeme Fowler chipped in with very great knocks of their own and made it a little easier.

As soon as we arrived in New Delhi, early in the morning of Wednesday, 31 October, we had a policy meeting – the manager, assistant manager, physio, David and myself – and then David and I came down to discussing the batting order. Now, I had grown used to being shoved up and down at everybody's whim, so being consulted on this was like being given a sense of dignity.

'What number do *you* want to bat?' said David, looking out over the city from our hotel window. 'Well, I've been batting 3 for Middlesex; I'd be *very* happy if I could do that.'

'Right,' said David. 'And I'll go in number 4. What we'll do is, we'll try it like that for the first couple of matches, and then if it doesn't work we'll drop you down the order. All right, Gatt?'

I looked at David, and I looked out over the city of New Delhi and suddenly I realized my life had changed. I wasn't going to be in and out of England any more. What this England skipper was saying, in effect, was 'You'll be playing in *all* the Test matches of course; now you'd better get to grips and make the most of it, and see if you can't do such-and-such.' Somebody believed I could put together a string of innings. Somebody had faith in me, that I had a role in the England batting line-up.

We had arrived at about six in the morning, and after our meeting we all crawled away bleary-eyed and jet-lagged to our respective bedrooms and went to sleep. I woke up, confused, at about 3 o'clock in the afternoon, and somebody was telling me Mrs Gandhi had been assassinated. I said, 'Don't be silly, you're pulling my leg'.

'No, no – it's true.'

And sure enough, the Indian Prime Minister *had* been assassinated and India was in uproar. People were being killed on all sides, and once again we were the innocent visitors in the middle of political turmoil and bloodshed. Fortunately for us, the Sri Lankan Cricket Board generously offered us sanctuary in Colombo for a few days, and that country's President, who had come to New Delhi for the funeral, invited the team to share his plane on the return journey. So, gasping and grateful, we loaded our belongings and ourselves onto his plane, and we escaped to Colombo where we had a few very nice warm days practising and getting acclimatized.

The trouble came much closer to our doorstep though, when we got back. On the eve of the 1st Test in Bombay on 28 November, they shot dead the British Deputy High Commissioner Percy Norris as he was being driven to his Bombay office just a little way from where we were staying. Mr Norris was a great cricket fan and had given a party in our honour at his home the previous evening to make us all feel welcome. After this it became clear that we too were actually in considerable physical danger. A lot of the players were very worried and feared for their safety, and I remember the following morning we were all sitting round wondering what was to become of us, and David and the tour manager, Tony Brown, were having high-level meetings.

The atmosphere was very tense and frightening, and a few of the younger players came to me and said, 'Tell us what's going on, Gatt? Are we going home or *what* are we doing?'

So I went and had a word with David and after a lot of comings and goings, and phone calls to the High Commission, Foreign Office and TCCB, it was decided that England should go ahead with their matches, with a slightly revised itinerary to avoid the worst flashpoints.

The day before the Test match in Bombay, for obvious reasons, we all wore black armbands. We had had a quiet draw in Jaipur against the Indian Cricket Board President's XI, in which we got our first sight of young Mohammad Azharuddin, out cheaply to Cowans in their 1st innings; and we had been outplayed by an Under-25 XI in Ahmedabad, when Azharuddin made 151, a bloke called Madhavan got the streakiest 100 I'd ever seen and their spinners bowled us out, one of them being eighteen-year-old leggie Sivaramakrishnan. I was run out for 52 when I'm sure I'd made my ground.

So the 1st Test began amid the usual cries of 'This is the worst side ever to come to our shores,' etc., especially after Vengsarkar got 200 not out against us for West Zone in a drawn game at Rajkot. Mind you, that had been a very flat wicket, and Fowler (116), Robinson (103) and Gatting (136 not out) made hay on it as well.

Anyway, we went in to the 1st Test at Bombay as happy as could be expected in the circumstances amid the odd uprising and 'worst ever side' headline. Sivaramakrishnan, thankfully known hereafter as Siva, won his first Test place, and was waiting for us when we chose to bat. I am afraid we made heavy weather of it, and a full toss accounted for Fowler, caught and bowled for 28, the first of the leg-spinner's haul of 6 in the innings (including me, for 15).

I think Siva had a little bit of help on the way, either from the Almighty or His White-Coated Representatives, but England were all out for 195. We were doing quite well in the field though, and we weren't letting them get away, until Ravi Shastri and Kirmani came in. India ended up with 465 for 8 declared.

Now, we *were* in a bit of trouble, and when we immediately slipped to 3 for 1, having lost Tim Robinson lbw to Kapil Dev, we were in very deep trouble indeed. Graeme Fowler and I put our heads together and decided to play it session by session. We were now into day four, and we had to bat for two days if England were going to come out of this. We survived until lunchtime and we looked set to survive until teatime as well, but then Graeme was given out lbw. He might have been out the ball before, but this one looked very dubious.

Then they began to go down like ninepins up the other end – David, caught Vengsarkar off Shastri and Allan Lamb, stumped – which brought in Chris Cowdrey, who was given out caught Vengsarkar off Yadav, but who was there long enough to see Gatting quietly reach his first Test 100.

I suppose that was the turning point of my Test career, right there. It's what they'd wanted of me. Oddly enough, when I finally got it, I felt that I had always known what to do. It was as though it had been there all the time, but I just couldn't get hold of it until now. Of course, it's one thing to know how to do something and quite another thing to do it, but it was a strange feeling of recognition that I had, and as soon as the three figures came up on that poor little Bombay scoreboard, I could feel some unspeakable pressure lifting off me.

I knew what it was: I had known for 6 years and 54 innings. People couldn't moan at me any more that 'Gatting hasn't got a Test 100' and 'He hasn't done that and hasn't done this.' Because I'd done it. And having had their say about that, they'd hopefully now turn their attention to somebody else, and leave me in peace to make some more 100s. I had two lucky charms tucked in my cricket case: little Care Bears, one from Elaine and one from little Andrew. I always take them with me wherever I go now, and not just from superstition either.

Unfortunately, Chris Cowdrey was out when he was looking nice and set, but then Paul Downton came out, looking surprisingly cheerful, and we put together a stand as he made his way to 62. Having got to 136 myself, I played a very very silly shot, departing from my custom in this innings and whacking one up in the air to Patil at wide long-off. If I had stayed where I was and been less impetuous I reckon Paul and myself could have saved the match. As it was, England didn't last out much longer. Siva took another 'sixfer' and we lost by 8 wickets. Mind you, I think even the Indian skipper Sunil (Sunny) Gavaskar was slightly embarrassed by some of the decisions that went their way.

We got some terrible stick in the newspapers. We were *definitely* 'the worst side to visit these shores' and 'Why did we bother to come?' etc. So it was very important that we then went on to beat India by 4 wickets in the first one-day international in Pune – England's first win since 2 June (when we'd won a one-day international against the West Indies at Trent Bridge).

Poor David Gower had had a very bumpy ride as England skipper, taking over in very difficult circumstances, but it was nice to be on top for a change. We had looked like we were going to lose, replying to 214 for 6 (Vengsarkar 105), and sinking to 129 for 6, but then Paul Downton and myself (with my first one-day international 100) managed to steer us home with 1½ overs to go.

There were several interruptions from the crowd, who, when they realized they were going to lose, started hurling bottles and rubbish on to the ground. Sunny told them he would take his side off the field if they didn't stop it, and I went and had a word with them myself, but was warned by a police superintendent to go back in the middle. Fortunately, Paul and I managed to duck and weave between the empties and to knock off the winning runs.

The 2nd Test at Delhi, whatever the critics thought, found us in a very good frame of mind. David lost the toss, they batted first, and we managed to limit them to 307 (Richard Ellison bowled very well there, taking 4 for 66) and we had them 6 down for 140 at one point. It was still a fairly good wicket, slow and turning slightly, when after an early flutter of terror when we were 1 down for 15, Tim Robinson took command and struck a superb 160 to inspire us to 418 all out. I was bowled blocking out Yadav when the ball spun back on to my stumps, for 26, but Paul Downton hit a very solid 74, and Siva took his regular haul of 6 in the innings.

In their second knock, Kapil Dev and Sunny were having a few cross words for some reason, and Sunny got out uncharacteristically, dragging it on to his stumps, and after Phil Edmonds had removed Amarnath they seemed to cave in with 235, so we were left to make 125 in 59 minutes and 20 overs. I was quietly collecting my 30 not out when Allan Lamb came in and started smashing it over the sightscreen and the scoreboards and we won by 8 wickets.

It was a great fillip to the side and a tremendous team effort, and on a high note we went off to Gauhati just before Christmas and crushed East Zone with a day to spare. I was actually captain in that game, because young David had gone off up country to do some tigerhunting (he doesn't shoot them; he only looks at them).

At Cuttack we won the second one-day international on a faster scoring rate, in complete darkness, after Srikkanth and

Shastri put on 188 for the 1st wicket (I ended up doing my bowling act and got both of them out) and we replied to India's 252 for 5 off 49 overs with 241 for 6 off 46 – our overs were darker. Which brought us to another visibility problem in the 3rd Test at Calcutta.

It was one of the few Tests I have ever played in that has actually been delayed because of *smog* – and rain as well – and the story of that was that the England bowlers including myself toiled away, Azharuddin and Shastri putting on 214 at a run a month for the 5th wicket; India batted until lunch-time on the 4th day and the crowd, having fallen into a light doze, woke up to throw an assortment of fruit and veg at Sunil Gavaskar.

It was a farce and a nonsense, with Phil Edmonds reading a newspaper on the pitch, Allan Lamb taking 1 for 6, the crowd periodically threatening to riot, and all of us bored out of our minds. Sunny vowed that he would never play in Calcutta again, and the match was no good to anybody. Then after a drawn game against South Zone, at Secunderabad, it was on to the 4th Test match.

Madras, famous Madras. I'll never forget it, and neither will Graeme Fowler. Not only did England win by 9 wickets; not only did we go 2–1 up in the Series after being 0–1 down – the first England team ever to come back from the dead in the Indian Subcontinent – but Foxy Fowler and I got our names in the record books for a rather special achievement.

I remember Sunny Gavaskar winning the toss, and reluctantly saying he'd have a bat. He was right to be worried. Neil Foster, bowling his heart out for 23 overs, took 6 for 104 and with Cowans and Cowdrey reduced India to 272 all out in just over 5 hours to set us on the warpath. We had a nasty couple of minutes at the start of our 1st innings, which Graeme Fowler and Tim Robinson negotiated safely, and then the pair of them laid into an attack that included Kapil Dev and put on 178 for the 1st wicket. Unfortunately Tim then got out, shortly after tea, on the second day, caught Kirmani off Siva for 74. So then it was Fowler and Gatting.

And Gatting and Fowler. And Fowler and Gatting. We were there at the close of play, plodding along. We were there the next session, and the next, and the next, talking to each other, and nudging each other to keep ourselves concentrating. I watched Foxy with genuine admiration up the other end, batting so well in very difficult circumstances (it was very *very* hot and humid) and I thought, Well, this is great – I could bat all day with this bloke.

On and on we went. Graeme got his 100; I got my 100; I hit a 6 off Shastri that went up into the stands and bounced two or three rows in front of the England chairman of selectors, Peter May, who just happened to be taking a holiday in Madras; then I hit another one up there that didn't go quite so far; then Foxy hit some of *his* three 6s, and his 21 4s and on and on we went.

It's quite a tiring thing, batting; it's quite gruelling keeping your concentration going for that length of time, because the Indians had set the field very defensively and it was hard to penetrate, so you had to keep running for 1s and 2s. Our instructions were to Carry On Batting, so you just had to look forward to drinks intervals, and changing your gear at lunchtime and having a quick shower, and guzzling water, and generally keeping yourself fit and alert, talking to yourself to make sure you did what you set out to do.

At close of play on the second day, Foxy and I had taken the score to 293 for 1 and that was nice, because you could have a rest. Throughout the Test match I was in my hotel room in the evenings, very rarely going downstairs. I just stayed in my room having my meals there, watching films on the television, listening to music, or perhaps popping along to the team room for a little while.

On the third day Graeme and I were still at it, trying to keep each other going, as David, in the pavilion, was taking his pads off to rest his legs. I watched Foxy complete his double-century and become the highest-scoring Englishman in the Subcontinent and then at last, after 565 minutes and one of the greatest knocks I've ever had the privilege to watch from the other end, Graeme was out, caught by Kirmani off Kapil Dev, for 201. Which brought in Allan Lamb to replace him, going very well for *his* 62, before he was bowled by Amarnath, and on and ever onwards plodded Gatting.

I had got to about 190 by now. I might have practised the reverse-sweep once in the nets, I think, but I had never played it, or dreamed of playing it, in the middle. It so happens that Ravi Shastri was bowling to a 7–2 leg-side field; now, the left-arm spinner would normally have a 6–3 *off-side* field, but Shastri had 7 players on the leg-side with just a mid-off and a squarish cover. And he was bowling into the rough. This is stupid, I thought. If I can get it round the corner here, it's going to go for 4.

It seemed a fairly safe shot too, because the ball was spinning that way so I would be hitting with the spin rather than against it, and even if I got a top edge, there was no gully or slip or anything, so even that would go for 2. So I played my first reverse-sweep in a match. I didn't time it quite right, but I got down and punched it out to square-cover, and I remember Ravi the bowler giving me a funny look. The next two I managed to execute better though, and they both went for 4 and I got up to about 199; and then I nudged one for 2 and I had made 201.

So Foxy and I joined the illustrious ranks of Test players who had scored twin double-centuries in the same innings – Ponsford and Bradman, Barnes and Bradman, Hunte and Sobers, Lawry and Simpson, Mudassar Nazar and Javed Miandad – and Fowler and Gatting! Sunny Gavaskar was kind enough to describe my innings as 'Most magnificent – he batted with a confidence which I did not think this England side possessed' – and you always greatly value the praise of a fellow- professional like Sunny.

Graeme and I were the first Englishmen to do the 'double double'. So despite all your Mays, your Cowdreys, Dexters, Comptons, and Edriches – it took two little run-of-the-mill fellows like Foxy and Gatt, both of us with beards at the time, and both of us very hot and weary, to do it for England.

Anyway, it was fairly near the close of play, and there was a substitute fieldsman at long-on, Gopal Sharma, and I ended up whacking one up there – and he caught it just on the boundary. So I was out for 207. But the game was proceeding exactly according to plan, and having declared at 652 for 7 (England's highest total against India) we were now going to take some beating. In went the Indians again and Neil Foster came on and bowled quite exceptionally (I remember catching Sunny off him at slip) and they crashed to 22 for 3, having lost not only Gavaskar but also Srikkanth and Vengsarkar. Amarnath and Azharuddin stabilized, though, and plundered the spinners, and Shastri and Azha saw them through to the close of the 4th day.

Azha completed his 100 on the final morning but then Pocock got him caught at silly mid-off by David; Edmonds got rid of Shastri and then Norman Cowans, with the new ball, found the outside edge of Kapil Dev's bat and I took the catch. They managed to hang around for a bit but at last we got rid of them for 412, leaving us just 33 runs to knock off, myself and Tim Robinson doing the honours after Graeme was out, and the Test was ours by 9 wickets.

It had been a tremendous Test match, and you couldn't really describe the glorious feeling afterwards. 'Ten feet tall' and 'cloud nine' don't really do it justice. It was a great day for me personally, having helped England into the record books, and I am sure it was for Foxy Fowler too. Whenever we have a chat, that 1st innings in Madras invariably comes up at some stage of the conversation. We are both very proud to have done it, especially as we had gone on to win the game as well. The New Delhi High Commission even supplied us with a few bottles of champagne afterwards to celebrate, which was very kind. Oh, and I thought the two umpires, Mr Gupte and Mr Ramaswamy, did an excellent job as well.

England won the 3rd one-day international in the lovely garden city of Bangalore by 3 wickets. I got run out cheaply because I couldn't hear the call in the roar of the crowd, and once again bottles rained down on the pitch when it became apparent that India were not going to win. I am afraid I got rather cross at one point when a run out by a long way on the Indian side wasn't given.

At Nagpur, India avenged themselves by 3 wickets, but we won the 5th and final one-day international at Chandigarh at the end of January, to take that series 4–1. Which brought us at long last to the 5th and final Test match at Kanpur, in which we faced a massive 553 for 8 declared and Azharuddin got his 3rd century, then England batted all the 3rd day and most of the 4th for our 417, and after another declaration that left us 46 overs to see out, we managed to stave them off and save the Test match – once again the umpires, Reporter and Ramaswamy, doing a very fine job.

Which meant that England had won the Series. We'd been written off before we started and also after we'd started, and we'd obliged a lot of reporters to rewrite or recast their stories. It was a wonderful feeling and especially pleasing from *my* point of view to have been able to repay David Gower for having faith in me. It had been a great team effort from a young side.

We all managed to have a good old sing-song in Kanpur, with champagne courtesy of the Delhi High Commission, but we had worked unbelievably hard and were really exhausted when from India we had to drag ourselves over to Australia to play in a World Series – the 'Benson and Hedges World Championship of Cricket', it was called, to mark the 150th anniversary of the founding of the State of Victoria. The sponsors spent £3m on the occasion and they must have been a bit stung, hoping for a final between Australia and the West Indies, when they got India and Pakistan – because the crowds stayed away in droves.

England were a very, very tired side and we played some very tired cricket, losing all three of our games to Australia, India and Pakistan. When we had arrived in Australia we had four or five days off and, having been living on fairly spartan rations in India (apart from the victory champagne) and having enjoyed very little in the way of amenities, everybody dispersed and flopped out exhausted in various corners of Sydney. It was like going on holiday after 3½ months in the Subcontinent, and however hard you tried to think about dragging yourself into the nets, it was just like relaxing in paradise.

There were other factors, too, militating against us in the competition. We had to get acclimatized to playing on much quicker, bouncier wickets; a lot of the lads had never played under lights before, as we had to do here, and the rules took some getting used to after India, because they were very different, plus the fact that we were a very young and inexperienced side; we had some bad breaks, and we had some injuries – Tim Robinson broke his arm; Chris Cowdrey broke some bones in his hand; so we didn't play as well as we would have liked, and we didn't do ourselves justice. But we were very, very tired and peaked out. It irked me very much that the Press quickly forgot about India, and how we had just come from 0–1 down to win a Test Series.

Even the journalists who had traipsed round India with us for 3½ months were worn out from their flights and long journeys, and they didn't have to play! So when the Press saw our three losses in the World Championship competition and said, 'Oh dear, it's back to square one,' I was very cross. I don't think Gatting was back to square one: I had fallen just 19 runs short of Kenny Barrington's record Test aggregate for England in India (with 575 at an average of 95.83) and I had had the local carpenters in Kanpur shave a couple of slivers off my new bats to match the one I had used in Madras, and I think I was now heading for different pastures altogether.

CHAPTER TWELVE
Glory to Gory
1985–86

Possibly because I felt more a part of the England side now, my major innings in the summer of 1985 were not for Middlesex; they were for England. Having played with David Gower in the successful Test Series in India and mastered the art of the long Test innings, I had a little more self-belief and it was just a question of translating that self-belief into runs. In fact I managed to top the Test batting averages that summer.

I was more at home in the England dressing room now. In my young days, because I'd been so nervous, I used to keep bouncing the ball on the bat, as Brearley points out, and keep whacking my bat on the floor because I just had to be doing something. Now, it wasn't so bad. I might have a wander round to stop my legs getting stiff, but that's just because I'm not a very good sitter-downer. If I want to watch a duel between a particular batsman and a particular bowler, I'll sit on the balcony and study that, and then probably talk to the batsman afterwards, to ask him the whys and wherefores of his innings. But I'm not a good spectator generally. I'm accused of having ants in my pants.

Of course, you have to be careful not to offend the team superstition I mentioned before about going out to watch. It so happens, you see, that on a number of occasions when players have gone out to have a look at the action after having been watching it on television, or reading, or playing cards or backgammon, or just trying to relax, a bloke has got out. Beefy Botham is very particular about this. He says at the start of a session, 'I'm not going to watch. Those of you who are, go and watch now, and those who aren't, stay where you are – so we don't lose a wicket.' I remember, certainly, in the Birmingham Test in 1985, I wasn't allowed to venture outside because I had been watching on television and reading the newspaper. The same at the Oval.

I don't mind obeying the rules; anything to keep people happy. Botham will sleep for ages in dressing rooms if he can. He's probably just a very tired person. Philippe Edmonds is another one who kips during the day because he's a bit of an insomniac at night. The bowlers generally have a sleep because they need to conserve their energy, whereas some of the batsmen will go out and play squash and Goochie will go for a run if he hasn't batted particularly well. Some will just stretch out with their eyes shut, relaxing. Some will be reading books or newspapers – I have a fetish about sitting down doing the *Telegraph* crossword. There's a lot going on, and a fair amount of mickey-taking and abuse – 'What were *you* up to last night?' etc. – to put it delicately.

At Lord's, before a Test, somebody wheels in the tea-trolley at about 10.30, just as the captains are going to toss up, so if you're the skipper and you're a bit tardy with your heads and tails, you might be unlucky. There are normally twelve cups, but then you've got the scorer and a couple of selectors in there as well, so some will go wanting. At most grounds tea is brought at 10.30 or even earlier.

At the Oval a lot of us don't bother having breakfast; we just send one of the lads out to get the toasted bacon sandwiches. People like to get to the Oval early because you never know what the traffic's going to be like on Vauxhall Bridge, so you set your sights on about nine o'clock, which for me means getting up at eight, having a shower and shave, and leaving myself half an hour for the journey to the ground and the bacon sandwiches. At Trent Bridge there's a cafe just down the road. Being a regular member of the England team, you are privy to this sort of information!

Our opponents this summer were to be the Australians. England had their banned rebel South African tourists restored, and having Graham Gooch and John Emburey back in the fold obviously helped. The Aussies were still a bit depleted and may have had a few internal squabbles over money, according to reports, so on paper they might have been slightly the weaker side. But you can never really tell in cricket who the stronger side will be until you go out and play them. The only thing we knew for certain was that Geoff Lawson was struggling – he was wrapped up in a lot of clothes and was rumoured to have bronchial problems.

The one-day Series for the Texaco Trophy got underway at Old Trafford in May, and England lost the first one by 3 wickets: I got 31 not out before I ran out of partners, Beefy got 72, and I do recall taking the catch to dismiss Wayne Phillips off Norman Cowans at short third man, which he actually hit quite hard, because I caught him again off Norman's bowling in the second Trophy match, so he must have thought I was giving him a hard time.

But again we didn't really get enough runs at Edgbaston despite a goodish pitch and we paid the price, losing by 4 wickets. Gooch had hit 115, but Lamb slowed us up a bit spending 21 overs on 25 runs. Allan Border played exceptionally well, which signalled his form throughout the summer, but then he's a very good player. We did however manage to win the last one-dayer at Lord's, despite being set a pretty stiff target of 255. We weren't worried because Goochie and David were both due for some runs, and both hit brilliant centuries to get us home in style with 6 overs to spare. It was a nice way to go into the 1st Test.

Headingley was a dodgy wicket and would generally help the bowlers. We knew it was going to be a rather difficult Test match. We weren't sure who the Aussies would play, and I don't think we really knew who we were going to play either. We ended up picking Peter Willey, John Emburey and three seamers, and hoping that would do the trick. Australia won the toss and from ball one we bowled extremely badly. There were far too many short balls, wides and half-volleys, and Hilditch capitalized with 119 of their 331. Botham having cleaned up on the second morning, our 1st innings was built very much around Tim Robinson, after we'd lost Gooch and Gower early on. Tim and I managed to put on 136 for the 3rd wicket.

The Aussies bowled as badly as we did, playing to Tim's strengths – his legs, and short or wide deliveries around his off-stump. With Both we managed to clatter it around at an amazing striking rate, for 533 and a huge 1st-innings lead. Then, having bowled them out for 324, we were left needing 123 on a none too friendly wicket.

Chasing this kind of target there was no real certainty (witness Headingley 1981), but we got off to a reasonable start, and then as the target came down our confidence went up. After a few minor tremors we won by 5 wickets. Obviously it was a great delight, having just won a Test Series in India, to go one up against the Aussies in an Ashes Series as well, and there was excitement in the camp. It was the first time we'd really had anything to celebrate at home, and being vice-captain now as well, it was all the nicer for me personally.

Well, at Lord's, in the 2nd Test, we managed to go and undo all the good work at Headingley. This was the scene of the famous incident in which the villainous Gatting supposedly threw the ball up in the air and dropped it again when Allan Border was on 87 – he went on to thunder 196. They had included Bob Holland in their attack, a 38-year-old leg-spinner. We were a pretty settled side, David having been confirmed as captain for the rest of this Series. Border won the toss and sent us in. The outfield, like the outlook, was sopping wet. We managed just 290 first innings, although we had them in a bit of trouble as well at 80 for 3; but they had added nearly 100 more runs for the loss of only 1 more wicket when The Incident occurred.

Border went for the pull off Edmonds and the ball flew at me, fielding at short-leg. It was a reflex action really: the ball having struck my hand I knocked it up in the air and tried to clutch it to my chest. People got the impression I was throwing it up in triumph, but in fact I was simply trying to knock it upwards, to give myself time to catch it properly. I didn't really have a grip on it at any stage, unfortunately, and it just sailed off into the middle of nowhere. The umpire quite rightly gave Border not out, saying I never had control of the ball.

So Border went on his triumphant way, and with Ritchie's 94, soon after lunch on day three they were all out for 425, to give them a very useful 135 1st-innings lead. We lost Gooch and Robinson, and that evening we sent in *two* nightwatchmen, and when you do that, very often somebody ends up stranded with no tail-end partners, and unfortunately that somebody happened to be me.

Both and I had added 131 to our 98 for 6, when for some unknown reason, with Holland bowling round the wicket, Both tried to hit one over long-on which just held up, and it sailed to Allan Border backward of point. Both had been playing very, very well, and we were just getting on terms, and now we lost 3 or 4 quick wickets. I ended up 75 not out and England had to settle for 261, setting them 127 for victory.

They got a bit rattled and were 63 for 4 at one point, and I am sure it must have flashed across Border's mind that they had collapsed chasing 130 on a previous occasion, but he got them home to beat us by 4 wickets. Bob Holland, their leg-spinner, had done them a very great service and proved a match-winner in our 2nd innings. I think the only good thing to come out of that from our point of view was that they were obliged to play him at Trent Bridge, which was a different sort of wicket, and he didn't do us much damage there.

As for my juggling act, I said I wouldn't talk about it afterwards because I didn't want to cause any trouble either for myself or umpire Bird. I told the Press, 'You saw it. Draw your own conclusions.' They all gave me some stick, saying I *was* trying to throw up the ball in triumph, because that made it more sensational, you see. Unless you have actually fielded at short-leg you can't possibly know how harsh the pressure is there, or the speed at which you have to react. So I was condemned, I thought unjustly. Perhaps it was my own fault for not talking to them about it, but I was a bit upset over the whole thing. I wasn't very good at knowing what to say at press conferences, and I found out that being guarded and saying nothing was just one more way of putting your foot in it.

The Trent Bridge Test was drawn. It featured splendid knocks from David (166), Wood (172) and Ritchie (146) on a very flat wicket. I was out 1st innings backing up David who had drilled this one past Bob Holland; but the ball hit Bob's finger and then rebounded on to the stumps at the non-striker's end, and I was run out for 74. David went on to play quite magnificently, though I'd have loved to have got my first home Test 100 there for the simple reason that the Trent Bridge crowd always used to give me a hard time, seeing me at the crease instead of their local hero Derek Randall. It wasn't my fault if I was selected and Arkle wasn't, but the murmur went round the ground that perhaps I was well in with the selectors or something, and although you shouldn't take any notice, it's very hard *not* to hear comments when people walk past your face saying, 'Why isn't Derek playing? You're no bleeding good'.

Beefy was in a spot of trouble up there as well, and he was later disciplined for what happened during the Australians' 1st innings. Both very rarely bowls no balls, and I think the point was, that he'd been called for a couple by Alan Whitehead before, and he was really charging in here because the Aussies, from doing well, had taken a tumble, so Greg Ritchie's wicket was quite crucial. He had chipped a couple off Emburey and then Both had come roaring in, and had Ritchie caught at 3rd man off what Alan Whitehead decreed a no ball. Beefy didn't see what was wrong with his ball, and there was a bit of an interruption, after which Both started bowling bouncers and Alan Whitehead turned round and gave him a warning.

I couldn't really tell from where I was what was going on, but I saw David go over to try and calm things down. Beefy got a lot of criticism in the papers afterwards which I thought was unjustified. He was just bowling his heart out to get us some wickets, putting all he could into shifting Ritchie on a very flat and unhelpful wicket, on a very hot day and in a very frustrating situation.

Unfortunately, that summer two other past or present Test skippers were also disciplined for dissenting with the umpire – Keith Fletcher, a very tough character, and Imran Khan, a very proud man as well, who won't be talked down to. I was just an on-looker in all this; though in general I think the umpires have a hard job. In India and Pakistan they seem to get carried away by the crowds a little bit, but it must be very difficult being an umpire, and although I've always maintained that we have the best people for the job here, they do it day in and day out, week after week, and after they've done it for a long time I think possibly they need a break from the pressure, like the pilots in the Red Arrows.

Players *are* more forthright now. Instant replays *do* put umpires' decisions under the microscope. And because they are only human, they do make honest mistakes. To give but one example, in 1987 at Headingley, England were batting against Pakistan, and Chris Broad dropped his hands and the ball went through the crook of his elbow to the keeper, whereupon the fielders all appealed for a caught behind. The umpire couldn't see from his angle exactly what happened, and he gave Broad out, because he assumed the bat was in his hand at the crucial moment. From the umpire's point of view at the front, that's what it looked like – and that's what I call an honest mistake.

Another extremely difficult decision is when the ball was missing leg and nips back. That's a case of personal judgement. It even happens that some umpires may appear slightly biased towards the opposition because they want to be sure that they are fair to them, a criticism which cannot be levelled at umpires in Pakistan.

Old Trafford was the venue for the 4th Test, and England took the initiative until the end, when Allan Border batted extremely well amid rain stoppages for 146 not out and saw them safely to the draw, despite the sterling work of our spinners on a dead pitch. Gower had won the toss and stuck them in, and between showers we bowled them out for 257. In reply we assembled 482 for 9 declared, so I think it was always going to be a draw really. We were 142 for 2 when I came in and joined Gooch.

Unfortunately, Goochie got out shortly afterwards for 74, lbw to McDermott who was to take 8 of the 9 wickets to fall in the innings. But Allan Lamb and I managed to put on quite a few (156) for the 4th wicket and I eventually got out playing a very tired shot to McDermott when I was really in control and should have gone on to 200. I had made 160. It was just a question of England batting for two days really and I tried to bat all the way through.

It was a great thrill to get 100 in England (it was in fact my first 1st-class 100 of the season) but then I felt a lot safer anyway, having already managed to break the 100 barrier in India, and I knew I was in good order from Trent Bridge. Hopefully this might silence the remaining critics who said, 'Ah! but Gatting hasn't done it *in* England,' and the biggest sceptic of the lot, Robin Marlar, who'd been saying, 'It's all very well for him to get runs against India, but if he gets runs against Australia, *then* you can call him a Test player'.

Alas it wasn't to be, because even after I'd done that, he started saying, 'When he gets runs against the West Indies, you can call him a Test player'. I must say it *was* nice to keep those sort of people at bay if only momentarily. My other great critic, Henry 'Blowhard' Blofeld, had written that it was a disgrace that I should have been taken to India instead of some other youngster, and after my centuries there, he was saying he'd always 'been a fan of Mike Gatting' and how marvellous it was to see him doing so well, and other such rubbish. There are three or four people who have stuck by me loyally among the Press corps, for which I am very grateful. The others write what they will.

A lot of Tests had finished in four days at Edgbaston, despite it being a good wicket, and we were hoping for a result in the 5th Test. Into the England side came Les Taylor, who had been getting a lot of wickets for Leicester, and Richard Ellison, who had done so well in India – a shrewd selection, as it turned out, because his swing was to take 10 wickets in the match – a tremendous effort which I feel won us the game.

Rain kept trying to interfere, and it was cloudy when we won the toss and inserted Australia. A very good run out by David Gower off the first ball of the third day prevented Australia's tail from wagging even more energetically than it did, and they were all out for 335. Once again, England had a big batting assignment. Jeff Thomson removed Gooch (his 200th Test wicket and his 100th against England) which brought together Tim Robinson and David Gower for a quite unbelievable partnership of 331 for England's 2nd wicket, David compiling a tremendous 215, and Robbo hitting 148.

I was hacking away as best I could, having been asked for quick runs, when Both came in, hit his first 2 balls for 6 and 4, hit another 6, and got out for 18 on the deep square-leg boundary. By which time they were just waiting for me to complete my 100 I think. We got a signal from the dressing room, and I managed to nudge 1 to bring up my 100 not out – quite quick as Test tons go, because it was off about 120 balls (England's striking rate this summer was a phenomenal 60 runs per 100 balls).

I had been given a free rein to do as I liked really, so I just enjoyed myself. We declared at 595 for 5 – and then in the hazy evening light Australia were reduced to 37 for 5 by Ellison, who bowled Border an absolute Jaffa that pitched about off- stump and came back through the gate.

We didn't want play to close. It was an evening of frustration, of longing to get at them. We were almost celebrating, but we were a bit worried it might rain on our parade and save them. I remember having dinner with a friend of mine who had come over from Australia, Ray Gallian, and we were agreeing it didn't really matter one way or t'other, we would surely win the Test tomorrow. All we had to do was prise out

Greg Ritchie and Wayne Phillips, their last two recognized batsmen.

Well, it rained and drizzled down till lunchtime, with England noses pressed against dressing room windows, and it wasn't until 2.30 that we at last managed to get out there, by which time we were having silly fields – 6 slips at one time, and for Wayne Phillips we had 4 slips, 3 gullys and a mid-off, because he likes to hit it through the gully. Didn't matter about the runs, of course, because they were never going to get those anyway.

Well, after about an hour of this, we weren't making too much headway. Ritchie and Phillips were still there, battling away. On came the spinners next, and Emburey had Ritchie, caught at silly mid-off by Lamb. O'Donnell came in, and was clean bowled by Botham. But we were still having trouble with this Mr Phillips, and so now came the incident that Allan Border says cost them the match. Philippe Edmonds was bowling; we had two silly mid-offs; Wayne went back to cut – and the ball hit Allan Lamb on the side of his instep, flicked up off Allan's foot and was caught by David Gower. I was fielding at short-leg, close by, and my immediate reaction was 'That's out – catch it!'

Afterwards we replayed it over and over on the video, and in slow motion, and the ball really didn't touch the ground. I don't know what David Constant, the square-leg umpire, could see, but I know what I saw and we were all delighted when Phillips was given out. All except Allan Border, who stated that it all happened so quickly, the umpire couldn't have been sure. It's a shame that England went on to win from that controversial decision, but we surely had done enough throughout the match.

So we were 2–1 up going into the final test at the Oval. It was a very good wicket and very flat and dry, and fortunately David won an excellent toss and we batted. Our innings of 464 had as its highlight a masterful 196 from Mr Gooch and a spectacular 157 from Mr Gower. The two of them put on 351 for the 2nd wicket – which really finished them off. I went in and got the only ball that turned all day, and I got caught at slip by Border off Murray Bennett, the left-arm spinner; it was a poor shot. By lunch on the 3rd day we had bowled them out and they were asked to follow on.

Then there was a lot of rain, which took us on to the 4th day, in a nightmare repetition of the previous Test pattern. But this time we had them corralled. Only Allan Border offered resistance to Ellison (with 5 wickets) and Botham. The rest crumbled meekly, all out for 129. So by the 4th day we'd drubbed them by an innings and 94 runs, to take the Series 3–1 and the Ashes. Goochie got Man of the Match and rightly so, and David was named Player of the Series.

We had a nominal celebration at the Oval, whooping it up till 6.30, and then some of the players had to get back to their hotel to pack up all their gear because we hadn't expected it to finish so abruptly. I went home to Enfield for a shower, and then we all went out to dinner that evening.

You can imagine my feelings. Not long ago I had been in and out of the squad and up and down the order, the bloke with no 100s, who had simply tagged along. Now here I was, vice-captain and top of the Test batting averages, a real part of the England team that had won a memorable victory. It was one of the best Test series I've ever played in, and despite the rain, what a great summer it had been for English cricket, as well as for me.

Middlesex won the County Championship in 1985. I was absent on England duty for ten of my County matches, not reaching a 100 there until September, and they were without Paul Downton, Emburey, Edmonds, and Cowans too for much of the time. Great credit for Middlesex's triumph must go to the younger guys and regulars like Wilfy Slack; Graham Barlow; Keith Brown, when he came in as our opener; Neil Williams; Jamie Sykes and Simon Hughes who battled it out in a crucial game against Hampshire; young Angus Fraser, and especially to our stalwart Clive Radley, who skippered in my absence and did a marvellous job keeping us in the points. All credit too to the senior players, because most of our victories came when we had a full-strength side. It really was an incredible effort. And let's not forget Wayne Daniel either, always steaming in and trying as hard as anybody.

We didn't do particularly well in the one-dayers. The John Player was yet another disappointment, and in the Bensons, where we got to the semis, we lost by 62 runs to Essex, as was our wont in the limited-over games around this time, on the very slow Chelmsford wicket. I got out to one of the most amazing catches I've ever seen, to Lilley at point. I launched into a big square drive, and the bloke didn't see it – then when he *did* see it, he launched himself to his left and stuck out his hand. Unbelievable.

Essex also stopped us in the second round of the NatWest, again at Chelmsford, by 84 runs. The wicket just got slower and slower. Keith Fletcher, who was injured and missed the match, was caught saying, 'We didn't want a wicket where the ball whistles round your ear'oles off a length when Daniel, Cowans and Williams were bowling. We are not here to prepare a wicket for Middlesex's benefit.' Which is fine, but you're not supposed to prepare a wicket for your own team either, as we felt they had, so there was still some needle against Essex I am afraid.

But we had won a trophy every year for our supporters, and this year it happened to be the best one of all, the County Championship. Whether they were happy about that, we don't know. You never know whether they're happy or sad because they don't say too much.

Without us Test players, the lads drew a crucial game against Hants at Bournemouth in June; we were up the top of the table having won a couple against Worcester and Sussex and we'd got quite good bonus points, and benefited from other counties' unfinished matches and what we *didn't* want was Messrs Marshall and Greenidge rolling us over: we needed our under-strength team at least to draw. Fortunately, though we were struggling, Simon Hughes and Jamie Sykes fended off Marshall to save the day. That enabled us to keep a few points ahead of Hampshire in the table.

Really, while the Test players were away, we were satisfied if the lads managed draws – which they duly did. A big win against Notts at Trent Bridge by 10 wickets with the full-strength side, thanks largely to our ton-up twins of the season, Wilfy and Graham Barlow, helped us roll right along and then the lads beat Worcester by 3 wickets, with the help of a young bowler called Graham Rose who took 6 for 41 for us there. We were full strength for our drubbing of Northants at Northants, by 141 runs (Phil Edmonds took 9 wickets in the match). It was very important for us to score these big wins with our full complement side, because Hampshire were still winning, and Gloucester were in the hunt as well.

Unfortunately then, the lads lost to Notts, and drew against Somerset, although Graham Barlow got another 100. He'd been to a faith-healer that summer because his back was giving him dreadful pain and he didn't know what to do. It seemed to work, and apart from putting faith into his back, it seemed to put faith into his batting, and with Wilfy he played magnificently well. When your openers can regularly put on a 100 it takes a lot of pressure off everybody.

We were able to play our full side at Uxbridge against Northants, where Clive Radley got 200. He had never got a double-century before, although he'd done most things and got hundreds in every sort of cricket including Test matches. He was as pleased as Punch, and so was Paul Downton, who got his maiden 1st-class century. Middlesex needed to get rid of 9 of them on the last day, and I managed to prise out Allan Lamb, who was proving troublesome. We won that by an innings and 161 runs, and this victory put us back at the top of the table, partly because we had a game in hand over Hampshire. Rain washed away a very good start against Lancs, but we salvaged 4 points from that; and then I was on Test duty when they lost to Essex (we kept losing to Essex in 1985).

Against the Aussies we had an experimental four-day game, which ended in a boring draw. We had lost a lot of time to the weather and I tried to talk Geoff Lawson into making a game of it, but they didn't want to know. The only good thing was that Slacky got 201 not out and Keith Brown chipped in with a 100 on his Lord's debut, and their 213 stand was the highest against the tourists to date. I had a bowl and managed to knock 3 over. I had David Boon lbw for 4 and we thought that might have finished his Test career!

Middlesex were ticking over with draws while we were away, but then a full-strength side went and lost to Sussex at Hove at the end of August, having been set too stiff a target, basically. We had chased 292 off 58 overs – they knew full well we would go for it because we always do when we are poised near the top of the table. So we lost our top spot now, and I told the lads that we would have to win two or three of our remaining three games. If we did that, I said, we could still win the Championship. Now our next game happened to be against Leicester, and as you know Middlesex beat Leicester at their peril in the Championship fortunes but this year we broke the curse and broke all the rules, and we swept Leicester aside by 10 wickets, thanks to some terrific bowling from Cowans and Wayne Daniel. This win restored us to the top of the table, and we were now steaming in.

But then came Essex at Lord's. Gooch didn't open the batting. Where was he? He was in the pavilion, talking to the TCCB about whether he would go on the imminent West Indies trip and whether or not they would let him in after the South African adventure. At about 12.20 Essex were 4 down, and our bowlers were roaring in, and out to the wicket strolled Mr Gooch, his meeting having been cut short. Fortunately he didn't last long and they were all out for 92.

In reply we amassed 279 and I managed my first century of the season for Middlesex. Then in their 2nd innings Goochie, looking very tired from his exertions, nevertheless hit 145, and got out lbw at last to me, and they set us 275 in 51 overs. We ended up having to hang around to see out the draw. Fortunately Hants had done no better. Which meant that in our last game, against Warwickshire, we needed 4 bonus points, because we were at this stage one point in front of

Hampshire, and Hants or Gloucester had to win their last game with full bonus points.

So we went to meet Warwickshire at Edgbaston very excited. I was spluttering and coughing with a chest infection, so I was hoping it might be over in two days if possible, then perhaps I could last out. Imagine our delight when we found they had produced the perfect wicket for Middlesex: dry and turning. We had the two finest spinners in the world, and they'd given us a Bunsen Burner. We bowled them out for 187, after they had won the toss, and we never looked back really. Slacky, Brown and Ernie were all in the runs; I managed 76 and we crushed Warwickshire by an innings and 74 runs.

We were the Britannic Assurance County Champions and myself and Rad, who said he hadn't given us a price at the start of the summer, were squirting champagne over the balcony at all the supporters who'd taken the trouble to come up and see us. I was 28, I was captain of a champion side, and I was grateful to every one of them for making it possible.

It had been a very close-run thing right up to the final whistle. It meant a lot to me particularly, because although it was very pleasing to have led Middlesex to victory in two limited-overs competitions, winning the County Championship was obviously what it was all about. As I told the Press when it was all over, Middlesex is not the easiest team to captain. There are some very experienced senior players who have their own individual views on how things should be done. Which is fine – they have every right to air their opinions. My own position as skipper is that everyone should be allowed his say, although in the end it has to be me that makes the final decision.

Sometimes, senior players found this hard to accept. Philippe Edmonds, for example, would occasionally get quite stroppy and upset, saying 'Right then – I'm not going to bowl', and so you'd send him down to the boundary, where he would mess about with the crowd to make himself feel better. I would say to him afterwards, 'You acted like a schoolboy,

Philippe,' whereupon he would turn around and laugh at me. He knew he was in the wrong but he wouldn't accept that he'd been childish, and if you treated him accordingly he simply got upset. He likes to try and lead people on – a bit like my brother Steve when we were little boys – to see how angry they can get, and how far they can be pushed. So I would try never to get very cross with Philippe, because that's exactly what he was trying to achieve, and he was very clever at it.

I never lost my temper with him. I'd tell him if he'd been an absolute idiot and on occasions we would have our to-dos, but to his credit, Philippe would never bear any grudges. You'd have an argument and that would be it. Some people are crafty and save things up whilst being outwardly nice to you; not Phil Edmonds – he'd have a row with you and that would be the end of the story. But you had to be very clear in your own mind what you were trying to do at the club, and be fair to the rest of the side. You couldn't have one rule for the senior players like Philippe and Embers, and another rule for the rest. You had to keep an even balance, and if you had to tell the youngsters to pull their fingers out occasionally, you also had to take them into consideration. That was always my aim – to be fair to everybody.

Another little focus of attention when we won the Championship was that people had begun to criticize Middlesex for having a contingent of five native West Indians, including principal spearhead bowlers and batsmen like Wayne Daniel, Neil Williams, Norman Cowans, Roland Butcher and Wilfy Slack. They were what we called our All-Black Attack and we were very proud of them. The criticism arose because of the current feeling that Englishmen should be given a chance in the counties, but in our case it wasn't quite fair.

Our overseas player was Wayne, who was eligible to play for the West Indies, yet you'd think Wayne was born and bred in Middlesex, he's so loyal and hardworking. As for the others; well they may have been born in the West Indies, but they've been in England since they were little kids. And what's more to the point was that Wilf, Norman and Roland were all to play for England. Perhaps Butch and Norman are the most Caribbean-orientated. Slacky got carried along with it occasionally; Neil is very quiet, and Wayne is very much Wayne.

I was once accused by one team member, who shall remain nameless, of being a 'racist'. In a team with no fewer than five black members, you couldn't afford to be a racist. I soon straightened him out on that one. Our team is a good combination, and we've always got on brilliantly. There are naturally little cliques; some drink and some don't, and some like to do their own thing. If they're happy why try to change them? As long as they do their best with their cricket, I don't care two hoots what they do, to be honest.

So there we were, cock-a-hoop over our Championship win. Unfortunately we couldn't get drunk because we had to drive back down the motorway, which caused rather an anticlimax. It's a funny feeling when you've toasted your victory with champagne and then you have to doggedly pack your bags and trundle all the way back to London; it definitely takes some of the fizz out of it. Still they were saying nice things about me in the papers: that at last I'd stepped out of the shadow of Mike Brearley, and so on, and Peter Smith even headed his piece in the *Mail*, 'Ghost Buster', which happens to be one of my favourite films!

The rest of the year, I had a rather violent time of it – especially that winter in the West Indies. I'd had a taste of things to come on my birthday, back in June, when I was at our Worcester hotel and was roused by a phone call asking me to attend a charity disco in a Worcester social club, to help raise some funds for the Bradford City Disaster Appeal. Roland Butcher and I went along, with a few of the Worcester lads as well. Two young lady organizers asked me to draw the raffle which I did, and then we were having a drink, and I was playing with their little kiddies, because I love children.

I was just going out to order a cab when the ex-husband of one of these young ladies suddenly came out and punched me on the nose. I found myself sitting there on my bottom, having been taken completely by surprise. Apparently this man had a reputation for threatening to thump people talking to his wife or playing with his children. When we realized what was going on, one or two of the cricketers and I chased out after this bloke but a few people grabbed me and said, 'Don't be silly'. The girls apologized profusely, we players went back to our Worcester hotel and had a nightcap. I only got a bloody nose, so it wasn't too bad and next time we were down there, I got a letter from the man who'd hit me, saying he was terribly sorry; he had got the wrong impression, and all this sort of thing.

Elaine Gatting:

Mike phoned me that night to warn me that I'd see something in the Press in the morning. It was quite amusing really. He was not allowed to retaliate, but then he has a very, very long fuse anyway and I've only ever seen him in a temper once. We had been out to a dinner and had had a fair amount of wine, and I started to have a go at him, and so did Mum, and he actually put his fist through the kitchen door. Whenever he gets cross now I tell him, 'We've still got that hole in the door you know'.

My nose had got back to normal by the time I flew out with the England squad to the West Indies. Well, 'normal'. It had been broken in Auckland, when Geoff Howarth padded one away and it flew straight into my nose, and that was when Bernard Thomas had stuck the tweezers up and straightened it out as best he could. And then when I was in Australia, playing for Balmain, we were doing some catching practice and I was fielding in the slips next to this huge man called Chris Fitzgerald, whose nickname was 'Moose', and he stuck a hand out and deflected the ball on to the end of my nose. There was blood literally everywhere but we managed to stop it and I ended up bowling 30 overs. Apart from being a bit blocked up, it was OK to play with.

Then in another fielding accident I got it broken back the other way, I think, as it tended to wobble about a bit. I had had a glancing blow on the side of the head from Imran Khan at Hove one year, and another bump on top of the head from Sylvester Clarke at the Oval, from a ball I didn't pick up until the moment before it hit me. Now, that last one was John Emburey's fault really, because when Sylvester had been batting, Ernie was in the slips saying, 'Come on, lads – bounce him!' And Sylvester had thought it was me. Thank goodness I was wearing a helmet, because it was very murky when he came charging in, bent on revenge.

Anyway I think everybody was in quite good heart when England arrived in Arnos Vale, St Vincent, to play the Windward Islands, in February 1986. We thought, provided we could get good pitches and reasonable practice facilities, we stood a fair chance of competing. Unfortunately, we weren't to get either of them. I was captain for this particular opening match and because I had played there on the last trip, I knew it was going to turn square. And I'm afraid we lost, because we had fewer spinners in the side than they did. Edmonds and Peter Willey did what they could for us, and secured us a 1st-innings lead, but in our 2nd innings we collapsed for 94 to their off-spinner Hinds, bowling over the wicket to a 2–7 field. If Emburey had played, I am sure we would have won.

So with me having deputized for David, we hadn't got off to a very good start. Nobody had practised for about three months; it seemed to me we could have done with a bit more planning and preparation for the tour as a whole. We'd found some decent practice facilities in Barbados, but there were none to speak of in St Vincent, and there weren't going to be any adequate facilities in Antigua either.

We drew our second game, against Leeward Islands, at St John's, when again we should have won. We needed just 116 in 70 minutes and 20 overs and we ended up saving the game on 94 for 8, which was stupid. Richie Richardson had bowled us out with his little in-swingers after they'd really given up the ghost. So here we were, having presented the Windward

Islands with their first-ever victory over foreigners, and drawn against Leeward *without* Viv Richards to lead them (Viv was to captain West Indies succeeding Clive Lloyd), and ill-prepared to take on Jamaica at Kingston, because of the worrying lack of nets there as well.

The Press had begun to get stuck into us for being a lazy lot, saying Both and Gower had gone off sailing, etc. I'm a great advocate of practice myself, but without proper facilities there's not a lot you can do. Here in Jamaica, we had only one wicket to practise on and that was a middle wicket. It had no enclosure so we had to do our own fielding. It was very hot and the practice took a long while due to the fact that we could have only two batsmen at a time. We did have our bowling machine and a few of us stayed on for more practice, because our own bowlers had had enough. We really wanted to do more but everybody was hot and tired.

In fact, England won in Kingston, by 158 runs, and that gave us a little boost. Michael Holding had been injured in the 1st innings, which put him out of the attack for the West Indies as well, so that would probably be a help. Jamaica had Courtney Walsh bowling at us instead, and we were 56 for 3, but Lamby and myself put on 147, and our 371 total set up the victory. It wasn't very easy batting on that strip, with the ball flying off a length, and one very, very nasty delivery from Walsh actually hit David Gower three times as he fended it off his nose. One bowler we weren't to see in that game was Patrick Patterson. The West Indies were keeping him up their sleeves.

We watched the pitch dry out at Kingston, ready for the one-day international and the 1st Test a few of days later. We could see how uneven it was, and we were wondering whatever it was going to do. We picked a side, and got underway, and I remember the game fairly well, for obvious reasons. The West Indies had drawn up their heavy artillery: Patterson, Marshall, Walsh, Garner, Harper. In we went, and we were 2 for 1, and 10 for 2, having lost Robinson and Gower for ducks. Now, Malcolm Marshall bowls at 90 mph.

He has a very fast arm, and he is altogether very, very quick, and with bowlers like him, even if you can see the shine on the ball, you don't necessarily know which way it's going to swing, because sometimes they wet one side and it swings the opposite way, and sometimes even the bowler himself doesn't know the swing direction.

When you first come into the game, you don't bother to watch the bowler that closely, but you soon learn that your survival may depend on it, so you notice everything, and you watch the bowler's hand as he's running in to see how the ball is positioned. You watch him from the non-striker's end as well, to pick up any little mannerisms about his action, and how he holds the ball. Of course there is also the danger that if you look too hard, you may come to expect a particular delivery and find yourself playing down the wrong line and looking a complete fool. So basically, whatever conclusions you draw from your observations, you've still got to play the ball on its appearance and merit.

Anyway, I'd made 10 runs, and I watched a couple go by from Malcolm at about head height. I'd already played one right in front of my face, and nudged it, if that's the right expression, for a single through square-leg. The odd delivery was a bit unpredictable and you were having to take care of yourself as much as think about scoring runs. Marshall walked back to his mark, turned, and in he came; it was short and I got into line for the pull shot, but in that split second I realized it wasn't quite short enough, and I got caught in two minds, half back, half forward, thinking I might turn it round the corner instead. It must have skidded on a greenish patch because it fairly flew, and the next thing I could see was the ball coming across my last lines of defence, the top of the bat, the top of the gloves, heading for my face. I watched it all the way, though obviously you close your eyes on impact; it was a bit like running into a wall. And then I felt it hit me.

It didn't hurt very much, oddly enough, though I could feel the blood pouring down as I trod backwards – and to add insult to injury the ball apparently bounced off my face onto my stumps. My nose was literally flattened. I couldn't see what it looked like but my shirt front was covered with blood. Laurie Brown immediately ran out on to the pitch to see how I was, and somebody gave me a towel. David Gower told people, 'I've seen a few blood-curdling injuries, but this was one hell of a blow'. I was helped back to the dressing room and sat down. Malcolm, meanwhile, had picked up the ball and, finding a bit of bone embedded in it, threw it down on the pitch in disgust. Somebody else had actually to pick the piece of bone out, because Marshall felt quite queasy. He told reporters, 'That has to be the most awful sight I've ever seen in any sort of cricket. I've hit quite a few batsmen, but I can't recall inflicting such a nasty-looking injury as that.'

He had indeed hit quite a few. Yashpal Sharma, concussed in 1983; Amarnath, hit in the face in 1983; Dilip Vengsarkar, also struck in the face in 1983; Andy Lloyd, hit on the side of the head in 1984. His fellow West Indians had done a spot of damage too: Graeme Wood was hit on the head by Holding in 1983, to say nothing of various broken arms and broken fingers.

I knew something must be fairly radically wrong, because when I went to blow my nose, blood was gushing out of the top, and the lads were quite distressed about that. It took most of the afternoon to stop bleeding, and my eyes, which began to resemble those of a panda, closed up with the swelling. It was actually a good thing that it bled so profusely, because it took the swelling down fairly quickly. Even after it had been stitched up there was still a horrible trickle down the back of my throat. Both was very good and came to the hospital with me, and he sat by me while I was being stitched. I must say the doctor did a good job: I think he's gone off to Florida now to ply his trade over there. His chief medical concern had been to find out whether fragments of bone had been driven backwards into my skull, but unfortunately the X-rays showed that they hadn't.

I went back to the dressing room and sat there for about an hour and a half, and England batsmen kept coming and going, so I said, 'Can I go back in?' and they told me, 'No, you were bowled and you trod on your stumps'.

'Oh hell!' I said, and we lost by 6 wickets, and there wasn't a lot I could do to help. I went back to the hotel and stayed in bed for the next couple of days, telling myself, It's not that bad – you've only broken your nose. My eyes were really puffing up by now and I couldn't breathe through my nose at all. That was probably the most uncomfortable thing, having to rely on my throat for breathing, because of the blood which kept trickling down the inside.

I can remember waking up in the night thinking, *What if something gets stuck in my throat*! And I came out in a bit of a sweat because I couldn't breathe properly and had to calm myself down a bit. For two or three days I was like this, and for the first day or two I couldn't actually see out of one of my panda-like eyes. I was given some painkillers, and told *not* to try and blow my nose, but just to keep dabbing it. I was going to have to fly home and have some operations.

I had to sit and watch the 1st Test, which wasn't very nice. I could see it was going to be one of those unpleasant affairs that would be over in 3½ days, though by that time I was on the plane home and into hospital. When I arrived in London, with steri-strips crosswise across the bridge of my former nose, one reporter stuck his mike out and said, 'Where did the ball actually hit you?' I laughed out loud, because it cheers you up, listening to really stupid questions, and I pointed to the cross of steri-strips and said, 'I think "X" marks the spot actually.' Elaine was rather shocked at the sight of me.

Elaine Gatting:

Generally, unless Mike is totally disabled, he will play on – like he did in Australia. On that occasion they said he should go into hospital but he wouldn't, and I get very cross with him sometimes and cross with the authorities for letting him play on when he's not fit. He would go out in a plaster-cast if he could, and I think someone needs to be firm when players are like that, and say 'You're not fit so you're not playing'.

I was shopping in Waltham Cross when I turned on the car radio and heard about the Marshall incident. First of all the report was rather vague, something about an accident to one of the England players. It was later on that I heard that Mike had been hit in the face with a ball whilst batting and I thought, Oh dear – another broken nose, without being particularly concerned. Then when I came home and put the teletext on and saw 'Gatting had been led from the field with blood pouring down his face . . .' it all began to sound rather more dramatic. My brother phoned and told me of a different radio report, and later on that evening the tour manager rang and gave me all the gory details.

Mike did ask the Press to hold up on the pictures until I had been properly informed, though one woman journalist actually rang my grandmother about *that* to ask if Mike was 'always so caring' – trying to make a story out of *it*. I met Mike at the airport. He wasn't wearing a bandage, just strips of plaster, with some stitches. There wasn't a nose really – just a bump in the middle of his face. And of course these two black eyes.

As soon as I saw the surgeon, the first thing I wanted to know was, 'How long will it take to heal?'

'Probably about three weeks.'

'Fine – can I get back for the Barbados *v* England match?'

'Well, we'll see.'

So I went into the operation about 10 o'clock in the morning and I was in the theatre for about two hours while they were trying to rebuild. Malcolm Marshall had in fact done me a favour, because my nose hadn't worked properly for years and had urgently needed rearranging. Because it had been broken on previous occasions, they found a stray fragment of bone and used that towards a bridge. A bit of the new nose has since collapsed down on the left side, but it looks reasonably normal now. I woke up from the anaesthetic in the early evening, and talked to someone for half-an-hour before falling back to sleep again.

My neck and shoulders were unbelievably sore, because I'd been in surgery with my head scrunched right back and a block under my neck. I had wire up my nose and about 17 yards of yellow gauze padding, which all had to be removed in another operation. That wasn't too bad, although I felt a bit queasy. So two days later they let me out, with instructions to give it a week and see what happened.

I looked at the England itinerary and worked out that I could get in about three days of indoor nets if I was lucky before returning to the West Indies. I phoned the TCCB and said, 'I'd love to go back out there, if they still want me' – which apparently they did. I had a very lively indoor net for the first time on the Wednesday night, with two Middlesex bowlers, Neil Williams and Alastair Fraser, running in very quickly. I wore a full visor, on medical advice. I also had two nets using the bowling machines, to get me going. I felt rather wobbly, partly from the operation and partly from the shock of balls whizzing past my nose at 75 mph, but I told myself, if you want to go out there for England again, you're just going to have to get used to it. I had to get straight back on the horse that had thrown me off.

After a three-week interval I was back in the West Indies. England had lost the Kingston Test by 10 wickets and were on their way to a famous West Indian blackwash. England had all sorts of problems apart from having lost an in-form batsman. Newspaper reporters were hiding behind bushes and there had been reports that Both was up to all sorts of things in Barbados with model Lindy Field in his bed and so forth. The fact that we were losing seemed to excite the newsmen, and prompt them to look for interesting whys and wherefores to explain our lack of success. There were photographers in every nook and cranny, and in the end everybody was pretty worried about who was doing what. The Anti-Apartheid lobby were holding noisy demonstrations about the players with South African links, and they were to give Gooch in particular a rollicking, especially in Port of Spain. The England team had police escorts on every island – though that's by no means unusual in the West Indies.

So back I went into the fray, arriving the night before the Barbados *v.* England match in Bridgetown beginning on 14 March.

'What do you want to do?' said David Gower.

'That's up to you,' I said. 'I'll play if you want.' They did want. So on the morning of the match, to get the drowsiness out of my system, I went for a run around the little golf course near our hotel. I seemed reasonably OK, so I had a net – and that made me feel slightly weak, but I said, 'I'll be all right.'

Fortunately, Barbados were without Marshall, or indeed Haynes or Greenidge. We won the toss and decided to bat, and we were going along quite nicely, myself on 36, having hooked one for 4, getting behind it and quite enjoying myself. I knew they were going to bring on their quicker bowlers to try and shake us up a bit, and I was fully prepared for any eventuality. On came this bowler called Vibert Greene and bowled me a couple of balls quite sharply, and suddenly one seemed to rear off a length. I managed to fend it off, pushing it out to cover, but the next one did exactly the same thing, except that it came through a bit quicker. It hit me flush on the thumb of my bottom hand and flew to second slip.

As I went off thinking, That really hurts, I took off my glove and there was blood coming through the nail. As soon as I got back in the dressing room, I knew that the thumb was broken. I stuck it in some ice and it was throbbing away, and they took me to the hospital where a clean break was diagnosed, straight through the thumb. And I am afraid that wasn't all the bad news either, because when I got back to the ground England were in desperate trouble. A few shooters, a few lifters, and we were all out for 171 – a situation from which we never recovered. I had to watch miserably as Barbados beat us by 3 wickets.

I was wondering what would be the third disaster to befall me personally because these things are supposed to happen in threes. Every time I walked up the stairs I was pretty careful. I tried to be philosophical about it all, but it was just another heartbreak really. I'd made all the effort to get back, and now here I was, sidelined again. Looking back, it may not have been such a bad thing. Perhaps I'd gone back a bit too quickly into the firing line, and if I'd been hit in the face again, it might have destroyed my confidence totally. I don't know – you never know.

Possibly, Somebody up top was saying, 'Now you'll *have* to sit down and have a little wait, won't you, at least until the final Test.' But the waiting was hard. It was hard to see England stuffed in the 3rd one-day international at Bridgetown, *and* the 3rd Test at Bridgetown, *and* the 4th one-dayer at Port of Spain in Trinidad *and* the 4th Test, also at Port of Spain, which I tried hard to get fit for, but I simply couldn't hold a jarring bat with my bottom hand. I hated to see the lads struggling, and I didn't know which was worse, sitting in the stands or going in the dressing room. Both were pretty depressing.

It seemed as though everything had turned against us: the wickets were fearsome, the photographers were peering into everything, and the practice facilities, apart from Barbados, were appalling – we ended up at one point in an army ground; at another point we were in a cow field with grass about six inches tall.

And then there was Frances Edmonds, doing a book about the tour. Philippe, her husband, kept giving her inside information which shouldn't really have been divulged, and you kept on having to look over your shoulder to see if Frances was coming to collect a few facts about us. However brilliant she might have been with her degree and so on, she wasn't writing about the cricket, she was writing and publicizing things about us; tasteful bits about my being a plumber and the right man to fix your toilet, and suchlike. It doesn't worry me personally; if she thinks that's funny, fine. If other people get a laugh out of it, great. But when a touring side is struggling like crazy to fight off the best bowling attack in the world, and fighting a lot of other additional pressures, the last thing you need is one of the wives out there doing a gossip book.

I felt particularly sorry for David Gower. He was in a very, very difficult position, because he had his friends, the Big Three, to contend with in Both, Allan Lamb and Bob Willis – who was Assistant Manager. I thought Willis should have given David a bit more support instead of being 'one of the lads'. I think he should have been out there doing some overtime and trying to find us some decent wickets to practise on. At least, that's how it seemed to me in my helpless state, and as I've said, practice facilities were scarce. In fact, nil. This was borne out by an incident on our arrival in Antigua when we'd toddled along in the morning with our gear, only to find the wicket soaking wet. They'd known we were coming, but they told us a cow got on the pitch and mashed it up, so they had to water it to try and roll it flat again. Members of the team who didn't enjoy practice may have heaved a sigh of relief, but some of us really wanted to have a knock-up and get the feel of the bat on the ball, so we were a bit upset.

We lost the final Test in Antigua. We shouldn't have done but we did. The wicket had hardly any life in it. The ball skidded along the ground. West Indies, put in, amassed 474 all out, with 131 from Haynes. Then Slacky played very well, and we got off to a good start, thanks to him and Goochie, but then it all seemed to fall apart. I was out for 15, our batting crumbled, and then their batsmen murdered us – Viv Richards hitting 100 off 56 balls. Botham bowled and bowled, looking for the wicket with which to overtake Lillee's record, our batting folded again as we were trying to save the match, and it was all over. England done for by 240 runs. My only consolation was that Marshall was bowling when I went in, and though he gave me a fairly rough reception, I managed to get through it without too many hiccups. It was in fact Joel Garner who got me out.

Our darkest dreams had come true. There was a Trinidadian Festival going on at the time, and the popular calypso song doing the rounds was called, 'Captain, the Ship is Sinking'. We could hear this refrain echoing all round the ground, and just after tea when we died the death, it was blaring out from the stands. We'd gone down with the ship 5–0, and it was eventually to lose David Gower the captaincy. The tour had been a nightmare, and it had reached a sort of climax of misery in Antigua where you thought, 'Thank goodness we're going home'.

CHAPTER THIRTEEN
Captain, The Ship Is Sinking
1986

Botham was suspended for most of the summer. He'd done something naughty, talking to newspapers about having smoked 'pot' and talking in public about gin-sodden selectors, so they decided to ban him, and he played in only the last Test match. All in all 1986 was a very unsettling year where England was concerned. We had lots of people in and out of the squad, and a lot of questing to find and try out new players, inspired by the Palmer Report on the standards of play in English cricket. The Report made me very cross actually, saying we had to change this and we had to change that, we didn't have enough talented young players coming through, we were doing things wrong – and generally spreading panic through the system. OK, we'd lost to the West Indies *in* the West Indies, but we had beaten India and Australia, and the captain, David Gower, who had managed so well in difficult circumstances, was under immense pressure coming up to the three-match Series against India and New Zealand.

Beefy's suspension in May for cannabis admissions, and the introduction of drug tests trying to fall into line with new regulations in other sports, led to a general hoo-ha about drugs. Painkillers, such as Paracetamol, were suddenly banned, and so were other remedies you had used all your life. We thought it was stupid really, although you could understand the authorities' concern over mood-altering drugs that might enhance performance. We read reports in the newspapers about the serious misuse of steroids, blood-doping, etc. and about beta-blockers being banned in snooker, so some poor bloke who was taking them to slow his heartbeat down was forbidden to use them.

I think drug-taking in cricket is more or less non-existent. Perhaps there might be the odd case but I am sure it's very rare. Cricketers take sleeping tablets, yes, for the simple reason that if you are flying in and out of time zones around the world and getting up at unearthly hours to travel and play you end up not being able to sleep, so you take a couple of pills to knock yourself out. It isn't to enhance performance – it's just to give you some sleep. As for cannabis, which is what Both's trouble was all about, I wouldn't really be able to tell you the first thing about it – or indeed any other drug. There are apparently some that you smoke, some that you sniff, and some you inject. That is the limit of my knowledge and that's how I intend to keep it. I wouldn't want to get involved with the subject.

Both around this time had apparently taken out writs against a couple of newspapers – I think possibly in the aftermath of the New Zealand effort there was a raid on Beefy's house, and he was convicted for possession. It wouldn't be fair for me to comment: I didn't want to get mixed up in that sort of thing and so I stayed well out of it. Both might have asked me what I thought and I might have told him, and that was about that, though I felt a bit sorry for him, having his home invaded by the drugs squad.

I *did* have to do with Botham's tremendous walk to raise funds for Leukaemia Research, during the winter. I walked for a day with him from Cadbury to somewhere in South Devon and my feet were in a dreadful way because I didn't have a pair of proper walking shoes, just trainers and socks. I think I must have had them on the wrong way round, as well, because I had three or four big blisters and no 'Soft Soap' to rub on my feet to stop the chafing. It was a great day though, with a lot of atmosphere. Both had been walking for quite a while, and the time limit had to be extended because they couldn't go on doing 25 or 30 miles a day. We did 15 or

16 I think, up hill and down dale. Lovely countryside, and a bit of spirit to keep up your spirits.

The worst bit was having to walk right past the hotel where we were staying and up a huge steep slope for another mile and a half to a farmhouse which would be their starting point for the following morning. That was the killer. I don't know how Both's feet were, but mine were certainly bad for a week-and-a-half afterwards – I had to see a chiropodist. Both told me the first seven days had been quite hard, but then he got immune to it. He put surgical spirit on his blisters and the skin hardened up. He really looked quite fit, like the young Ian Botham again, and it was an amazing feat with his feet, if you'll pardon the pun.

When I crawled back to my hotel I got in the bath and lay there, too tired even to go out for liquid sustenance. It's amazing the fluid you lose by walking. I had had two or three layers of gear on because it had been fairly chilly, and when I had taken them off they were all soaked through. Both lost two stone comfortably. It was really worthwhile though, and people were so grateful that you had come along, which is why early in 1987 I did another trek with Both – six out of his seven days in Ireland. I was a bit better equipped for that one but it was still very painful.

Not as painful as the England cricket season. We had our South African rebels all right but we didn't have Both, and it was a very difficult summer. We had begun with two Texaco Trophy one-dayers against the Indians, and although we had lost the first fairly comfortably, the second was a very good match. David, Man of the Match and of the Series, played a captain's knock of 81 and we beat them by 5 wickets. Nevertheless the selectors told David that they were going to give him one Test at a time.

Despite the obvious uncertainty, the dressing room atmosphere for the first Cornhill Test against India was excellent. You couldn't have had eleven people trying any harder, and perhaps in the end we tried too hard. It was a funny sort of game – it felt from the start as though England were doomed to struggle. When we were batting it was grey and overcast; when they batted the sun came out. This happened all the way through. We lost the toss. We were put in and soon after lunch Gower, myself and Allan Lamb had fallen victim to Chetan Sharma. Gooch's 114 and 63 from Pringle saved appearances and we finished with 294, but we had never looked comfortable.

Still, things didn't seem too bad when India finished just 47 runs on after we had knocked over the tail cheaply – it had looked very much worse when Vengsarkar was getting support. But then we batted very badly in our 2nd innings. Kapil Dev was fired up, the ball started swinging, and we were 35 for 3 before we knew what hit us. Allan Lamb and I managed to put on a few, but we were both out in the space of 5 runs, and England, on the Monday evening, were all out for 180, setting them 134 to make on the last day. We gave them a bit of a fright, because they were 5 wickets down in the end, but they got them; we lost.

I didn't think they were going to sack David, I honestly didn't. I thought everybody had tried so very hard, they couldn't blame him for what happened. Of course, we knew that David had only been given tenure for one Test match, so we were slightly on edge, thinking something might be in the offing. But it still came as a shock. David's record stands up to scrutiny: he had taken over from Willis and unfortunately the first blackwash occurred. Fair enough. But then we'd gone to India, missing key players like Botham, and we'd won a Series there, and then we'd come back and beaten the Australians too.

We had to go back to the West Indies after that, where unfortunately we lost to the best team in the world again, but in between these two maulings we had won two very good Test Series and the Ashes. I think David's reputation had been tarnished in some way – he had been labelled 'laid back' in the Press, though the selectors could scarcely sack him after his very good Texaco Trophy performance. But after this lost Test match it was a case of counting out his money.

I'd barely sat down in the dressing room, having come off the field, when our physiotherapist came up and said, 'Would you go and see Peter May? He's in my room.' I thought, 'Oh no, they haven't done anything today, surely.' I hustled along, opened the door, and there was the chairman of selectors, looking his usual immaculate sober self, sitting in the physio's room waiting for me.

'Bad luck,' he said, because losing a Test match isn't very nice. After a few more words of commiseration he asked me whether I would like to be captain of England. 'We think you're the man who can do a good job for us.'

He said this in a rather matter-of-fact routine sort of voice, 'and the best of luck' sort of thing. He's fairly straightforward, is Peter May; he likes things to be done correctly. He's a very easy-going character, and wouldn't go out of his way to offend anybody, but he likes results. Whereas I thought the situation warranted careful consideration.

'Could I have a bit of time to think about it?' I asked him politely.

'We'd like an answer now,' said Peter May.

'Have you told David?'

'No.'

I didn't know what to think of it – I suppose if they had told him and then I said no, they'd have been in a very difficult position.

I really would have liked some time to look at all the pros and cons. I'd just come off the field from losing a Test match after all, and that's not a great frame of mind in which to make important decisions because you are still very preoccupied. Though obviously, if you are suddenly offered the England captaincy, you're not really going to say no.

'OK', I said, 'I'll do it.' What else was I supposed to say? It is a very great honour to be asked to lead your country. It was just that I felt the offer was badly timed. I'd rather we had been allowed to go away and put this Test match behind us; I'd have preferred it if Peter May had said, 'Give me a ring on such-and-such day,' and then when I phoned him, he could have said, 'Look, we'd like to change the captain – would you do it?' That would have been slightly easier for me. It was all a bit sudden.

I didn't know how the rest of the team would take it – though I knew everybody had been solidly behind David. Shaggy, as we call him had, after all, done a lot for England and I'd hoped the selectors would thank him accordingly. I think looking back, perhaps he knew something was in the wind, because when Peter May told him, Shaggy didn't seem particularly surprised: he came up and said, 'Well, best of luck, mate, we'll give you a hundred per cent.'

There had been comments in the Press at the end of our winter tour to the effect that England needed a captain who looked firmly in charge, and who was a touch forceful, rather than one who kept in the background (one comment was that David was 'so laid back as to appear horizontal'). So a friend of David's had had some tee-shirts printed, one with 'I'm in Charge' on and the others with 'I'm not'. Obviously, although that was David's jovial way of passing it off, he must have been very hurt and upset, and he was asked to lend me the 'I'm in Charge' shirt posing for Press photographers. He had just been sacked from a job he'd done rather well and I didn't like it. I didn't think, at the time, that it was particularly tasteful.

I'd been given a two-Test trial period as England captain and I was asked by the Press how I felt.

'Well, to be honest with you,' I said, 'it doesn't really worry me. For the simple reason that I'll try and do the job and if they don't want me after that, fine. Playing for England is what I'm happiest doing.'

I had begun to feel a part of the side; I'd got some runs in India and done well against Australia and I felt I belonged in the team at last. I was one of the lads. Botham had given me a nickname. I was now called 'Jabber' after a vile creature in *Return of the Jedi* with a bowl of froglike things which were his staple diet. And because I now belonged in the team, it had brought the best out of me, and that's what I was going to try to make the rest of them feel.

Unfortunately, selection for the 2nd Test at Headingley was difficult: we had a lot of injury problems and we didn't seem to get the side I'd hoped for. So we ended up losing my first Test as captain of England, I'm afraid. And in 3½ days – which wasn't a great performance, I must admit. The wicket wasn't particularly clever and they won the toss, and as Peter May said afterwards, 'We were outplayed in every department.' Gower was absent with a shoulder injury; so was the suspended Botham. We had brought in 37-year-old John Lever in our seam attack and India batted respectably rather than brilliantly, putting together 272 and 237. Whereas we collapsed – twice. Gooch and Slack didn't do their usual opening number, and we managed just 102 and 128 so we lost by a depressing 279 runs.

I was just feeling my way really. I wasn't sure in my own mind what approach to take, though I could see dressing room morale had plummeted. I was trying to think what David would have said and what Brears would have said, and I phoned Brears for a chat, though in the end of course I suppose I knew the best thing, as with Middlesex, would probably be just to be myself. I just had to do what I thought was best and hope that people would respond. Anyway, I had the unenviable task of sitting in the hot seat at the post-mortem press conference, telling them how we had lost the Test match. The Press really got stuck in as well.

I was very cagey and non-committal at the press conference. The last thing I wanted to do here was to say anything that would be blown up, so I gave them straight basic answers. There's a fine distinction between what journalists say and what they write. The idea of press conferences is that we help the Press by giving them a little more information about the match. Now, they don't give *us* any help when we're out in the middle. If anything, they put us under more pressure. Yet they like us to help them write their articles and they want quotes that make them a little better reading. What they would really like is for you to say something emotional because they ask you how you *feel.*

'How do you think I feel?' I replied. 'I'm sad we lost. Can't you just write that?'

But no, they want a hint of something sensational. They want to be able to write, ' "Kapil Dev's useless and the Indians are a bunch of no-hopers", says England skipper. "We can murder these blokes or heads will roll." ' They must think I'm stupid if they believe I'm coming out with rubbish like that. I'll tell them details of the cricket, but they're not getting quotes out of me like 'We'll rub their noses in it'. It may sell newspapers but it's ridiculous.

And then when you *don't* tell them how you feel or give them headline quotes, they ask standard questions about the cricket such as, 'Will the captaincy affect your batting?' etc. My reaction to that is to trot out standard answers. I think, haven't they got a few different questions they can ask me? They're all the same. I could give you a list of 90 per cent of press conference questions beforehand. So I give pat answers to the pat questions, and I avoid falling into the trap of saying things that can be turned into silly banner headlines.

Still, they're not a bad bunch of blokes, I suppose; apart from one or two phases and one or two individuals, we've got on reasonably well and a few of them have been very good and decent to me. I just don't like press conferences.

I was still finding my feet when we went up to Edgbaston for the 3rd and final Test against India, trailing 2–0. I felt something was missing; something needed to happen. I won the toss and we batted first on a goodish wicket, though the conditions were slightly overcast. And what did we do? We lost Gooch and Athey and suddenly we were 0 for 2. So there was I sitting in the dressing room, thinking, What's going on? I'd had this feeling that something was about to happen and this was it. A disastrous start.

Thank goodness, David and young Mark Benson steadied the ship and we lost our 3rd wicket at 61 which brought together myself and David. 'Will the captaincy affect your batting?' they had asked me at Headingley. Well, it was make or break now all right. Somebody had to make some runs, and in the dressing room we always talk about 'batting for two days', meaning batting for as long as possible and piling up a big score. The two things Test matches revolve around are: No. 1, discipline, and No. 2, 'If you get in, you stay in'.

I didn't mind batting at Birmingham: I'd got a Test 100 there the previous year, and I felt pretty much at home. Chetan Sharma had gained a lot of confidence this summer and was bowling very well, but I kept prodding away, and everybody down the order gave me great support, so I managed to get 183 not out and we put on 390. But as fate would have it, India got exactly that as well, so we were back to square one. Well, we suffered a mid-innings catastrophe and put together just 235 second dig, Chetan Sharma and Maninder doing the damage after Kapil Dev withdrew injured. (Chetan took 10 wickets in the match.)

India looked to be strolling away with it before Phil Edmonds got amongst them, and there was a terrific catch from John Emburey in the gully to get rid of Ravi Shastri. They were 5 wickets down for 174, when bad light stopped play. I think we could have bowled them out actually. So that was quite gratifying: a moral victory, if you like, because we'd actually put them under a bit of pressure, and I had succeeded in getting my 180 odd not out. So it felt, dare I say it, as though things were beginning to come together for England again. Little did I know what was round the corner.

I was given the captaincy for the 3-Test New Zealand Series, but first there were two Texaco one-day matches. At Leeds, New Zealand beat us after we'd been unable to capitalize on a good start. We failed to meet their target of 218 to win. We went to sleep frankly. I was very annoyed. Our cause wasn't helped by three run outs, one of them involving myself and Allan Lamb.

Then we went up to Manchester for the 2nd international. Manchester – I'll never forget Manchester. That was the first time I was ever booed off the field playing for England (I'd suffered the booings at Chelmsford for Middlesex of course). It was an unbelievable feeling. What happened was this. The New Zealanders were batting remarkably well on a very flat wicket, Martin Crowe cracking an undefeated 93. He hit two 6s and eleven 4s in 74 balls, with his brother going well up the other end and the runs were coming at an alarming rate.

The last 4 overs actually produced 71, as the Kiwis murdered the bowling, and for the last over, with Hadlee ready to whack it about, I tried a bowling change. Graham Gooch went for 26, including 5 wides. Their final tally was 284 for 5. The crowd had erupted in a storm of boos and catcalls at England's performance in the field. It says in *Wisden* that the crowd's displeasure was 'warranted but crudely expressed!'. I don't think it was warranted. If a side bat magnificently on a very true wicket it's always going to be difficult, whatever field you set them.

To make matters worse, the lads had gone out the night before, and after the match we got wind of the fact that a reporter from one of the Sunday papers had caught four or five of them in a wine-bar drinking champagne and with a girl on each arm, on the eve of a fairly important match. So I was a bit worried about that as well. The Press always go prying into things when England aren't doing well, and although I can't say I've never had a drink after midnight, it was a bit silly and unprofessional of the lads to go to a fairly extravagant and well-known wine-bar like that so publicly before an international match. We weren't running a school, so I didn't think fines would be appropriate. I just told the lads it was unprofessional.

Anyway, all was not lost in this match, because England had got their batting sorted out, and Bill Athey, with a quite magnificent 142 not out, and Graham Gooch with 91, put on a match-winning 193 for our 1st wicket, and we won the 2nd Trophy match in the end with flying colours. The boos turned to cheers, and for the first time in my life I felt very cynical. I felt like turning on the crowd and saying, 'What are you up to? It was a flat wicket; we've just proved it was a flat wicket. So what was all the booing about?'

I managed to avoid going off at the deep end, and it's just as well, otherwise there might have been a few more juicy bits in the papers.

We came away from that victory with a rather better attitude for the 1st Test against the New Zealanders at Lord's. I'm afraid there was a lot of discussion over selection for this, however! The team chosen was: Gooch and Martyn Moxon to open, then Athey, David, myself, Peter Willey, Philippe, Bruce French as wicketkeeper, Dilley, Foster and Radford. Though Emburey was injured, and Pringle was picked but declared unfit just before the match, I felt we hadn't selected our strongest side. But then selectors have different ideas, and you have to arrive at it democratically.

It wasn't until the 3rd Test that I felt satisfied with the selection: I'd wanted to stick with the people who had just scored 286 against New Zealand in the one-day game. That wasn't to be.

What was to be was a rain-interrupted draw. We owed our first-knock 307 largely to Moxon, David, Athey and Peter Willey, Hadlee's 6 for 80 having done the damage, and Bruce French was hit on the helmet by one of his bouncers, which put him out of action for most of the match. (Four people actually wore the gloves for England at various times, including, at one point, Bill Athey.) We managed to keep New Zealand within striking distance, 35 ahead on 1st innings, Dilley and Edmonds being our main wicket-takers.

And then it was Graham Gooch, cutting and carving, who constructed our 2nd innings with a truly marvellous 183, which was just what we needed. It enabled me to declare fairly safely on the fifth day at 295 for 6, the fourth day having been ravaged by rain. Dilley and Foster had a quick bout at them, and David took a couple of catches at 3rd-slip, and we had them 2 down for 8. But they'd reached 41 for 2 when we called it a day. I thought our people were playing reasonably well, though they still seemed slightly on tenterhooks, slightly unsure.

More selection problems. Nottingham was next on the agenda, and our bowling line-up looked very different. Foster and Radford were dropped in favour of home Test newcomer Greg Thomas and Test debutant Gladstone Small – Derek Pringle replacing the injured Dilley. This gave us a very, very raw pace attack and it wasn't very easy for me as captain to generate any sort of team spirit with such a turnover of staff, particularly as the changes happened to be bowlers. You've got to get to know bowlers and develop a working relationship with them so they can find their rhythm. At Trent Bridge, Hadlee would be bowling on his own stomping ground in front of his own County crowds. They would probably be more on New Zealand's side than ours.

We still lacked our equivalent, Ian Botham. Although his ban had elapsed the previous week, he wasn't picked. So we got underway to a mediocre batting production from England, with Athey and Gower making the bulk of our 256. It wasn't too bad on that wicket, but we could have done better. The Kiwis' 1st innings was a bit of a killer. We'd kept them down to a fairly civil 144 for 5 but then Gray made a ponderous 50, Hadlee had had a bit of luck and then gone for his shots, and Bracewell, who is a steady batsman but not exactly your average century-maker, played well along with Gray and made a very important 110. They raised the score to 413 which gave them a formidable 1st-innings lead.

And then, what with a couple of questionable decisions, some bad luck, and some rotten weather (we had had flying ants, storms and rain), England stumbled to 230. If it hadn't been for a magnificent knock from John Emburey, now happily restored after having his nose broken, we'd have stumbled to 155. New Zealand knocked off the runs and the crowd cheered Hadlee's Man of the Match Award to the rafters. So we faced the 3rd and final Test 0-1 down.

I must say there were a couple of times in that Trent Bridge debacle when England lost a wicket and then we came off for bad light, which really disappointed me because if we had come off earlier we might have avoided losing a wicket. The light is a very difficult and contentious subject for the umpires, players and crowd, and often very frustrating. I actually reached exasperation point when we were losing our grip on everything, and took David Gower to one side.

I said, 'What do we do about all this? What really happens? I've never known it like this, either for England or Middlesex. Is there anything more I could be doing? What do you think, David?'

He was very good and told me there wasn't much I could do. He said, 'Things just aren't going our way. People aren't playing as well as they can; you keep having key players left out of the side. Just keep doing what you think is right – that's all you can do.'

He was right of course, but after the match I still felt deeply depressed and unsettled in my own mind. I was very unhappy about what was going on, and with my family I'd gone into my shell, worrying about the situation. Elaine and Jean, my mother-in-law, say there are times when they simply can't get through to me, and this was certainly one of the times. Nothing seemed to be going right, and I was afraid I was taking my depression home with me.

I would be thinking about the cricket all night and all day, brooding. I felt terribly worn out and tired. I'd recovered from my illness and the gallstones, but for some reason I felt unbelievably drained and played out mentally. I'd go home and stare at the television, saying nothing, and go off to bed. If people tried to talk to me I found it very hard to make conversation. I wasn't nasty to anybody. I just found it very, very hard to communicate for about two months – it lasted that long. I kept it all inside.

Elaine would say softly, 'Mike, what's the problem?'

'Oh, nothing. Nothing really.'

'You're ignoring us.'

'I'm not ignoring you. I'm relaxing. I'm under a lot of pressure at the moment. Just leave me alone.'

I'd been playing for England regularly for a couple of years now, and I suppose this was another stage I had to negotiate. I had to learn to cope with new mental pressures, of the England captaincy, the Press and so on. I was mentally exhausted.

To make matters worse, I was worried about Middlesex as well. Although we were successful in the Benson and Hedges Cup, we were doing badly in all the other competitions, especially the Britannic Assurance County Championship where we languished at the bottom of the table. It was a very difficult stage of my career and self-doubt had begun to creep into my thinking.

Was I doing the right things? Why was the dressing room atmosphere so terrible now? What did the rest of the team think of me? I just couldn't work it all out. I was so very depressed about the cricket. England and Middlesex were both losing – they never looked like winning. It didn't seem as though things were about to change either.

In one of my rare utterances at home, I told the family, 'If it doesn't work at the Oval, the next few weeks are going to be very depressing.' I'm sure they must have thought, That will make a change. Clearly I had to go and talk to somebody. Being captain of the ship wasn't all plain sailing at all. The waves were mounting up; I had to learn to cope with it and I didn't know where to start. I phoned Brearley again and had a little chat with him, and then I went to see an old friend of mine from my Brondesbury days, Mike Sturt.

Mike Sturt:

I had to go to Lord's because Mike wanted to know, in the event of Middlesex granting him a Benefit in the future, whether I would join his Benefit Committee. I remember walking into the Middlesex office and being introduced to David Gower, who appeared rather unshaven and dishevelled, as though he'd been on the toot all night (and who could blame him: he'd just been sacked as England captain). I offered my commiserations. Gatt had obviously and very sensibly taken the earliest opportunity to talk with Gower. A few days later, Mike telephoned me and asked to come and talk to me, saying, 'I'm a bit depressed about things'. Having given up the chairman of selectors job at Middlesex at the end of 1985 I was not as closely in touch with events as I had been in the previous six years; however Don Bennett had told me that Gatt was really at a pretty low ebb and not in his usual bubbling form. We arranged to meet at my house in Regents Park when Mike was on his way to practise at the Oval prior to the New Zealand Test. Mike's car turned up laden with cricket kit and with blazers and suits on hangers, and since we had agreed to meet for an hour or so, I enquired if he planned to stay for a fortnight! I did not attempt a Brearley-type psychological exploration – we just talked. It was my view that he was feeling somewhat exposed, and that possibly he wanted a shoulder to lean on. I remember saying to him, 'Look, the selectors have chosen you; there is nobody else, so this is an opportunity to stamp your personality on the side, and don't take any truck from anybody. They've tried Botham and Gower. You can't let things drift on the same way. Don't be worried about comparisons in the press. Do what you think is right. The selectors will welcome some positive attacking cricket.'

Having had tea and biscuits with Mike Sturt, I went and had a chat with Ian Botham. He'd just come back from suspension, having been doing all sorts of things, and he said he was ready for this Test match. I said, 'Well, Both, obviously there's going to be a bit of opposition to you coming straight back into the side, because you haven't had any cricket for seven or eight weeks' – although probably Both could come roaring back into a Test match even if he'd had no cricket for seven or eight years, but it wouldn't have been fair to the others to have picked him for the 2nd Test if he'd performed badly.

'Are you OK?' I said. 'You're sure you're ready to go?' He was raring.

Anyway in the 3rd Test we all sat down and talked hard about our side and in the end we finally, in my opinion, had got our strongest side onto the field for the first time that summer, which was Gooch and Athey to open, David at 3, Allan Lamb at 4, myself at 5, Both back at 6. Our bowling attack, apart from Beefy, consisted of John Emburey, Dilley, fit again, Gladstone Small, who'd taken to Tests like a duck to water though he had been unlucky at Trent Bridge, and Phil Edmonds. The wicketkeeper was Bruce French. Right, we were set.

The morning of the Test, everything seemed suddenly different. There was a buzz in the dressing room. It felt as though we were about to go out and paint the town red. Well, I won the toss, and on a goodish wicket, New Zealand having been put in, John Wright decided to play one of his speciality knocks, batting the whole day for 119. But we managed to wind them all up for 287, which, with respect to that wicket, was a great effort. Now we had to 'bat for two days' – certainly most of the second and a bit of the third.

We had a great time. David got in on his favourite wicket and hit a magnificent 131, I managed to get 121, and then Both came in and smashed it around and got 59 not out off 36 balls. Old ball, new ball, it was all the same to him, and went flying round the ground. A youngster called Stirling came on and tried to bowl quick at him – disappeared to all parts! It was a phenomenal knock, and we had done what we set out to do. At 388 for 5 we'd got a tidy lead.

And then what happened? We'd never seen anything like it: the skies opened and it rained and rained and rained. We got out for less than half an hour on day five, I think, before the light went out. Still it was a good note to finish on. The England spirits were back to normal. We'd played very well and certainly for me it was a landmark getting my first 100 against New Zealand. They'd given me an awful lot of stick in the Press about Richard Hadlee. 'Hadlee only had to walk up and bowl Gatting an orange, and he'd get out.' I'll admit he does that to quite a few people otherwise he wouldn't be the world's leading Test wicket-taker. But still. It was nice to finish on a high note, and it was nice to tell the Press: well, the New Zealanders were always going to be a tough side to beat, but we got our best team together at last, and that felt like the way cricket should be played.

You had only to walk in the dressing room to tell the difference. There was a bit of a 'bubble' in there now. Before, it had been terribly flat, with new people feeling their way and no doubt very nervous. India and New Zealand these days are not the pushovers they used to be. They've got some very good players now – people like Kapil Dev and Richard Hadlee who are quite capable of winning matches on their own. And with England's experimental sides, and players coming and going, it was hard to generate any rhythm or galvanize an attack. Now, we felt solid. We had a balance of fresh talent and experienced players like Both, Lamb and John Emburey who knew what it was all about. With this squad going to Australia in the winter, I reckoned we might do something special. By the way, for those interested in standard questions: no, the captaincy hadn't affected my batting.

Poor Middlesex though. They were having really quite a silly season, with many Test absences and no continuity. I don't really remember a great deal of it either, because my mind was so taken up with England. Middlesex had a lot of injuries, and suffered a major loss in Graham Barlow, for whom we had to find a replacement. Neil Williams and Angus Fraser both sustained early injuries. Wilfy Slack was still a bit shell-shocked from the West Indies trip, and it took him some time to start producing the form that got him on the tour of Australia. He probably found it hard being without Graham Barlow up the other end saying, 'Come on, Wilfy!'

We had signed on Andrew Miller, and I think Wilf felt some pressure from that quarter too, because Miller was very much a Wilfy-type player. So what with losing our precious opening partnership, that had loyally built us platforms over the years, and losing a couple of bowlers, and fielding youngsters like Andrew and John Carr when the Test people were away for much of the time, we had a very 'iffy' season. One of the few bright spots was some very fine bowling from Simon Hughes, whose variation and tidiness was a great bonus.

We tied for 9th in the John Player, after our usual intermittent spells of success. In the NatWest we were knocked out in the 2nd round by the Yorkies, not by much, but by enough, and the County Championship – well, we were actually bottom of the table until July, but pulled *one* sock up to finish 12th. I had ended up coming down the order in the last three or four games, to give young John Carr and Keith Brown a bit more responsibility as they looked very promising, and also, it must be said, because I was feeling the strain as well – it had been a very hard summer for me.

Our last game, at Canterbury, it rained, and I was doing a little bit of promotion work for Austin Reed, the gents' outfitters. They had wanted a few London people to help advertise their new lines, so there I was, a man who had never been a good fit for a pair of trousers, parading about in the old double-breasted pin-striped suit, and highly polished shoes, and having my photo taken to a chorus of catcalls and whistles from the Middlesex dressing room. This all took place on the outfield at Canterbury.

That, and a few jars with the Kent lads, was about the best thing to happen in our whole gloomy County season . . . . That and the Benson and Hedges, which really was a silver lining, because in that competition we played some of the best Middlesex cricket of my career. We bowled, we batted, and we fielded at every stage as well as I can remember us doing, and if we didn't win it on our 1986 effort we would surely never win it. We'd started off extremely well against Surrey, brushing them aside by 6 wickets. I'd enjoyed myself for a 90 not out and got a Gold Award for my batting, bowling and slip catching! Butch got 65 and our bowlers did us proud as well.

The Hampshire job was even better. Weather having reduced our second attempt at a match, we hit 80 for 3 off 9 overs, chasing their 77 for 5 off 10, and I hit 60 not out off 30 balls for another Gold Award – I'll never forget that little knock.

We rolled over Oxford and Cambridge Universities next, and went on to a trouncing of poor old Kent by 134 runs and by now the Gold Awards were coming thick and fast. Everybody chipped in with the bat (258 for 8) and our bowlers crumbled Kent for 124. Quite magnificent, to give us 4 out of 4 in our Group.

We had a fairly good quarter-final against Sussex at Lord's in which they ended up 84 short, due to Norman Cowans bowling fast and straight and to Philippe, who removed three of them. Our semi-final was always going to be tough, especially after Notts got off to a very good start – 115 for 1, and we had to let Wayne off his leash again straight after lunch. The turning point was probably Emburey's caught and bowled dismissal of Richard Hadlee for 1. We needed 190 to win, and Mr Slack got 65 of them; I was run out for 3 (I think Wilfy did me) and then Clive, Butch and Emburey carefully knocked off the remainder to see us into the final. This had been our wobbliest one, no doubt about it.

It was a smashing final, against Kent, and as everybody probably remembers, Kent finished up batting in darkness and pouring rain. It was their own fault really for having bowled so slowly early on – that's why it went on so late. They'd inserted us because it was swinging about, and we'd managed to gather 199 for 7. Graham Dilley was hitting his straps and so was their other Test quickie, Richard Ellison, who took 3 for 27, but Rad as usual kept us ticking over, and the tail picked up valuable runs.

So they had 200 to get. It was a funny situation because although in Lord's finals, 'them as bat first usually win', 200 wasn't much to bowl at. It was going to be nip and tuck. Anyway Wayne Daniel tore out of his trap and put them under pressure, and with Norman bowling tidily up the other end, they didn't seem in any particular hurry. When tea was taken, at the ridiculously late hour of 5.50, they were on 71 for 4.

Then Graham Cowdrey began to go for his shots. Baptiste took fire as well and by about seven it was getting not only dark but very tight. 116 for 5. They were offered the light; they declined. I'd have totally understood if they'd come off. They could all bat, the men of Kent: the only one who couldn't was Underwood, who thought he could as well. Simon Hughes had bowled very well in the one-day competitions for Middlesex: now he was both sensible and tidy, and with Emburey he pegged them back.

So it came to the penultimate over, and Philippe Edmonds got rid of Ellison. Philippe had been bowling earlier to attacking fields, I remember, and was being whacked for quite a few, but Ellison's was a valuable wicket and in this his final over Edmonds gave away just 5 runs.

So off the last over, Marsh and Dilley, with just Deadly to come, needed 14. Now you may think that was easily gettable – I didn't. The last 3 overs, I felt we'd won it. I trusted Simon Hughes and Philippe, and I felt it was now in our grasp. Well, Marshy hit a 6. It had been raining for 20 minutes and now it was bucketing down, and you could see the lights on the scoreboard like beacons.

Simon composed himself, having been launched straight into the crowd off that full toss on Marsh's off-stump, he kept his head, and a ball or so later, and a furious swipe by Graham Dilley to try to bring up the winning runs, they finished 3 short of their victory target.

So Middlesex won the Benson and Hedges Trophy by 2 runs. It wasn't a 'jumping about' sort of occasion like the day we had beaten Essex; this victory was more like meeting an old friend and was tempered with a bit of sadness for Chris Cowdrey. I had told him in the preliminaries, 'We'll see you in the Finals then, Chris.' I felt sorry for them because they'd not had a very good season either and they'd played their hearts out to qualify for this. I think Middlesex were the better side and deserved to win – somebody's got to – but it seemed hard on Kent.

More exciting for me was that the day before the final, Elaine had given birth by Caesarean section to James, or Jimbo as I called him. I had him in my arms as Elaine was recovering, because having had a Caesarean, she was under anaesthetic. So as happened with Andrew, I saw baby Jimbo even before his mother did. I must admit I think kiddies are absolutely great. When they're born they're amazing; they look horrible, wet, mucky bits of things, but they're wonderful little people really. Elaine and I had planned it virtually to this date, so I could be there, and it was a terrible wrench when I had to go with England to Australia soon afterwards, leaving Elaine to cope with a baby and little Andrew.

I was still missing my kids terribly, going away. When I was home, sometimes I'd think, Oh dear, why don't they shut up! All right, Andrew, I'll come out and play with you in a minute! When you're home you sometimes want to flop down and have a rest, and especially in 1986 I was under terrible mental strain as well. But then when you're away you realize how much you long to see them. I miss Andrew tugging at my shirtsleeve, saying, 'Come on, play with me, Daddy.' All credit to Elaine for bringing them up on her own. All I could do was to go and see her in hospital two or three times when she had James. It was nice, because I could see the little fella getting more awake and alert, and Elaine seemed to recover a lot quicker the second time around.

We were having one or two problems with our Andrew though; in many ways, as my wife says, he is frighteningly advanced, and you had a job to keep him amused because he could work anything out in five minutes flat. He had an exceptionally large vocabulary. He had had his eyes tested too, and was found to have astigmatism, so he wears little glasses these days which make him look very studious. He obviously missed me desperately, and got upset whenever he saw me on television.

I'm basically a little boy myself. I love going to amusement arcades, and watching TV and reading Tolkien and science fiction. You can always be young at heart if you want. Funfairs, ball games – I love them all. If you get too old and serious life becomes boring.

Mike Brearley:

I think my happiest memory of Mike was during that summer of 1986: I'd gone to Lord's with my eleven-year-old son, who was captaining Brondesbury CC Under-11s. And we were watching a Middlesex game and Mike Gatting was on the balcony. Middlesex were batting, and he was out and we waved to him. He jumped out of the pavilion and came running down wearing his shorts, and he said hello and shook hands and was very friendly to Mischa, my son.

And then Mischa and I had a tennis ball and Mike said he'd walk round the ground with us – we were going away I think – and we walked behind the Tavern towards the Grace Gates; Mike was playing catch, jumping and throwing the ball with Mischa, and though there weren't many people around, I think that was very nice, unselfconscious, boyish and friendly and not at all concerned with what people might think of the England captain playing catch at the back of the pavilion at Lord's with a tennis ball and an eleven-year-old boy. He was very nice with Mischa, and interested in his cricket, and that's a warm memory I have of Mike Gatting.

CHAPTER FOURTEEN
The Triple Trophy Tour
1986–87

In my book, *Triumph in Australia* (I have to give it a plug!), I have given a very detailed and dramatic account of the winter tour of 1986–87 with day-to-day reports on all the matches that we played with my on-the-spot impressions and analysis. Because that tour was obviously a very important part of my life, and one of the high points of English cricket. What I have to say about it here, while it may be less detailed, will have the benefit of hindsight. I can tell you, for example, that a lot of thought and hard work went into it – from selection on day one.

A lot of people thought Both shouldn't go. But though he wasn't an automatic choice in their minds, I felt it was very important to get him in the team. He always seemed to me to want to prove something in Australia, and with rumours rife that this would be his last tour, he would undoubtedly want to go out on a high note. Plus there was the small matter of his very great talent as easily our best all-rounder. So I went and had a chat with him before the tour, and so did Micky Stewart, our assistant manager. And we both came away with the impression that Both was in the right frame of mind; that he wanted to do the job, and was ready to fit in with the team. So we backed him, and persuaded other people that he was a good choice.

I wouldn't describe myself as a stickler for practice, but I do feel that, if a team is going to practise, *everybody* should do it – Both included. He hadn't really played that much cricket during the summer because of his suspension: he'd played in one Test match and a couple of odd games at the end. So, as much as anyone else, Botham needed a net or two. When people are naturally very gifted like Both and David Gower, they tend to find practice a chore. Both will only go and have a net out of desperation: he will bat, but he won't bowl. David will only have a net because he feels he has to – he doesn't enjoy it. Yet one only has to look at the discipline Clive Lloyd has engendered in the West Indies team to see the good of it: I think that was possibly why they stayed at the top the way they did.

Botham isn't one of those practice-mad blokes at all. You'll see Richard Hadlee and Malcolm Marshall having tremendous loosening-up sessions, but Both thinks he can manage without it. David will come and have a knock-up or a run with the guys because he's been captain and he knows how important it is for everyone to join in. Both has a slightly shorter memory of his captaincy days, when he needed people to make just a little bit of effort. But considering we're professional sportsmen, we really do very little. Having a stretch never harmed anybody.

Botham's bowling has certainly declined in the last two or three years. Imran Khan and Richard Hadlee are both older than Both yet they're still fit and strong to bowl. Whereas Both's bowling has gone downhill. It's a great shame. Perhaps if his immense natural talent hadn't been granted him, he might have worked. It's quite fascinating watching films of Richard Hadlee when he first started – you can see the raw material he has had to hone and hone into the striking force he is now. Imran as well. He was about my pace when he began.

David, in his younger days, was extremely talented – flying rather than simply batting. No matter what the bowling attack, it never seemed to worry him. He had so much time. He had a way of playing which was all his own, and not because he was a left-hander. He couldn't really discuss what he was doing. People with that sort of ability would find it hard to define or explain. It just happens. I think he finds it difficult to think about batting techniques – he just does it by natural instinct. Critics these days may say, 'Oh, his feet haven't moved again – he's had a waft at a wide one'. But a lot of the time David wasn't moving his feet anyway, even for brilliant strokes that went for 4. Deep down, if he does get out, he knows, and he'll sit down and reflect on why for about 5 minutes. And then he'll forget about it, and I think that's fair enough – you can't be analysing all the time. But David will work if he has to.

Both, on the other hand, doesn't feel he has to do anything. He doesn't respond well to people telling him what he has to do, either. He'll take anybody on, including the newspapers. So it was particularly nice, when I had that little talk with him before Australia, to be able to persuade Both to commit himself and say that he was prepared to muck in with the rest of the team. He was as good as his word too, especially in the four or five days before our opening games began. He was really working terribly hard.

Both was keen – to me that was going to be a key factor in the tour. Another one was to secure the cooperation of other senior players with Australian experience – people like Allan Lamb and David, who knew the grounds, the fixtures, and the conditions. I had to get these key individuals on my side before we started, so I got six of them together for a sort of think tank. I told them 'We need everybody's input to give us background information on all the wickets, players, conditions, etc'.

It is possible for just one man to generate confidence within a team provided there's a background of support. But if there are a couple of people slightly undermining him, it doesn't matter what he says or does, the captain loses his credibility. The rest of the team can sense the doubters immediately. But provided you have that background of support, and provided you ask the possible rather than the impossible, and explain in simple terms how it can be achieved, your team will believe you and have confidence in themselves. But they have to be able to believe what you're saying. It's no good asking for impossibilities or they will lose faith in you. You tell them step by step, 'If we compete, if we do the right thing, we can pull this off'. And then it becomes a possibility.

I told the senior members of my squad, 'It's as much your responsibility as mine to engender this enthusiasm and confidence. We don't want any negative thoughts that we're going to lose. We need to be positive all the time, and we need you to be supportive in this because you are the guys people are going to be looking up to, and you're the people who are going to be making the bulk of the runs and taking the bulk of the responsibility. We have to engender that enthusiasm.'

Phil Edmonds was also experienced, but he had been a bit naughty before the tour, going on television and making unhelpful remarks. Botham had been forbidden to air his views on a sports programme, and the very next day Philippe had gone on the Terry Wogan Show, knowing full well he wasn't supposed to say anything before we went away. It was just one more example of how Philippe tries to take liberties and see how far he can push people. He knows he's in the wrong but he goes ahead and does it anyway. To be in the newspapers, to be different, to be noticed – who knows?

Despite the groundswell of positive thinking, and despite all the training and practising, we didn't get off to a great start Down Under, managing only to draw our first game against Queensland Country XI, winning a one-dayer against South-East Queensland Country XI, and actually losing the third, against Queensland (we were all out for 135 in our 1st innings). So we had to put up with all the 'This is the worst team ever to visit these shores' sort of caper from the newspapers. Well, I knew we were fulfilling all the requirements for success even if we didn't have the results to show for it. We weren't doing too badly anyway; we won two more one-dayers and we beat South Australia in Adelaide, on a turning wicket before drawing with Western Australia. But as David didn't seem to be getting many runs, we decided to rest him for a little while.

I knew what David must be feeling, because I had the same problem myself: 'I don't really want to play the warm-up games. Let's get on with the Test matches'. I also knew that whatever the preliminary hitches, it would be all right on the night. I did have a word with David about the batting order, and we agreed in a very few syllables that I would go in 3 and he'd drop down to number 5. Allan Lamb had been advocating this and we both agreed it was a good idea. We'd also developed a problem, in the State games, about 'left-arm overs' – young guys like Chris Matthews and Bruce Reid who bowled left arm over the wicket and kept getting us out, so Australia thoughtfully included these two in their side for the 1st Test at Brisbane, to try and upset us.

We lost the toss and Allan Border invited us to have first knock, which he lived to regret. After a nervy start and a little chat from me when I got in at first wicket down, Bill Athey plunged right into the occasion, hitting a very fine 76. The first day belonged to us, because I got 61 and Allan Lamb, looking every inch the key team-member I'd taken him for, was rattling off a few when we came off for bad light, England on 198 for 2. The new Aussie bowlers were nervous. Chris Matthews, in particular, wasn't sure where the ball was going, and Merv Hughes, the Victorian quickie with the huge walrus moustache, looked quite taken aback when Bill Athey responded to the usual stream of abuse about Pommie bastards, by tugging his forelock like a yokel as if to say, 'Yes, squire, sorry squire'. They don't have yokels in Australia.

Next day, though we immediately lost our two overnight batsmen, Beefy Botham came out and clubbed 138 along with David Gower who got 50, and with a sparkling 40 from Daffy DeFreitas in his first Test match we were sitting on 456. Not only that, but Daffy went out in the last 30 minutes and collected his first Test wicket as well. And from there on out the Australian Press turned their critical attention away from the worst-ever side to visit their shores, and started getting stuck into the Aussie players instead.

The whole Australian side were deeply demoralized because they'd psyched themselves into believing that all they had to do was turn up to knock us over, and suddenly having been forced to follow on, and having been unable to cope either with Graham Dilley's speed and accuracy or Embers and Philippe turning the screw, they found themselves 0–1 down. England celebrated at a Chinese restaurant, and when I got back to my hotel room, I found a message from Peter May. It said simply, 'Congratulations. Delighted'.

England were in fine fettle apart from all the hairy inter-State flights. We'd had a truly terrible one over Wudinna in South Australia. Three of us got off as white as sheets from that, because the little plane kept dropping 100 ft and toiling back up again, and when it wasn't doing that it was banking sharply, so you felt as if you would fall out, and what with the dropping and the banking, Bill Athey was sick, the manager was sick, Neil Foster was sick, and I nearly saw a rump steak breakfast disappear into an air bag as well. I'd been casually playing cards up until the last 20 minutes, but then it got so rough that I was having a job keeping my mind on the pips because I could feel this steak coming up and coming up.

I went on a deep sea trip with Both and the lads before a one-day game in Lawes, having had to get up at 3.45 am for the privilege. We travelled out a fair way for about an hour and a half and it got very choppy so I was seasick as usual. But I enjoyed watching all the fishing. I love all those underwater documentaries by Jacques Cousteau and the like, and seeing all the dolphins and marlin was the brilliant part for me. Whereas Both was definitely bent on catching something. He did as well – he hooked a marlin. Had a tremendous fight with it. I was quite happy watching – it looked very hard work to me.

The 2nd Test in Perth was hard work, but rather amazing as well. We'd lost to New South Wales at Newcastle just before, where we'd been flattened both innings for 197 and 82, so the Press had come back with renewed cries about the worst team ever to visit the shores, saying, 'The 1st Test was a fluke', etc. Whereas I thought it was all going extremely well. Allan and Both, Philippe and Embers, Graham Dilley, Gladstone Small, Daffy and Neil Foster were all gearing themselves up. I won the toss, and Bill Athey and Chris Broad couldn't have got us off to a better start.

The Aussies had recalled Geoff Lawson in their attack, who I didn't think was fully fit, and Chris and Bill lambasted him, putting on a mighty 223 for the first wicket. I didn't last long with 14, Allan Lamb didn't trouble the scorers at all, and even Both ended up wandering about with a rubber duck's bill on his nose, a joke present to Allan Lamb from his 'Mrs'. But David and our wicketkeeper Jack Richards seemed to go from strength to strength out in the middle, pushing the field further and further back. They ended up with 130 *apiece*, which was quite phenomenal and I declared our innings closed at 592 for 8.

The Aussies, thanks to an imperturbable knock from Allan Border, managed to avoid the follow-on, and we went in again 191 in front, looking to add another 170 very quickly as I was hoping to slip them in for half an hour before the close. That was the plan. But we lost a couple of wickets and had the brakes put on us, so I changed my mind. I wasn't running the risk of declaring and leaving them 300 to get with a day to bat. Despite critics who thought I should have declared sooner, I wasn't handing it to Australia on a plate after we'd worked so hard in the 1st Test.

Besides, on a wicket with half-inch cracks, I thought that if we were going to bowl them out, we'd do it in a day anyway. I was wrong. Despite a first-ball wicket, they managed to stave us off. What bothered me though, was not so much the draw, but the fact that when Ian Botham had been bowling, he had pulled up suddenly, dropped the ball and walked off, telling me he couldn't continue. He had badly strained a rib muscle.

It was just as well that the next Test match would be at Adelaide – one of the flattest strips in Australia. Just prior to the 3rd Test, though, we had to play a 4-day State game versus Victoria at Melbourne which was being billed as the 'Sir Robert Menzies Memorial Match' with a lot of dignitaries and officials present on the opening morning. You may have heard about that one. Captain Gatting slept in.

A very close friend of mine, Peter Spence, had moved from Sydney to Melbourne and invited us to dinner. Now, we had just flown across from Perth, and I was dog-tired but I went along and we shared a bottle of port and it was 12.30 or so before I got away, needing matchsticks to keep my eyes open because quite apart from all the travelling, I hadn't been sleeping very well either. I'd promised to phone home that night as well, so I got through to Elaine, and she remarked that I sounded as though I was nodding off. I was nodding off.

The next thing I knew, there was a pounding on my door. It was light. I was spreadeagled on the bed in my boxer shorts and socks and a rumpled tee-shirt, and with the phone half on the hook and half off. From the depths of my dreams I could hear Chris Broad's voice shouting, 'Gatt! Come on – we're starting in 10 minutes!' I was totally confused.

'What do you mean?' I said, letting him in with my hair standing on end. 'It's about eight o'clock, isn't it?'

'No! It's half-past-*nine* nearly!'

'Oh no!' In the shower, gear on, rushed to the ground.

Meanwhile, the Press had started sniffing, particularly since this match, with its early start, was in honour of somebody. David had tossed up for me and lost, and I was to be the 3rd seamer as well, along with Fozzie and Gladstone Small.

'Where's the captain?'

They had bowled about 5 overs, I suppose, when I pelted into the ground and ran on to the pitch 20 minutes late. They couldn't get hold of me because my phone wasn't on the hook, and somebody had said, 'Oh, I think Gatt must have gone already.' They'd gone to the ground in three or four cars, but when the last car arrived and no Gatt had got out, there had been a bit of a panic and somebody was sent back to bang on my door.

It wasn't worth lying to the Press, saying I'd been indisposed. I told the truth. It's not as if I'm the first cricketer ever to oversleep. It's been hushed up on a number of occasions.

There have been times when nameless Australian players in the West Indies have not even made the plane for an Island game. But me pitching up 20 minutes late gave the Press something to write about.

Things had been running far too smoothly. There were no scandals; Both was quietly installed in what he calls his 'bat cave', and there were no drink or drugs parties they could get their hands on. The fact that I had a very good day in the field with 4 wickets for 31 didn't make much difference. Neither did the fact that we won the match by 5 wickets. It was all my fault for sleeping in – I fully accept that, but I didn't do it deliberately. I told the team, 'I'm terribly sorry for what happened,' particularly as I was the captain and had been trying to get people to toe the line and turn up on time.

And then it was on to Adelaide, for the 3rd Test. We were without Both. He'd thrown his bat down in practice, in disgust at the pain from his injured muscle, and walked sadly back to the dressing room, and I am afraid Daffy and Dilley (which sounds like a nursery rhyme) didn't bowl particularly well because they'd had four or five days off and lost their rhythm. The Aussies were rock solid all the way down the order and put on 514 for 5 declared, having won the toss and elected to bat.

But we in turn showed our mettle on that wicket, myself and Chris Broad getting hundreds and Ath hitting 55, and it looked at one stage as if we could overhaul the total and perhaps gain a 150 lead. But it didn't materialize. We lost our bearings against the new ball that night and had to content ourselves with 455 on the fourth morning. They got in and eventually declared at 201 for 3, playing it fairly safely and not wanting to go 2–0 down. And with interruptions from the weather we weren't rushing either, to be fair. We managed to get out of it with a draw. It wasn't bad, considering their huge 1st-innings total.

From here we took in Tasmania at Hobart (turning them over even without the injured Both), and a Prime Minister's XI in Canberra, on 23 December. We were getting into a

Christmassy mood, having dinner in a revolving restaurant in Hobart on top of the Wrest Point Hotel, with Peter Lush plunking out his touching rendition of 'Greensleeves' on the bar piano, and England having their timehonoured Christmas fancy dress, celebrating a little win over Bob Hawke's XI *and* the season of goodwill. I went as a musketeer, Bill Athey went as a wicked schoolmaster, and Phil and Frances Edmonds went as convicts; the Fosters went as *Animal Farm* pigs with reporters' notebooks, and Jack Richards was an Indian chief; but Daffy DeFreitas put us all to shame with his moustacheoed Diana Ross, complete with fetching slinky dress. Not that we didn't work over Christmas: we had a serious net on Christmas Eve, chaps!

I think you may know what happened next, in the 4th Test at Melbourne. Because when we eventually got back home all sorts of delighted-looking English folk kept coming up and telling me how they'd been up at all hours watching it on television. The match that was to make me happier than anything since my first England cap began on Boxing Day. Three days later, it was over. The Aussies had collapsed in a shambles, and we'd got the match, the Ashes, and Elton John in the dressing room pouring champagne over our heads.

It began in a fairly orderly manner. Graham Dilley decided he wasn't fit: he was having trouble with his knee, and didn't think it would stand up to a 5-day Test pounding. We brought in Gladstone Small to replace him, although Neil Foster was terribly disappointed, and had been hoping his batting might swing the decision his way. As it turned out, Stoney went for broke and bowled magnificently well, and I'll never forget, as long as I live, the sight of Gladstone getting Allan Border out 2nd innings, off a remarkable catch by Emburey at 3rd slip. Because the next batsman came out looking completely bewildered by it all and it was at that point that I knew they were a beaten side.

The story of the match is fairly simple. I won the toss and stuck them in, and there were all sorts of hoo-has about that because England captains did this at their peril. And

Australia, with a little resistance from Dean Jones, staggered to 141. Gladstone removed 5 for 48, and Both, who was by no means fit, bowled off a short run and conned the other five into getting themselves out – with Jack Richards leaping this way and that and taking amazing diving catches.

Chris opened *our* account, making his third 100 in a row, and we all chipped in a bit but made silly mistakes, and we needed our tail to bail us out. We put together 349 runs – and it was then that I thought perhaps we'd blown it and left Australia a chance to get back into the match. I saw no reason why they couldn't clear the 208 arrears and then set up a quick target to put us under some pressure.

That's what I was thinking about on the last morning. But I needn't have worried. Daffy, Gladstone, Emburey and Edmonds all clicked with the ball and by half an hour after tea Australia had struggled and slithered to 194 all out. Bubbly was about to flow. The team forced me to lead them off, which was very nice but very embarrassing. We had won by an innings and 14 runs. It was the first time I'd ever seen Phil Edmonds drunk.

We had the old Union Jack draped around us, and hardly knew where we were, and a bloke with strange sequinned bins and a little trilby poked his head around the dressing room door – it proved to be Elton John, a keen sports enthusiast who'd been watching all day from a box and happened to be in our hotel as well. Elton, it was, who led the celebrations – I think he was more thrilled even than we were – and it was nice to have a down-to-earth superstar in our midst; Elton acted as DJ at one of our parties afterwards – I think, blearily, it was the one in Botham's room – so he must either have recovered from his throat operation or he hadn't had it yet. A few of us had been to one of his concerts in Perth so we knew a bit about Crocodile Rock, and he knew a bit about cricket.

The partying went on and on till very late, and we all woke up with fairly large headaches. We still had one Test match to play, and more immediately, we had the Perth Challenge, a four-nation one-day competition to celebrate the start of the America's Cup. For our opening match, against Australia on New Year's Day 1987, I won the toss, to enable us to bat in daylight, and Ian, Lamby and Chris Broad blasted away to give us an unassailable 272 for 6. We won that by 37 runs, to keep the Aussies in our psychological grip.

But next up were the West Indies, and this was to be our first big test. So the lads and I went into a huddle. When I had taken over the Middlesex captaincy I gave the team a little confidential questionnaire, to see what their feelings were and what we could do to help the cause. I'd been influenced by Rudi Webster's Positive Thinking in *Winning Ways* and the same psychology was to help me as England captain in Australia because although we'd been beaten 5–0 in the West Indies, I believed we were playing wonderfully well as a team, and could beat the West Indies here. I read little extracts from *Winning Ways* that seemed to me particularly relevant, because I wanted a more positive approach.

At that time, when you mentioned the West Indies, they would say despairingly, 'We haven't beaten them for ages'. So it had to be got over to them, in simple and convincing terms, that we were going to go out on the field and beat them.

'Look, lads,' I said, 'we've got the best chance we've ever had of knocking this lot over. They've come over fairly cold, whereas we've been firing on all cylinders. We're disciplined and we've got to stay disciplined.'

It gave my own and Micky Stewart's team talk all the more credibility that the West Indies had in fact just thrown away their opening match to Pakistan. West Indies came out against us with their full-strength side, including Marshall and Garner, and we were playing on a new, quite lively wicket. But again, thanks to fine knocks by Allan Lamb and Jack Richards, we managed a respectable 228 for 9 off our 50 overs. And then it was just a question of convincing the boys that if we kept our heads, and our self-discipline, we could run through them.

Well, our bowlers were keyed up, and steaming in, and we caught everything, and we had them out for 209; a fantastic win for us by 19 runs, and an enormous boost to everybody's confidence.

Then after beating Pakistan by a rather wider margin than the 3 wickets on paper suggest, we simply had to beat Pakistan again in the final, and that was rather one-sided really, although Chris Broad's dismissal raised a few eyebrows, and we had another flutter of panic, sinking to 7 for 2. But then David, Allan and myself steered us into port and Ian gave us a final flourish to secure a 5-wicket victory with nearly 10 overs to spare.

Now we had won two things, the Ashes *and* a very handsome trophy featuring a cricket ball in a ballooning silver sail, and I must say that the support for the team out there in Perth was quite unbelievable. There may have been four or five thousand English people, but it sounded like fifty or sixty thousand cheering us on. It's so lovely to hear people yelling for you – and in Australia!

Our confidence was sky-high for the 5th Test in Sydney. People had said, 'How will you motivate the side now you've won the Ashes? It doesn't really matter now, does it?' Of course it mattered. It mattered to all of us. Australia, having won the toss, had gone in, finishing the day on 236 for 7. We might have dismissed them a lot sooner, had Dean Jones been given out when he was 5, but I suppose that's cricket. He went on to 184 not out, a sizable chunk of Australia's 343 total, their tail having defied us as well. So I was very depressed when England plummeted to 17 for 3 at tea, and I wasn't much happier when we finished the day on 132 for 5. Elton John cheered us up over dinner.

Next day, thanks to John Emburey, limping with a groin strain, and Jack Richards, we closed the gap to a 68-run deficit, and had a couple of them out in the final session as well. After the rest day (I played golf with Richie Benaud, and some of the lads went on a trip across Sydney), we had a series of disasters in the field.

Graham Dilley, Philippe Edmonds and John Emburey were all either secretly or undisguisedly injured. Yet Ernie insisted on bowling, groin strain or no, and it was his heroic effort with 7 for 78, his best Test figures, that pegged Australia to 251 all out, leaving us 320 to win in just over 7 hours. I thought that was a reasonable target. And although we lost the wicket of Chris Broad caught and bowled that evening by leg-spinner Peter Sleep, I still felt we should go for it. I had a chat with David and because of the rough around the off-stump getting progressively worse, I suggested he went in at No. 3.

The newspapers were saying England hadn't been successful at chasing more than 300 since 1929, but we got off to a decent start before they began pulling the legs from under the chair. I was still in, but at lunch we were frankly in trouble: 101 for 3, and it got even worse when we lost Allan Lamb, caught at silly-point by Waugh, and Both caught at mid-wicket, both of them off the bowling of the off-spinner Peter Taylor. That left us on 102 for 5.

I *still* thought we could do it, and when Jack Richards came out to join me I told him, 'We've got to stay out here till tea. Then we can see where we stand'. We survived a couple of chances and some huge imaginative appeals, especially from Zoehrer the keeper, who eventually made me a bit cross. By tea we had got the target down to 133, Jack and myself still battling together. The last 20 overs – 90 wanted, and the new ball an hour old. Jack thought we should get 10 overs nearer home before letting rip, and advised caution. Border set the field more defensively, and I was out attempting to play Waugh through mid-wicket, caught and bowled 4 runs short of my second tour 100. As I walked back, I told the incoming batsman Emburey, 'It's still on'. But then we lost Jack and we were obliged to abandon hope and look for the draw.

I couldn't bear to watch the last few overs after Phil Edmonds was out lbw. We lost Gladstone, and then John Emburey very nearly managed to keep them out, but fell in the end to the last ball of the 19th over – with just 1 over to go. So we failed to save it by 7 balls. It had been one of the best Test matches I'd ever played in, and you couldn't have had a tighter finish.

Most of the Press praised us for having tried so hard to win it. Only one bloke thought it was stupid, and that was Geoff Boycott. He would have blocked it all day long, had *he* been given the choice, as it was a Test match against Australia, and 'you shouldn't give them a hope in hell'. Their victory gave the Aussies a tremendous lift, and there was talk of them having 'turned the corner', which wasn't perhaps quite realistic. OK we didn't win, but we didn't deserve to lose either – at least, that's how most of the lads looked at it.

The last leg of our Australian tour got underway at Brisbane. This was the World Series, a three-cornered one-day competition between Australia, England and the West Indies. Our first match, on 17 January, was against the Blackwash Brigade. It was a sweltering 100°F. Phil Edmonds was out of our attack with an injury, but Ernie and Graham Dilley were in the side. We'd beaten the West Indies in the Perth Challenge, but the question was, with a little of Rudi Webster's Positive Thinking, could we make it two in a row?

We could, and we did. Having bowled them out for 154, and won by 6 wickets, we made the front page, the back page and all sorts of pages! We outplayed them really. But unfortunately the *next* day we had to play *again*, against Australia. Very, very hard work! Very hot, very humid. Dean Jones got a fine century and we came up 11 runs short of their 261 for 4.

We tried our best: Bill Athey got 111, but everybody was totally annihilated because we'd had no break at all. Then it was off to Sydney, to play the Aussies again – and this was the famous match in which they had us on the ropes at the beginning of the final over, looking for 18 runs. Bruce Reid was the bowler, and he looked on in increasing horror as Allan Lamb stood up and hit 2, 4, 6, 2 and 4 to get us home with a ball to spare. England won by 3 wickets.

With renewed energy we went back to Adelaide and beat

the West Indies by a convincing 89 runs, having piled up 252 for 6, courtesy of Ath and Broad, which they were never in any danger of getting with DeFreitas roaring in. We had handed them their third defeat in a row. They had always had mutual confidence in each other, and had the personnel to carry it off. Now they'd lost a player here, a player there, and there were a few chinks in their armour. Whereas we were supremely confident. We weren't going out on the field thinking of losing to them any more. We were going out there to win, and if anybody wasn't of that opinion, he could stay in the dressing room. You always have to want to win, and believe that you can. Otherwise there's no point.

It was Australia Day, 26 January, when despite our unbounding confidence we lost our next match – to Australia at Adelaide, by 33 runs. They were playing 'Waltzing Matilda' round the ground; they had been 35 for 3 and Allan Border chipped a dolly catch to Graham Dilley which he somehow couldn't get a hand to, so they managed to total 225 for 6. And then – to make matters worse – we were cruising along needing about 100 off the last 20 overs and we collapsed in a heap. We lost by 33 runs. So now Australia had beaten us twice in three matches – three times in four with the Test match.

Well, we got to Melbourne to find ourselves on a rather fresh wicket. The West Indies, for it was they, slipped us out for 147 after we'd won the toss. We then took a quick wicket in their innings, but Viv managed to hold them together with 58 to beat us with 1.3 overs to go, by 6 wickets.

We were getting very tired, and when Australia thrashed us yet again, in Melbourne, by 109 runs, we were a very weary England indeed. It was now a question of qualifying for the finals, because Australia had now overhauled us in the points chart and we had to play the West Indies in Devonport to see who their opponents would be. We were not only tired but hurt. Wilfy Slack had fainted in the nets and was rushed to hospital for tests; Chris Broad was carrying a hamstring injury all through the World Series, and Both couldn't move his side without wincing. So we were strapping and patching people up just to get them on the pitch.

The Devonport wicket didn't make life any easier either, doing all sorts after Viv had put us in, but Chris Broad played an heroic knock, 76 of our 177 for 9 – that being all we could muster. Now, we did have a stroke of luck here: West Indies were without their openers, Desmond Haynes and Gordon Greenidge, and that gave our walking wounded a glimmer of hope. But it wasn't until later that I knew we had them, when Both managed to induce Viv Richards, who had curiously dropped himself down the order to number 5, to drag one on, attempting to cut.

With John Emburey bowling splendidly as well, they were all out for 148 runs! Both had been an inspiration both on and off the field, telling people they didn't want to go home yet as it was very cold in England. He took 3 wickets, and the others bowled their hearts out too – it was pointed out to me afterwards that five out of my eight bowling changes got us a quick wicket. I didn't know that. We were in the finals.

Our opponents were Australia, who had finally put West Indies out of the reckoning. I had got round to the unusual idea of opening with Botham. In Devonport he had said, 'You've got to let me open,' referring excitedly to the rule of only having two men out of the circle in the first 13 overs. So in he had gone with Chris Broad – voted 'International Player of the Year'. The new formula hadn't worked at first, but here in Melbourne in the first Final, it did.

The game was shortened by morning rain, and the England bowlers oiled their weary bones and strapped up their injuries. And they went out and produced a tremendous performance, restricting Australia to 171 for eight. I was in the pavilion listening to the crowd roaring and cheering, thinking, oh no – don't say we've lost a wicket!

But no, it was sheer appreciation of Botham clubbing the bowlers mightily all around the ground, for 15 overs. Well, we cruised home by 6 wickets, Both hammering 71 and David Gower gliding to a classic 45. So the lads were dead keen not to mess up the second final either, because we'd played very badly against Australia all the way through, despite having beaten them in the Test Series, and if we lost this one we'd have to play yet another final match, to decide the winner.

It was another important toss to win and I won it. England went in on a dampish Sydney wicket, and Both gave us another blistering start, despite his left foot being swollen and bruised, but it was a horrible dead wicket and we fell away in the middle – 187 for 9 off our 50 overs. It would have to be enough, because Both was struggling and we couldn't face going down to Melbourne: we were on our last legs. Graham Dilley asked me to have a few looseners with him. Daffy DeFreitas sat in the dressing room examining his damage, and I said, 'Are you going to have a bowl with "Picca" then?' (Picca – Dilley, you see.)

'No, I'm not,' said Daffy.

'Fair enough,' So I went out with Dilley and the next thing I saw was Daffy, trotting down the steps, looking at the injured Dilley bending his back.

'He's serious, isn't he?' said DeFreitas. 'Right. I'll be with him,' and I promise you, on that slow Sydney wicket, Daffy DeFreitas bowled very sharply indeed.

The Australians struggled, managing only 20-odd runs off their first 14 overs but we desperately needed a wicket. On came Botham. He got 3. He had Allan Border caught behind, Marsh plumb lbw, and Ritchie caught in the covers. It was a superb piece of bowling, Both finishing with 3 for 26 off 10, and when John Emburey struck with a magnificent return catch to dismiss Dean Jones, they were really going to struggle in the closing overs. Dirk Wellham smashed one to David at cover, and David threw it up many a mile. It was the first time I'd seen David get excited on this trip. They needed 18 off the last over – which Allan Lamb could have managed for them. I put Neil Foster on.

'You pick some right times,' said Fozzie – and they tried, but they ended up 9 runs adrift. England had won. England had won the Ashes, the Perth Challenge, and the World Series. It was worth a tear or two.

We were staying in some apartments in Bondi Junction and Elton John threw a huge party for us on the roof, with a barbecue, with lots of food and booze because he was thrilled as any of us. I was close to tears in the dressing room. We were the most successful England touring team in history. The lads had been superb – not once had they let me down, and I hope that I hadn't let them down either. We'd lived out a sort of fairy tale. It could never happen again I don't think, that England would take three trophies in Australia. It was the first time England had won the World Series, and the Perth Challenge was probably a one-off anyway. It's rather strange that people never give credit where credit is due, though, because they commented afterwards that Australia were a pushover. Yet the same side, with perhaps one change in 1987, won the World Cup.

We came back to a heroes' welcome, from one of the most punishing schedules of any England tour. Our flight to Heathrow was our 35th of the tour – we'd flown nearly twice round the globe, 44,000 miles. It had been a fabulous trip, played very hard but very fairly, and we were rather overwhelmed by the strength of feeling back home. I was invited to dinners down south and dinners up north, and everybody was so effusive I was a bit embarrassed. They said, 'You kept us up all flipping night watching it on telly!' And people had apparently gone to work all excited and happy, clutching transistors to their ears. It was probably one of the happiest England winters of all time, I should think.

I was awarded the OBE, and although I was on tour and not allowed by the TCCB to return for the actual presentation ceremony, I did go to lunch with the Queen. Apparently she has one of these sort of lunches fairly regularly, and there was a lady there in charge of a women's prison, and the Minister of Trade and Industry or something, and a few others as well as myself. The surprising thing was how down-to-earth and easy Prince Philip and the Queen made the occasion. It was a fascinating lunch and the only thing that made me feel uneasy was dining off the 1854 crockery, in case I broke something. It was lovely to receive the award, though, and I feel it was an honour for the team as much as for myself.

Had I needed to be brought back to earth, a trip to the Worcester ground shortly afterwards did the trick. The previous visitors – the Leicestershire lads – had left a message for me posted up on the dressing-room door: 'Congratulations on the OBE, Obese Branston Eater'! Getting the OBE is a great honour, but I must admit I find it slightly embarrassing, like having a road named after me near one of the County grounds.

CHAPTER FIFTEEN
Press on Cap'n Cock-up
1987

After we'd won all three trophies in Australia, a sense of deflation set in. I should have started 1987 jumping up and down, as happy as Larry. Yet I was just glad that it was all over, frankly. We'd been under the most tremendous pressure to keep going, keep going, keep going, and you were putting in, putting in, and giving and giving, and once you'd finished, after that initial half-hour burst of jumping about and celebrating, you woke up the next morning and thought, Well (sniff) yeah. Great. It's over. And that's really how I felt after our triumphant tour of Australia. My mind knew: I don't have to do it any more. I can't do it any more. Leave me to sleep.

It was nice, the winning. And that's it. Because you've sacrificed so much of yourself; you've driven yourself to a standstill. You *can't* do any more. You don't *want* any more. And then you get back to your family and try to become a normal person again, and you totally withdraw, because they want you to give and give and give as well.

I reckon it takes about a week to wind down from the sort of intensive cricket we play. If I get a four-day break from our year-round schedule, it takes me two days to settle down and recharge my batteries, yet the kids are still at you all the time, and it's only after about day three that I'm totally back to normal. I have to change gear from being the man's who's trying to control things to a man who's simply part of things again.

Elaine Gatting:

To us, because Mike is so busy, when he's 'relaxed', he's comatosed at home. He's literally lying down asleep. He'll fall asleep in his chair. Either that or he watches television, and if you ask him a question you don't get an answer. I don't think he's really watching the television, even. For 'home' games during the season, people think, well, he starts playing at eleven and finishes at six, six-thirty, so he must leave the house at half past ten. He doesn't.

He leaves here at 8.15 and he never gets back before eight at night, and generally not until nine, weekends included. So when he gets in, I give him something to eat and then he usually goes to sleep. If we do go out, it's usually to a cricket function, of which there are a great many, rather than somewhere private to simply enjoy ourselves. We don't get many holidays: we had five days in Sussex last October.

We walked along the beach, Mike and Andrew searching for crabs. There was a little pleasure park with a waterless swimming pool filled with plastic balls, and we took some photos of our little boys messing about in there. That's all we want to do – something quiet.

We don't socialize very much with the other players, apart from the Dilleys and the Emburеys – we've always been friends with them. But the things Mike is expected to do outside of his playing hours take up most of his time: committee meetings, selectors' meetings, speaking engagements, club dinners. Mike finds it awfully hard to say 'No', and if he *does* say no, people get upset and complain, 'Who does he think he is?' People think we lead such a glamorous life, you see. They ask me, 'What's it like being married to a famous man?' I always reply, 'Well, *that* isn't the man I'm married to,' yet there are times when I think perhaps I'm married to that man after all!

Nobody who played a part in the Australian tour will ever forget it, but the party was over now and it was back to work.

What had happened since we returned had been absolutely marvellous: non-stop invitations to join in one celebration after another, and the lads deserved every glass of champagne they were offered. But now we tried to put it all behind us. Looking after Pakistan was going to be no mean feat in the coming summer, and I was especially concerned about Middlesex, who hadn't had the greatest of seasons in 1986.

They started badly again and got very sloppy in the early Championship matches. I had hopes that we could launch a realistic challenge before the start of the Benson and Hedges and before myself and the other Test players were called away; but that scheme was shelved. We lost to Yorkshire, were forced to block out for a draw in Manchester and we batted so badly against Northants that I kept the team locked in the Lord's dressing room for 25 minutes, reading them the riot act. Northants went on to beat us by 10 wickets – and really that was the sad story of Middlesex in 1987. There doesn't seem much point in giving you the gory details.

We decided at the beginning of the season that we wanted our 'Finals man' Clive Radley to play, and to bat in the Sunday games, and then we would reassess the situation. Sadly this was probably going to be his last season, after long and sterling service. We had a couple of youngsters coming through, so it was a season of sorting out. We got knocked out of all the one-day competitions, and we lurked around the bottom of the Championship table.

We had some very promising young cricketers coming along like batsman Mark Ramprakash, who was still at school but who played on Sundays for us to give him a taste of what it was going to be like. John Carr was batting well as one of our openers, and we gave the other youngsters their heads – Mike Roseberry, Keith Brown, and Wilfy Slack opening. Jamie Sykes played a bit towards the end, and when we left out Phil Edmonds, who had outside commitments, Philip Tufnell replaced him.

As the season went on, and we found we weren't getting anywhere, we rested senior players in favour of youth; we tried to give them some experience. So, a rebuilding sort of year. The hardest one to leave out was probably Roland Butcher, but we had given Butch a very long run and after an early flourish he just wasn't striking his form. It was very tough for me, as captain, to make these changes and ask senior stalwarts to step down.

We didn't think Philippe Edmonds was going to accept the contract we had offered him and we were quite right. He was always being reprimanded for something. He'd have a business meeting to go to and at some stage he might let you know: 'Oh, sorry – can't play Sunday – going off for the weekend'. He had European trips, I believe. He didn't bother to tell you until the last moment: it may just have been a failure of communication, though I think in his heart of hearts it was because he felt we'd probably say no. We had our differences, but I think they only came about because he got himself into trouble. The final crunch came when he did some writing for the newspapers, and though he said they stuffed him out of sight with misquotations, it was his own fault and it really was quite a serious matter. So he got suspended. To tell you any of the details, I would have to rack my brain, and I don't like racking my brain over Philippe.

Another twilight season was that of Wayne Daniel. Having given ten brilliant years to Middlesex, and always given a hundred per cent, last year Wayne couldn't quite get it right, and with Norman Cowans injured, Angus Fraser recovering his fitness, Neil Williams not able to find his form, and Simon Hughes bowling below his abilities, there was probably a lot of added pressure on Wayne, and then towards the end of the season, after he'd had a few niggling injuries, there was a tragedy in his family back in Barbados and he went home because his mother had died.

He was terribly upset because his Mum had been very close to him. I think 1988 will probably be his last Middlesex season. He's only 32, but he's thickset and heavily built, and ten years is a long time for a welterweight to come steaming in. Wayne has been a true professional. He would run in and bowl his best all through his career: no-one could have tried harder. He's been a genius – the best overseas player in the land, a great team-mate, and a very funny and humorous person, dropping into the old West Indian lingo to tell us beautiful stories about Hammy the village batsman back in Barbados. We'll all be very sad to see our Diamond go. He has been the man behind Middlesex's success over the last decade.

For England, 1987 was always going to be a tough summer, because Imran's Pakistanis were here (Abdul Qadir, however, had stayed behind because his wife was ill). For the three Texaco one-day internationals, I felt it was important for us to get stuck in straight away. The first one was at the Oval. I was hobbling with a poisoned toe and in the end I had to have an ingrowing toenail cut out, so when I got whacked on it as well, I could hardly walk, let alone run. I also had a right thigh strain and had spent some time on the physio's couch having ice-packs applied.

Put in on a fairly good wicket Javed Miandad hit a magnificent century and got them up to 232 for 6. For our part, Graham Gooch, out of form, had been omitted and Chris Broad opened with Bill Athey – with myself coming in number 3. I hobbled about for a couple of overs for 2 runs before hobbling off again. But Chris, robbed of a century by a catch on the boundary, and Allan Lamb with 61, got us home comfortably. One up.

I couldn't play in the next game at Trent Bridge. I was hopping about in fur-lined bedroom slippers, John Emburey took over the captaincy and I'm afraid England played very badly there: Javed hit 71 not out and we lost by 6 wickets. So it was all eyes on the third game, at Edgbaston, and I was back. We managed to get off to a great start, nailing them 2 down for 0. Greg Thomas had been called into our seam attack and Thomas, Foster and Emburey restricted Pakistan to 213 for 9, with 6 ducks (Javed being their mainstay). We lost Ath to Imran, David to Mudassar (he often gets out to him) and Lamb to a great cover catch – also off Mudassar –

and then I came in, got to 41, and had an almighty whack at Mohsin Kamal that lodged somewhere in Javed's person, and I was gone.

Fortunately Daffy DeFreitas, in a spectacular display, took the attack to Imran, hitting a tremendous 6 over mid-wicket and we fought our way home with 3 balls to spare to take the match and the Texaco Trophy. There were two notorious features of that match. One was Pakistan's use of slow over-rates and substitutes, with bowlers going off and Jack Rabbit fielders coming on, and the other was the disgraceful behaviour of a section of the Pakistani supporters, about twenty of whom were arrested, and more than fifty ejected from the ground after running on the pitch and fighting.

Imran Khan deplored their behaviour saying, 'People should take cricket as a game and not get so carried away that they turn it into an emotional issue. It causes great embarrassment to us to see our supporters behave like this.' One poor chap had his throat slit by a flying broken bottle. The whole thing was horrible really. And because of all the dubious goings-on in the match itself, I got a bit frustrated and worked-up, and I was pacing up and down the dressing room. I do get quite upset when people push the laws to the absolute limit. So I was very glad we won – it was a good note to finish on.

So, on to Old Trafford for the Test match. Chris Broad had broken his thumb. Graham Gooch still wasn't getting many runs, so we brought in Tim Robinson who opened with Bill Athey, and Allan Lamb had also been omitted to give young Neil Fairbrother a go. Imran Khan, having injured himself weightlifting, was unable to open their bowling, and at the close of the first day, having been stuck in, we were going well on 145 for 3, with Tim Robinson progressing next day to a very determined 166 of our 402 for 7 (I contributed 42).

Rain shortened the evening, Pakistan having bowled very few overs, and the England team manager, Micky Stewart, observing all this, and the comings and goings of various

Pakistan fielding substitutes, commented, 'I can now understand why they needed to bring such a large squad.'

Replying to 447, Pakistan had a long fight in store to avoid the follow-on; Both had Javed caught behind and Fozzie and Daffy were putting them under pressure. We were ticking over nicely, with Pakistan 5 down and still 307 behind, with Imran and Mudassar in, when the weather ruined the fourth day and wiped out the fifth. We were really in line to have done something there, though the Pakistanis were moaning because they felt they hadn't had enough practice before the Test match, saying this was why they'd played badly. We had been on top from Day 1.

The squeegees were out for the 2nd Test as well, though again we got off to a fairly good start, at Lord's, because having won the toss and elected to bat, England established themselves, Chris Broad hit a 50 and Bill Athey justified his place with a weather-interrupted maiden Test 100. I ran myself out stupidly. I had pushed one round the corner and set off, and long-leg hadn't really started after it, so I thought, I'll try and nip through for a second here. But Salim Malik got there quicker than I anticipated and I was run out for 43. I should have shot myself – it was very bad cricket. We went on to 231 for 4 at the close, and next day nightwatchman Bruce French added a valuable 42, and we wound up with 368. And then it was rain, followed by more rain, followed by a draw.

The Pakistanis complained bitterly about the umpiring in that match. They thought I should have been given out lbw second or third ball to Wasim Akram. There seems to be a disagreement over the interpretation of the lbw law between England and Pakistan, because the Pakistan players don't seem to realize that if the ball is pitching outside leg-stump, they are not going to get a decision against the batsman. In Pakistan, the batsman is quite regularly given out in these circumstances (as was to happen to Bill Athey in a one-day game on the coming tour).

Haseeb Ahsan, the Pakistan manager, had written to the

TCCB earlier this month objecting to the umpiring of David Constant and Ken Palmer (they'd always complained about Constant and it dated back to an incident in 1982 when a short-leg decision involving Sikander Bakht went against them and they happened to lose a Headingley Test match) and Connie stood in the Lord's Test despite their official protest. Their objection had been overruled by the TCCB. Mr Haseeb Ahsan claimed the ball would have knocked back my middle stump.

Unfortunately the bad feeling engendered here may well have lit a very long fuse that went all the way to Faisalabad. At the time, it seemed to me the Pakistanis were complaining unjustly. David Constant is a good umpire – harsh yet scrupulously fair, and even if umpires do make genuine mistakes it's usually a case of swings and roundabouts, and the batsman is given the benefit of the doubt. I can think of one decision in that match where the England players thought a Pakistani batsman hit the cover off something and was given not out.

Anyway we took off our mackintoshes and went to Headingley, for the 3rd Test. I won the toss again, and chose to go in as I thought the Leeds wicket might deteriorate; they often do. I'd had a chat with a couple of senior players, because experienced people may hold different views about what the wicket is going to do, but in the end it's down to me, and if I say we bat, we bat.

When it's a bright sunny day at Headingley, the ball doesn't normally swing about. Today it swung. We were all out for 136, and if it hadn't been for David Capel's 50, we would have been in an even more parlous state. We had an evening to bowl at them, and we took two catches, and dropped three. Pakistan finished the day on 76 for 2, with Mansoor Akhtar and Saleem Yousuf in, both having been put down. If we'd have held on to those catches, we could have had them 4 for 40, a state comparable to our own.

Next day, Fozzie continued his work though, by getting rid of Javed for 0, but unfortunately Salim Malik and the tailenders contrived to hang around and wag. The nicks didn't carry. It was going to be one of *those* Test matches. They ended up with 353, and Fozzie, who had bowled unbelievably well without much luck, finished with a fairly remarkable 8 for 107. So we found ourselves 217 adrift, and we started off badly again.

All sorts of things went wrong. We lost both our openers; I got out for 9, playing forward to one from Wasim Akram that went straight to the only slip. Poor Chris Broad was unlucky on two counts: the wicketkeeper Saleem Yousuf claimed the catch from Chris's left hand, which he had already removed from the bat. Yousuf tried it on again, claiming a catch off Botham that he had clearly dropped, but this time he didn't get away with it, and Imran had a sharp word with him. You cannot defend that sort of behaviour. If as a cricketer you drop the ball, and it goes down, you don't just pick it up and claim a catch. You don't do that to other cricketers. It really gives the game a bad image.

They were on top and they were desperate to win, and prepared to go to any lengths to achieve it. And it was quite unnecessary as well, because Imran had bowled magnificently, and the ball had swung all over the place for some reason in that crucial first session that broke our backs. It was not to be our Test match, and by the third day it was all over, really.

We'd been skittled out for 199 and we lost by an innings and 18 runs, Man of the Match Imran's haul in the match being 10 for 77. He was 35 years old: I was 30 but at the press conference I felt 50. It was difficult to tell them much about it, because the simple truth was that we'd been outplayed. But we were also unlucky, and that happens in cricket. The ball seemed to favour the other side. At the Oval, it had favoured me with a bit of fortune. Here, the breaks all went to Pakistan. And as for the gentleman who writes to me saying luck's got nothing to do with anything, I'd like to tell him that in my book, he's certainly wrong.

The 4th Test at Edgbaston. Well, that *was* interesting. Again, when the coin flipped, Gatt guessed right, and this time I asked them to bat – it was a bit overcast, which augurs swing at Birmingham. Unfortunately, because we didn't bowl very well, nothing much occurred, and by the close they'd got 250 on the board for the loss of 3 wickets. The following day, the Friday, Fozzie and Dilley fired them out, Dilley removing Imran for 0, but Yousuf reached an undefeated 91 and Pakistan stood 439 to the good, after which we survived an awkward 45 minutes that evening without loss.

That was the cricket. There had been no play in the morning because of intermittent rain. After an early lunch we restarted at 1.25, and about 55 minutes later, as Dilley was bowling, the batsmen were offered the light and we came off. We'd just got in the dressing room, and people were changing their vests and shirts because it was a chilly day and they wanted to get out of their gear. I was in the toilet. The television set happened to be on and tuned into a film.

Unfortunately, no sooner had we got in there, than the umpires, Barrie Meyer and Alan Whitehead, reckoned the light had improved sufficiently for us to go back out again. So unbeknown to us, they'd gone out to the middle, put the bails back on, and stood there waiting for us. Then the light deteriorated again, and they came off. It was the Strange Affair of the Missing Team.

Nobody had let us know we were wanted, and Richie Benaud later cited the law in question, law 3 (8), which states quite clearly that after suspension of play 'The umpires . . . shall call upon the players to resume the game'. I think they said they'd had difficulty getting through the crowd by the gate, and that was the reason no-one had come to the dressing room. At Edgbaston it is just 15 yards from the ground – you don't have to go up any stairs or anything like you do at Lord's, and they'd had a reserve umpire, Kevin Lyons, who could have 'called upon us'.

Well, the Press went to work. Following huge headlines about my quite logical decision to put Pakistan in to bat the day before, such as 'Cap'n Cock-up' and 'Gatt the Pratt', we were now entertained with 'Gatting's Mug Punters' because

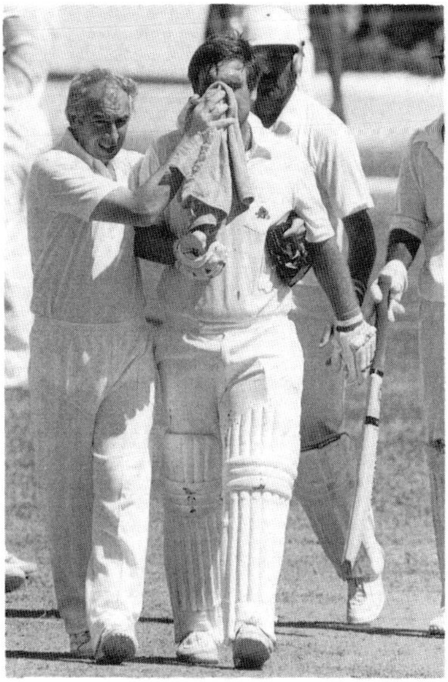

ABOVE Enough to put your nose out of joint: Malcolm Marshall, full bore *(Patrick Eagar)*

ABOVE Being led off the field noseless *(All-Sport)*

BELOW Treading on my stumps after the blow *(All-Sport)*

ABOVE Not in the best possible taste. Asked to pose with David Gower after the 'takeover' *(Graham Morris)*

BELOW Smiling through the blisters with fellow Leukaemia-walker, Kathy Botham *(All-Sport)*

BELOW Both relies on his genius. Could practice have helped? *(All-Sport)*

ABOVE The 4th Test: Gladstone Small getting rid of David Boon during our triumph in Australia, 1986-87 *(All-Sport)*

LEFT Well watered in Melbourne after England retain the Ashes 1986-87 *(All-Sport)*

ABOVE Jubilation in Bombay. For us, this was the final *(All-Sport)*

LEFT Allan Border and I before the big match in Calcutta *(All-Sport)*

RIGHT The 1st Test, in Lahore. Chris Broad is urged back to the pavilion by Graham Gooch *(All-Sport)*

LEFT Umpire David Constant. Was he the key to the controversy in Pakistan? (Here he shares a little joke with Both) *(All-Sport)*

ABOVE Eyeball to eyeball
(Graham Morris)

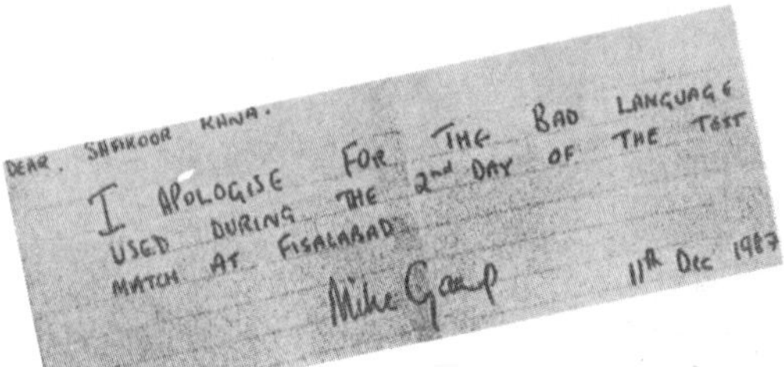

DEAR. SHAKOOR RANA.
I APOLOGISE FOR THE BAD LANGUAGE USED DURING THE 2nd DAY OF THE TEST MATCH AT FISALABAD
Mike Gatting 11th Dec 1987

LEFT The apology, written under duress

32 SPORTS GUARDIAN

Mike Selvey reports from Faisalabad on the second day of the second Test, where simmering tensions between England's captain and Pakistan's umpires erupted yesterday

A day of discord, dispute and disarray

CRICKET

Sun Sport

CHEATING PAKISTAN A DISGRACE TO CRICKET

It's enough to make poor old Gatt weep

ABOVE & RIGHT The Rana row – headline news

LEFT A British version of events

BELOW Pakistani eyeview: *The Nation* on the incident

ABOVE I received fantastic support from my family during a difficult summer *(Rex)*

BELOW Ramprakash did us proud in the NatWest final at Lord's *(Patrick Eagar)*

it was assumed that the England team had failed to show up on the field because they were glued to the horse-racing on television. Now, they'd had an interesting day's cricket. They'd had Graham Dilley and Neil Foster bowling very fast and intelligently, and they'd had some very good stalwart batting from Yousuf and the Pakistanis. And what do we get, but accusations about England not wanting to go out to play, letting things drift on, and being 'unforgivable', 'wimps', and 'jokers'.

At the press conference, I sat down next to Micky Stewart and muttered, 'Should we put our funny hats on now?' And then I got stuck in because I was very angry. I told them we'd been struggling along, and they'd not been interested in the cricket. All they seemed to have written about was the lads supposedly watching the horseracing. I asked what it was we were supposed to be watching – the 2.30 at Ascot. Well, Ascot was a couple of months earlier.

I said, 'There were all sorts of interesting things you could have written about Friday's play but all you were concerned about was this stupid little five-minute incident, and you haven't even got your facts right. We'd been out there trying our best, and you didn't give two hoots. We don't want to sit in the dressing room,' I said, with the sort of anger in my voice that most of them had never heard before. 'We want to go out there and play. What happened was a genuine mistake, first by the umpires and then by the team. Yet everyone seems obsessed by what happened in the dressing room, rather than what happened on the field.'

They said our manager had given them the impression that we were watching the racing – I don't think he did. In any case, they'd forgotten what they were there for.

The Press attacks on me brought forth an unusual ally in Bob Willis, who's very much for getting stuck into the Press when they attack players. He defended me very stoutly. What had hurt me particularly was the fact that they'd forgotten that we'd totally outplayed Pakistan in the first two rain-ruined Test matches. Yet as soon as we'd done badly at

Headingley, as soon as success and triumphs in Australia weren't forthcoming, they jumped on the bandwagon to slag us off. The Texaco Trophy, where we played very well; Old Trafford and Lord's, where we had played our hearts out and been on top – they were all history.

Now my honeymoon period as captain was over. I was Cap'n Cock-up. I believe the business of cricket writers is to write about cricket, not speculate on what the side might or might not be doing in the dressing room. If they want to speculate, there's not much point in having press conferences. They don't need the information – they can make it up. It was all rather puerile (I like that word – Philippe Edmonds taught me it).

As for England, we had a Test match to win. We had two days left in which to try to win it, and that meant either Both or myself had got to get 100 and we had to aim at getting 550 to 600 and then trying to bowl them out. Of course I was under a bit of personal pressure too now, because I'd only made a couple of 40s in this Series so far ('Is the captaincy affecting his batting?' 'Was Australia a flash in the pan?' 'Is he the right man for the job?'). The third day, England went to 273 for 5. I was 35 not out, Both was 16 not out. Tim Robinson and Chris Broad had ground out 119 for the first wicket, and David Gower had hit a cool 61.

Fourth day, here we go, we're 166 behind, 5 wickets left. Unfortunately Both got out fairly early in the piece, but Emburey and Foster helped and everyone chipped in, and I managed to get 124 and that calmed everybody down. England finished on 521. But then they started asking me, 'Was it the Press that spurred you on? Are you a bit piqued with the Press?' and suchlike rubbish.

I said, 'I don't care two hoots, and I'm not worried about the Press: I'm worried about the *side*. We're trying to win a cricket match here.' They found it rather surprising that I didn't say anything vengeful such as, 'There, you bunch of twits! That's put you in your place!' I'm not a vindictive sort of person. I like to be straight with people – I hope they're straight with me.

Well, we bowled out Pakistan for 205, to leave us needing 124 to win in 18 overs and we looked to be winning comfortably. And our batting let us down. At the close we were 109 for 7. But England certainly tried. It was a lionhearted effort by our bowlers on the final day. If it hadn't been for Imran's 37, Neil Foster and Graham Dilley, with Both roaring in, would undoubtedly have run through them and we'd have reached the target. It was against all the odds, and all the crucial decisions went against us, and against poor old Both in particular (I think there may have been a bit of atmosphere between him and one of the umpires). As for my 2nd innings contribution: I was run out for 8. It was that Athey – he absolutely did me!

Still, everybody had said the match was going to be a boring draw – at least it wasn't that. It counted as a sort of moral victory over Pakistan *and* the Press. I hoped in future they might be a bit more sensible and considerate before they started climbing into people. Anyway, we couldn't win the Series now; we could only hope for a draw.

The Pakistanis were already literally dancing and chanting with delight or some other emotion. I left the ground at Edgbaston in my car; it had been a long day and I wanted to get on the motorway and back to London. And for some unknown reason, I was suddenly surrounded by Pakistani supporters and one of them started kicking at the car and banging on the roof, and another one scraped a huge great mark down the side of the paintwork. I don't know whether they wanted autographs or whether they were expressing their fervour or their patriotism or what was the matter with them, but they were banging on the car window so hard I nearly got out and did something. When I got home, I was as cross as Elaine had ever seen me, other than when I put my fist through the kitchen door.

The last Test was at the Oval: on the flattest wicket of all time. We'd gone with a different opening partnership, in Broad and Martyn Moxon, and this time I lost the toss.

Mrs Vera Gatting:

I thought, Thank goodness – at least they won't be able to criticize him for that!

They elected to bat, and although we made a little inroad into them, 45 for 2, they proceeded to wallop us about. We had intended to go with four seamers here, but we ended up playing our two spinners, Edmonds and Emburey again – and quite rightly because it was always going to turn. Unfortunately we lost Neil Foster with hamstring trouble, and so we were left with just four bowlers – John, Philippe, Both, and Graham Dilley. That was another blow. Anyway, Pakistan laid into us, Javed getting a pulverizing 260 single-handed, Salim Malik and Imran helping themselves to centuries. All sorts of records were broken, John and Philippe didn't bowl as well as they might have done, and we were all very unhappy and worried about the state of things. Fortunately, Graham Dilley bowled very well to knock over the tail, and Both, though he had no luck, kept faithfully racing in and trying all the way through.

Going out to bat under the shadow of their vast 708, we quickly lost Chris Broad for 0, and also Martyn Moxon for 8. Avoiding the follow-on still looked a very, very long way off indeed. Tim Robinson was bowled by Abdul Qadir, who had been summoned to the fold by urgent appeals earlier on, and he accounted for me as well, trying to go down the pitch to drive him when I was on 61 – it was a very bad shot. Both and John Emburey braved it out for a while, before Abdul wrapped up the innings to leave us, mid-afternoon on Monday, a miserable 476 behind.

We followed-on. The leg-spinner was bowling round the wicket by now, having been twice warned about his follow through. They had a day and a half in which to bowl us out, and as if that wasn't bad enough, we began the last day fighting for our lives on 95 for 3, with Chris Broad and myself at the wicket.

I had a bit of luck! The first ball of the morning I faced from Imran, I played a very tentative stroke – a sort of early morning no-feet shot. And Salim Malik managed to drop it. Then just before lunch, I had a bit of a flurry trying to reverse-sweep the off-spinner Tauseef and it hit Miandad in the chest. It would have been a good catch, although I got a fearful roasting from a lot of people saying if I'd got caught, with us coming in on a wing and a prayer, I could have wrecked the whole effort. I should have been run out as well, probably, the same over; I came down the wicket and the ball turned, hit me on the pad and went straight to silly mid-off. I was stranded a foot out of my ground, but Mudassar's throw missed the stumps completely. I was on 58. So that was another bit of luck. And then I got an inside nick on one which went past the keeper for 4 – yet another bit of luck! But you do need a bit of luck, you know.

They took the new ball some time in the afternoon, and Imran came tearing in and bowled me a bouncer, which I hooked very hard. The unfortunate Ijaz Ahmed, fielding at short-leg, had to go to hospital to have his head examined. (Wasim Akram went to hospital as well, but that wasn't me, that was his appendix – so they were also a bowler short). They just couldn't get us out. Botham up the other end was as resolute as I have ever seen him, holding a watching brief, quite unlike Both. He was determined we weren't going to lose. We all were.

So with England unbowed on 315 for 4, the final Test was drawn. I was 150 not out; Both was 51 not out. We may have lost the Series, but we survived what may have been another heyday for the Press. The rubber had hinged finally on that first disastrous session at Headingley, where we'd lost by an innings. But we'd shown a lot of character, and instead of being criticized here we came out of it rather well with the newspapermen. The Pakistan manager, Haseeb Ahsan, a man of words, was still complaining about David Constant's umpiring, but because the Series had gone very nicely for them he threw in a few compliments as well, telling the Press I was 'a gentleman' and 'your best batsman'.

He said, 'If you want to build your side around Gatting, you must give him encouragement and not rubbish him. Help him, don't destroy him.' Mind you, he was also saying cheating is essential to the game:

> This has now become a technique for all cricket teams, that they must pressurise the umpire to the extent that they get one or two wrong decisions in favour of the bowler, in the match. So if Saleem Yousuf picks up a half-volley, all right, it is called cheating. But everyone is doing it. It has now become absolutely necessary in professional cricket today.

Well, that's up to them. We have certainly never done it with our umpires in England; we've never been able to. It has happened in India; although not recently. And it happens in Pakistan – they've got it down to a fine art over there. I felt very disappointed at the end, that we *weren't* able to win the Series. I didn't feel we should really have lost it – a draw would have been about the right result, but there you are – the weather wasn't on our side either. It always seemed to come down in stair-rods when we were beating them.

I was very honoured and privileged to be asked to captain the MCC side in the Bicentenary match at Lord's versus the Rest of the World. When you're playing with a host of stars of the calibre of Greenidge, Marshall, Hadlee, Gower and Gooch, you know you're taking part in something special, to say nothing of Allan Border's Rest of the World team, featuring the likes of Gavaskar, Kapil Dev, Imran and Courtney Walsh. We had four days of beautiful weather before the rain came down and spoiled the last day, and there was what you might call 'total cricket' played.

After I'd won the toss with a 1787 Spade Guinea and chosen to bat, the first day belonged to MCC, and to Graham

Gooch in particular for his fine knock of 117, before being run out by a most brilliant piece of lithe reflex fielding from Roger Harper. But there's a little story that can now perhaps be revealed, which was kept very quiet at the time.

Gatting didn't arrive at the ground until 10.25. This was due to the fact that the phone in my hotel room wasn't working, so I didn't get my morning alarm call. I opened my bleary eyes around 10.15 to find there was a rather large panic on. Fortunately someone had been despatched to collect me, and I got dressed very quickly and managed to be at Lord's for the toss at 10.30. I arrived out of breath, red-faced and acutely embarrassed that it had happened a second time.

It took a bit of pressure off me as captain to think of all the talent in my side, and although the game was played in a splendid sporting atmosphere, everybody was trying very hard. In the team I had, there was certain, total professionalism. I only managed to get 68 not out on that first day, and after Graham Gooch's spectacular shots, the crowd was giving me a slow hand-clap for plodding along. I was a bit upset about that because I wasn't that slow, really, and I was doing my best to hang around for the morning because we were out to score 400 if we possibly could. We were trying to play it very seriously you see.

Anyway, I thought it was a great day. You couldn't ever explain it in words: the full house, the brilliant sunshine, Lord's set out like a scene from history, the sense of nostalgia and grandeur about it all. And MCC were well perched, with 291 on the board, and six big names still to come. It was a tremendous feeling.

Next morning, I pitched up on time and had a chat with the lads. We decided to try and get to some sort of decent score as quickly as possible. So I went back out thinking, OK, we've got to go. With Clive Rice up the other end, suddenly everything seemed to go right for me. I hit one good shot early on which gave me a bit of confidence, and from then on it got easier and easier. They took the new ball; I didn't care. Rice and I were going strong, attacking the bowling.

Suddenly I found myself getting close to 100, and once I got past that, I thought, Now I can really give it a go. A warm day, an easy pitch, a capacity crowd. So it was chocks away! I added 111 to my overnight 68, 64 of them in boundaries to go with the ten 4s I'd hit the previous day, because at lunch our guys had said, 'You've got to try and get 200,' and I'd agreed with Allan Border that we'd declare at 450, *and* only bat for half an hour after lunch as well, so it would give them time to play sensibly and make a game of it. So that meant my trying to get 30 in half an hour, and with Courtney Walsh pelting in, it makes it slightly difficult.

I was finally bowled by Courtney for 179, and as soon as I got out we declared, 455 for 5, Ricey not out for 59. It was such a nice feeling because the crowd appreciated it, and then when you went in to the dressing room, to have people like Malcolm Marshall and Gordon Greenidge come up and shake your hand and say, 'Well played' – that was really rather special.

Well, we had to try and win it. We'd got our score, now we had to bowl them out – and Richard Hadlee and Malcolm were very, very keen. So you may imagine my feelings, as captain, being able to toss the ball to Malcolm Marshall and say, 'Go on, Malcolm. Have a bowl'. I suppose it's a bit like owning a Rolls-Royce. Malcolm is probably the best fast bowler in the world. Not only that, he plays to win. He is very professional, and a very, very deep-thinking cricketer – people don't give him credit for that. He really considers his bowling very carefully indeed.

I think Malcolm had Sunny Gavaskar lbw second ball before he had scored actually, but Sunny got the benefit of a lot of doubts, it being Sunny, about to retire, Bicentenary match, etc. It was given as a leg bye. And third ball I dropped a catch at 3rd slip that just about carried, to let off Haynes. But from then on, Sunny went on to play a fabulous knock, and ended up 80 not out overnight. Malcolm, whatever he may have felt about all this (he finished the day with 2 for 14 off 11 overs), sent down some nasty deliveries, removing

Haynes immediately, and roaring round the wicket at Vengsarkar who is not on his Christmas mailing list, to have him caught in the gully by Gooch. Clive Rice took a terrific catch to get rid of Allan Border – a bonus – and they ended the day on 169 for 3, still a long way behind.

We had quite a few beers that night, we MCC boys, and the following morning we were out having a net. Anyone who thinks there was no sense of camaraderie in the teams, with so many stars from so many countries, should have been there. MCC wanted to win. Another beautiful day, another full house, and Hadlee and Marshall steaming in at Sunny Gavaskar, bent on getting his 100. It was his last opportunity to score a century at Lord's.

And then Ravi Shastri made me laugh: 'I'll get him out, Skipper,' he said – and in fact he bowled extremely well. Now and again the batsmen got the better of him but he bowled very tidily at people. Marshall had nipped out Dujon, and in came Imran Khan, and Imran played some quite majestic shots for 82, including a soaring 6 into the President's Box, before Ravi removed him just before lunch. They eventually declared on 421 for 7, 34 behind, on the third night and Gavaskar had made a quite unforgettable 188 – before being caught and bowled by Ravi.

The fourth day was sunny and glorious *again*, and after we lost Chris Broad cheaply, Gordon Greenidge and Graham Gooch set to work in our 2nd innings. Goochie got out just before lunch, having hit a much-applauded 70, and Gordon was going steadily; it was just what the doctor ordered. After lunch, he unleashed himself and started going for his shots, and in the finish he was playing lots of reverse-sweeps, and people were taking the mick, because he was reverse-sweeping over fielders, and past fielders, and entertaining the crowd for five hours before Abdul bowled him for 122. He'd come down the wicket to one that didn't turn, and it went through the gate. I decided to let everybody see all our fine batsmen – I'm sure they'd seen enough of me – and David and Richard Hadlee having chipped in, we declared at 318 for 6. They had an hour and a day to get 353.

It began to cloud over and get rather dark, but not before Malcolm had stormed in to knock Sunny's off-stump out of the ground. In fact Gavaskar got out for a duck – to a very similar delivery to the one that nearly had him 1st innings, except that this time he couldn't get his pad in the way. Roger Harper, the nightwatchman, came in but then darkness descended, and very sadly on the final day the heavens opened. The game was so beautifully poised. We couldn't really have done any better, either for the spectators or the game.

It was a really historic occasion. And I think it's one cricket match that will always stay in my memory. The atmosphere had been exactly right: friendly, yet competitive. In the old days, before media and money and pressure and 'winning at all costs' took over the game, that's how cricket must have been played. I think you could play Test matches in that spirit. Certainly Richard Hadlee and Malcolm Marshall were taking it like a Test match; so were Imran and Courtney Walsh, judging by the way they tried to knock you over. But there wasn't any animosity or nastiness at all. It was a case of world-class cricketers competing against fellow world-class cricketers. There was nothing at stake, apart from the game of cricket, and that was enough.

My little son James, whom I saw very briefly before I joined the long long double England tour of that winter, was tottering about at home, wrenching himself out of his chair and constructing things with his plastic baby-builder kit. Somebody commented that he looks exactly like me, only smaller and clean-shaven. Apparently, while I was away playing cricket, he got hold of a photo of me because my Benefit brochure was being made up and I had to be featured on the back of the fixture list, and James was wandering around clutching this picture in front of him repeating 'Dada, Dada'. He carried it around for the rest of the afternoon. He has learned a bit more quickly than Andrew did about who is

Daddy, though I'm not sure he actually knows the picture is of me – he does and he doesn't.

It's funny really; it's difficult to know how the little lad's thinking. People say, 'Oh, you go off around the world and see the sights, and you get paid all this money,' but we really only see hotels and cricket pitches and it isn't a great deal of money when you consider it's for six months' work, and £12,000 basic tour pay for top professionals isn't what I would call excessive, not really. Not for what people have to go through, missing their families, and if you want to bring your wife and kids with you, you have to pay for them – air fares, hotels, everything – and that mounts up to a lot.

For an Australian tour, for example, with the wife and two children, with internal flights and all the hotels, you're talking in terms of £6,000 – and I'd rather spend that on my son's education. After all, you're not at the top for very long in this game, and you have to think ahead, and try to save and be careful. Obviously we enjoy the cricket – of course we do, and of course it's an honour to be out there playing for England, and we love it.

But it's very hard if you're a family man like me. The England football team have their wives flown out free of charge during the World Cup. I do wish the TCCB would consider helping us out a little bit, because we do spend *so* much time away these days. It's not like it used to be. With away games in England, Elaine and I have worked out that we actually spend, together as a family, about three months a year.

The greatest fear of my life is not of getting killed by a cricket ball: it is getting back home from the cricket and finding something has happened to my wife or my kids. I read a Jeffrey Archer novel recently, about a father waiting for the phone call from the Prime Minister to tell him whether he is going to be in the Cabinet or not; and he is playing football in the garden with his son. Dad is in goal and he goes to kick the ball, and just as it rolls into the road, the phone rings. As he turns to rush to the phone, the little boy says, 'No goal! I'll get the ball, Daddy!' and the man is halfway to the door when he realizes his son is running into the road.

He hurries out there and catches hold of the kiddie just as a big trailer comes down and hits the pair of them, and though the father recovers, his son is killed. That story preys on my mind. Fortunately our house is not near a main road but that is the thing that really scares me more than anything.

CHAPTER SIXTEEN
Cruel Sport in Pakistan:
The Winter Tour of 1987

Angela Patmore

Publisher's note: The following chapter has been written by Angela Patmore who was in Pakistan during the winter tour. From her vantage point as co-writer of this book Angela was able to supply a fuller version of the events that occurred.

It wasn't the right thing to do, he knows that now. He wouldn't condone people having arguments with umpires on the cricket pitch, and he has apologized to the authorities for his part in the row with Pakistan umpire Shakoor Rana, which pushed Reagan and Gorbachev off the front pages and boiled up into an international incident. But the circumstances, and the events leading up to those explosive closing minutes of the second day in the 2nd Test Match in Faisalabad, were quite unique.

Lots of people called for his head without knowing the full facts. To their credit, many who learned what really happened later apologized, or did an about-face. Other critics said that, no matter what the provocation he may have suffered, he should never have lost his cool or pointed his finger, because the Umpire is always right, even when he is clearly wrong. Those critics are entitled to their opinion, but they don't know what it feels like to be called a cheat by an umpire, and a string of obscenities into the bargain. Perhaps, too, they never paused to think what sort of man Gatting was, that he should have taken such exception to these insults. Hopefully, if they have taken the trouble to read this book, they may have come to know him a little better, and be less eager to condemn him without a hearing. Because throughout his career, he has always had the best interests of cricket at heart, and has tried very hard to play the game honestly and fairly.

He knows that, as England Captain, he has a tremendous responsibility to his sport, to make sure that it is played in a right and proper manner. He loves his job, and he has always regarded it as a great honour to play for his country. Even as the humblest member of the England XI, in and out of the side for a number of years, he did his best to play the game in the right spirit, upholding its laws and principles because he believes in laws and principles. He had never before been involved in a tour where an umpire's decisions had given rise to such open dissent (he didn't play in the 1981 Bombay Test in which Keith Fletcher, the England captain, was prompted by a decision against him to knock off his bails), and he had certainly never been on a tour where differences could not be amicably resolved for the good of cricket. The England team always got on and played the game in the best possible manner, even when bottles and lumps of concrete had been hurled at them; even when they'd had to barricade themselves in their dressing room amid riots and tear gas; even when, through no fault of their own, they had been made the subject of political storms and had to be given armed guards for their own protection. Through all this, Gatting and his team-mates had tried to behave like the professional sportsmen they are, for the good of their sport, and in the wider interests of the game. But they had never, ever, been faced with the sort of situation which confronted them on this particular tour, and reached crisis point in Faisalabad. Because here, for the first time, they felt that they were no longer playing cricket: that in fact they were now playing a different game altogether.

The plane took off from Heathrow in October, bound for the blackest tour of Mike Gatting's career. At the airport, some of the players' wives had waited until the actual departure, but Mike had sent Elaine away. She understood: she knows he finds all the fond farewells on these occasions too painful to bear. England were off to play in the World Cup in India and Pakistan, and to follow this up with a three-match Test Series against Pakistan. Having been to Pakistan before, Gatting had serious doubts as to how those parts of the World Cup would be organized, but to give credit where it's due, the BCCP did the competitors proud. The whole competition went off very smoothly, and the facilities were excellent. They'd gone to the trouble of building new pavilions, and everybody seemed to go out of his way to help.

When the England players arrived in Pakistan, though, Gatting still thought there was plenty of time for things to go wrong as they played their early matches. Things didn't go wrong. The Indians, too, had organized their fixtures very well, and preparations for the final and semi-final were beyond reproach, so they'd obviously done a lot of hard work to see that the competition was properly staged: it was the World Cup, after all. The only thing Gatting did find tedious and trying was all the travelling up and down – it seemed to him that the home teams had a sort of base, whereas sides like England and the West Indies were always on the move, with less time to practise.

England, lacking David Gower and Ian Bothan, who had preferred not to join the fateful party, nevertheless had a strong nucleus of players who had done well in Australia. The return of Graham Gooch was obviously going to be a bonus, and the in-form Allan Lamb would be another big plus, especially with all the one-day stuff coming up. And although some members of the Press thought England were a batsman short, John Emburey, Phillip DeFreitas and Neil Foster were all perfectly capable of chipping in with runs.

England's first World Cup game was going to be a tester, against the West Indies, on a fairly lively wicket in Gujranwala, and the England bowlers had a struggle to keep them down to a manageable score. And then when England got in they seemed to keep whacking it to the fielders, and they ended up needing 50 off four overs, and 13 off the last. Fortunately Allan Lamb was in cracking form, and the West

Indies had slipped up by making their spearhead bowlers swelter in for five overs straight off – three, in that heat, would have been plenty. Which meant that the last over was bowled by a very tired Courtney Walsh, and, 1-day cricket being the funny, unpredictable game that is, England managed to plunder the runs to give themselves a victory and a big boost.

So away they went to Rawalpindi, to meet Pakistan. And unfortunately, Gatting felt, they really threw that one away. They were facing a small target, with Allan Lamb and himself needing six an over, and Gatting played a reckless shot. Six wickets fell in 16 deliveries, and it ended fairly disastrously for England. This was also the match in which Javed Miandad aimed a punch at Gatting. The Pakistan batsman had stood around after being given out leg before to Phillip DeFreitas, fairly plumb, one might add, evidently hoping that Australian umpire Tony Crafter would have a change of heart. Gatt went to put his arm round Javed's shoulders saying, 'Come on, you've been given out, on your way', and Javed flew into a temper and Bill Athey had to steer the seething Pakistani away towards the pavilion. Javed says that Gatting swore at him. Gatting says he didn't. He can't say that he has never sworn at anybody but he certainly didn't swear at Javed Miandad, whatever the mutterings Javed may have heard from other people who had walked up to see what was going on. In any case, whatever Javed might have construed, this scarcely justified trying to aim a punch at the England skipper, saying 'I kill you!' with his bat up in the air. So far as Gatting was concerned, Javed was out, and that's all there was to it.

England proceeded to lose another game to Pakistan, won fairly convincingly against Sri Lanka, and then came to another crunch game against the West Indies, played in Jaipur, on another very lively wicket. If Gatt had won the toss, he would have had no hesitation in bowling first, and when the West Indies won it, this is what they did. But then they had to watch with growing desperation another of Graham Gooch's monumental knocks like the ones they'd seen in the

Windies. Everybody chipped in after Graham's assault, and England managed to get the huge 1-day total of 269 for 5 on what was after all a very good bowling strip. If you had asked the England captain before the toss-up what total he'd like, he would have said that on this wicket, 230 would be handy. Well, chasing 270, off they went, in typical West Indian fashion. There would be four very good balls, followed by two fours – it was that sort of pattern. Viv Richards was distributing a few, and they'd got the run-rate down to about 5.5 an over with wickets in hand, but England kept their composure, and in fact, once they'd got rid of Viv, the rest didn't resist them long. It was, Gatting thought, a tremendous effort from the bowlers – Eddie Hemmings, Emburey, Foster and DeFreitas – because they could easily have cracked up under the pressure. Gatting believed it was England's best game in the Cup so far. They then had to beat Sri Lanka again, and though it was by no means a formality, they were in the semi-finals.

Gatting didn't say much before the World Cup began about England's chances, but deep down he would have been very disappointed if they hadn't reached the semi-final. He considers it unwise to make predictions to the Press, but though there were three good sides in England's Group, he felt before they started that he had a good enough squad to get through. Anyway, playing rather than making predictions, they had now arrived in Bombay, to meet India.

Wankhede Stadium, Bombay, is a fearsome place to play cricket. It's not a very big ground and the crowd are right on top of the players in this terrific, terrible heat. It's rather like a cauldron. Gatting thought that, for a one-day game, the wicket was very poor. It was going to turn quite sharply from ball one, but what happened too was that it got lower and lower as the game went on. The England players had seen wickets at Bombay with lots of grass on them that were seaming wickets, so it was difficult for Gatting not to speculate that this World Cup pitch was intentionally prepared.

Kapil Dev won the toss, and the visitors remembered, as

they stepped out into the baking heat, that England hadn't in fact won all that many games in Bombay for a very long time. Gooch had been telling his skipper that it wasn't a very good wicket and that they wanted to bat first, and Gatting had replied that it might swing early on. To which Gooch responded by pointing out that if it did swing, India had two bowlers who were going to swing it, and if it didn't, they had two who were going to spin it. So if Gatting had won the toss, to this day he's not sure what he would have done. In the event, England were asked to bat. Kapil had been very apprehensive about his options as well. Anyway, it didn't swing. Graham Gooch, who had got his wish, and who had been in the nets for hours sweeping puzzled-looking left-arm spinners, set into them. It was a magnificent, commanding display, as Maninder and Ravi were swept to kingdom come, and Gooch went on to bludgeon and swipe 115. Gatting kept him company for about 20 overs for 56, and England put on 254 for 6 – about 15 or 20 short of what they would really have liked, though if they had been offered 254 at the outset, Gatting thinks they would have said, 'Right, we'll have that.'

When India went in, it was Daffy DeFreitas who gave England a lift by bowling Sunny Gavaskar in front of his fanatical supporters. In fact the Indians had gone about their work fairly sedately, cutting loose once or twice an over to frenzied applause, and it got to the stage where Azharuddin and Kapil Dev were well on their way, whacking England about. There didn't look to be any problem about India knocking off the remaining runs at just 5 an over, with Kapil on 30 and playing exceptionally well.

Suddenly he went for the sweep, off Hemmings. The ball sailed a fair way up in the air and Gatting was just in front of the square-leg boundary. He had plenty of time to think as it came down. It reminded him of his first Lord's Final against Glamorgan, when he'd stood underneath a similarly crucial skyer from Mike Llewellyn. On that far-off occasion, he'd caught it and some poor chap had rushed on the pitch with a beer for him, and when the police got a bit stroppy with the invader, Gatt had said, 'Oh come on – he hasn't done much', so it seems they just let the fan back into the crowd.

But that was then. This was now. The sky was much bluer here in Bombay, and Gatting was trying to focus his mind on the ball. As it got about halfway down, he was trying to tell himself to relax, wait for it, and watch the ball. Because if you get tense in that situation, it hits your hands with a smack instead of landing in a nice supple cushion. So Mike was telling himself over and over again that he was going to catch it, he was definitely going to catch it, and while he was hypnotizing himself the adrenalin was pumping through him at a terrible rate, and the ball got bigger and bigger and came down – plop – into his hands. Got it. 'Oh thank goodness!' you think – and you feel quite drained.

Anyway, England were still left struggling, because Ravi Shastri is no fool with the bat, and he and Azha put on 36 in just under 8 overs. And then Azha went for the sweep against Hemmings – and was out leg before for 64. A little bit of hope for England. A little window in the wall. Emburey came on now, and bowled a very mean spell, and not only that but he took a return catch to get rid of the dangerous More. England were through to the tail, but Ravi still looked as happy as a lark.

Fortunately for England, he was running out of support up the other end, and at last, just when they were thinking he'd never leave, he went for the big hit, underestimating Eddie Hemmings, and top-edged it. In fact, Gatting could have caught it at short fine leg, but Paul Downton the keeper ran in and laid his gloves round it, and India's last man was out, for 64. England had won, and although this was only the semi, in their minds, it felt like the final. This, to them, was the crucial game, the exciting one. They had beaten one of the favourites in Bombay, in fearful heat, in front of a huge, partisan, fanatical, fenced-off crowd. There had been many times during the match when Gatting had felt England might lose it. But when Kapil Dev was out, the game turned and the team's spirit seemed to soar. And when it was over, all he wanted to do was to sit down. It had taken a lot out of him, that victory. It had taken a lot out of all of them.

Gatting had told Allan Border, when he saw him in Madras, 'We'll see you in the final, then, Allan,' because the organizers were evidently hoping for an India *v.* Pakistan showdown in Calcutta – everything seemed to have been set up that way, with home ties for the favourites. Their plans got rather shot to pieces. It was to be England *v.* Australia. England had only one day to practise (they'd had three or four days to acclimatize before the semi-final). It was fairly cool here, compared with Bombay. The wicket was another slow turner, and Gatting would have liked first knock.

Well, Australia won the toss and went in, and England didn't bowl very well early on: the first 10 overs they went for way too many. Australia were able, with Boon's 75, to mount up 253 for 5 – batting well, to be fair to them. Gettable, but it would certainly put England under pressure, Gatting thought. Unfortunately, from England's point of view, towards the end of Australia's innings there were a few quick darts and nicks that went for four, which put 20-odd on the bill they could well have done without.

The knell of doom sounded in the first over of England's reply. They lost Tim Robinson for 0. Bill Athey, though, wasn't ruffled by this, and seemed to be going well. Perhaps Gooch could give them one of his spectaculars. Gatting had felt so happy for him in the semi-final, when he was their Star of India. Graham had had some dark days, and none more so than when he had left home telling the others that the Essex captaincy was affecting his game, and that he wasn't going to do the job next summer. Now England needed something special from him, and from Athey and Gatting, if they were to pull this off. Gooch was out lbw for 35 – a body blow. So now it was up to Gatt and Bill Athey. England were 2 down for 135, and the were stuck in a rut so Gatting was trying to push it along to get the over-rate down to respectable proportions. Allan Border was bowling, and the batsmen needed to make the most of it before the spearhead bowlers came back on. With Lamb still to come, Gatting felt that a few risks were justifiable. Well, as *The Times* correspondent put it,

> there was another of those confounded reverse-sweeps, this one costing Gatting his wicket.

It was the first time he had ever got out using the reverse-sweep. Over the last two or three years the stroke had got him a lot of runs, and in important innings. It has the advantage of putting the bowler off his rhythm, too, and stops him using negative tactics – part of the competition between batsman and bowler that goes on all the time out there in the middle. Anyway, this time, Gatting was out, and he knew well enough that if England lost from this position, he was going to get it in the neck. He had played the shot in the semi-final, when England had won, and nobody minded. It's just an improvisation born out of the pressures of the modern game, and Gatting is not the only batsman to use it, by any means.

Middlesex coach Don Bennett:

> Most of the criticism has come from people who haven't played limited-over cricket, where the pressures on the batsman must be out of this world, really, and they've got to think of ways to combat different situations and strategies. The reverse-sweep is a fairly recent development: I suppose Mushtaq Mohammad was the first one *I* ever saw playing it. Botham does it, of course, and so does Gatt – and Gatt plays it very well, in fact, usually!

Gatting felt that the one criticism fairly laid at his door was that he had chosen to reverse-sweep Border's very first delivery, but he knew it would be something down the leg side; it was just a little wider than he had anticipated. The reason he got out was not because of the stroke itself, but because the ball hit his shoulder – as had happened in Pakistan when he was dismissed playing an orthodox sweep. So he yielded a catch to Dyer, anyway, and was gone for 41 – ready for the newspapers to get stuck into him, if the worst came to the worst.

Sure enough, England ended up losing. Perhaps in the final analysis, it was because, as Gatting had feared, Australia got 20 or 30 runs too many, and then England didn't have Gooch in long enough to give them one of those solid starts that are so crucial in 1-day cricket. Gatting felt that his men made a tremendous effort to get as far as they did without Gower or Botham in the side. His own name may have been mud in the newspapers, but it wasn't a bad World Cup for England: at least it had been what you might call a friendly final, rather than the acrimonious affair it might have been, had India and Pakistan qualified for Calcutta. On the day, Gatting felt, England lost because the Aussies played better than they did, and deserved the trophy.

England had to play three 1-day internationals in Pakistan before the Test Series, which Gatting thought was silly planning and remarked on this before he left England. But he was told that this was what Pakistan wanted. He was prepared to concede the point, but he said that he didn't think the players were going to like it. As it turned out, the three 1-dayers were a total flop. There was very little interest, and some riddle or other concerning Javed Miandad as to whether he was fit to play or whether he wasn't. He had just been given the captaincy for the Test Series and decided he wasn't going to play in the third game, and Pakistan had all sorts of people in their side and lost the mini-series 3-nil. England won quite comfortably, so they were well pumped up for the 1st Test match.

The Pakistan manager, Haseeb Ahsan, said that they weren't worried about the 1-dayers; it was the Test Series that they really wanted to win. Rumours were rife that they were preparing the most evil turning wickets ready to receive England; well, Gatting thought, that was their prerogative. England expected to have to play on turning wickets against Pakistan. They had played for a day and a half on a turner at the Oval and survived Abdul Qadir's wiles there, and in the end he'd had to go off because he had bowled himself into the ground. Gatting is very much a believer in the theory that if one or two of the England batsmen can stay in and see off Abdul, the rest will take care of themselves all right. Because once somebody like that, who is spearheading a side, is blunted, the others tend to drop their heads very quickly.

The 1st Test was in Lahore, and it was obviously going to be a very good toss to win. Gatting won it. England didn't pick three spinners in their attack; they went with two. In fact Pakistan's *four* spinners did comparatively little bowling in the first innings, and it made their tail a little longer towards the end, as well. England went in, and by the twelfth over the Pakistanis had two spinners on – which Gatting thought had to be a fairly significant comment on the wicket on the first day of a Test match. The ball was turning sharply. England lost Gooch and Robinson, the latter having had a torrid time against Abdul which didn't allow him to settle. Chris Broad, though, seemed happy enough, and Gatting went out to join him.

The captain looked at the situation and decided that if Qadir was going to bowl like that, with three men round the bat, what was called for was a spot of sweeping. If he got his leg down far enough, he reasoned, playing outside the line of the off-stump, they couldn't very well give him out leg before. So away he went. First ball, Qadir tried to slip him a flipper: a quicker top-spinning delivery. Gatting sent that back down the wicket. Then Abdul had a little think, and a skip and a twirl, and threw the next one up outside the off-stump, so Gatting planted his foot well down the wicket, and well outside the line of the off-stump, and went for the sweep.

It was the leg break. The umpire, in his wisdom, thought it was the flipper, claiming to be able to read Qadir, but whether it was the flipper or not, Gatting's foot was outside the line and he was playing outside the line, and therefore he shouldn't have been given out in any case. Up went the finger. Gatting couldn't believe it, but you have to go, so off he trudged and stood in the dressing room wondering what was going to happen next. Contrary to tradition, umpires had been appointed *without* informing the touring team. It was becoming apparent why.

Gatting had had a feeling something like this might happen, and in fact he had warned the others, saying they'd just have to get on with it. But he was so angry about this particular dismissal, he had to go out and have a run. So he put on his trainers and an old tee-shirt, and ran twice round Gaddafi Stadium to calm himself down a bit. Unfortunately, as he was going round, word reached him that Bill Athey was out, and then on his second lap he was told David Capel was gone as well (there wasn't much cheering or roaring because there were very few of us in the stands). Gatting was mortified.

Emburey and Chris Broad were in, but then Embers was bowled, and Broad thudded one straight into silly mid-off's midriff which somehow was clung on to, so Broad was out for a very tidy and promising 41. One by one, the rest of the England batsmen plodded back into the dressing room and threw off their gloves, and they were all out for 175. If it hadn't been for Foster's 39 and French's 38 not out, they would have been in an even worse mess as well. The players stared at one another in bemusement.

'How did you get out?'

'The same way you did.'

In their opinion one or two had been absolutely sewn up. They looked at the replays on television with their eyes out on stalks. Qadir's figures appeared proudly on the screen – he had 9 for 56, an unusual tally.

Pakistan went into bat, and the England bowlers, in the shortish remaining session on that first day, were still a bit shellshocked by events to contain Pakistan properly and went for a few too many, notably down to third man, which Gatting admitted was his fault: he would post somebody there in future. England had their first glimmer of hope, though, the following morning – John Emburey took two wickets in two balls, to leave Pakistan 71 for 2. If England could steal another wicket very smartly, they might get amongst the longish Pakistan tail, even though Mujtaba did make 100 against them in the 3-day game in Rawalpindi.

But it wasn't to be. Mudassar was given not out when he was in the sixties. The close fielders had gone up for a bat and pad, having distinctly heard two noises, and Bruce French put down Javed Miandad off Nick Cook, to reprieve him until Cook got him out caught by Gooch at widish mid-off for 65. And then, in Emburey's first over to Ijaz, there was another bat-pad catch refused – this time with what the close-in fielders felt was a yawning interval between the sound of leather on wood and leather hitting the pad. The ball went straight to short-leg. How's that? Not out.

And that really made Gatting very cross, because a captain may be prepared to accept doubtful decisions to a degree, but when it's as marginal as that, and his batsmen have been dismissed in the way England's had, he reaches a sort of turning point. Had that wicket gone down, Pakistan's long tail would have been exposed. As it was, the home side went from strength to strength. England felt that Asif Mujtaba was out plumb lbw to Foster at the start of his innings, but in the end, having been 277 for 4 overnight and after Wasim and Qadir had added insult to injury, Pakistan were all out for 392; 217 runs ahead on first innings.

So now it was going to be a bit of a fight, the England captain thought. England's second innings was about four overs old, when on came Abdul. The *Pakistan Times* had said of his nine-wicket haul in the first innings, 'It is evident to the blind schools as well that Qadir is and has been in his elements'. Chris Broad, though, had played him very well first knock, and England were going fairly comfortably 'in Qadir's elements', when just before tea Pakistan brought on Iqbal Qasim, the left-armer, to bowl over the wicket into the rough at Broad. The batsman negotiated a couple successfully, but then Qasim bowled him a wide one, and Broad was very late on it, missing it by a long way. Now, to the surprise of players watching events on television, there was a huge appeal for caught behind, and lo and behold, umpire Amanullah Khan, in the words of the *Pakistan Times*, 'told him to go home'. Up went the finger without any hesitation – indeed, it was half-way up, Gatting estimated, before they had finished their appeal. The television replay suggested that Broad might have missed the ball, and the batsman also suggested that he might have missed it!

Broad and Gooch, it must be said, had gone out to the middle very hyped up, because their team-mates had all been saying, 'Come on, lads, get us off to a good start and we can still do this!' And what with all the unbelievable goings-on of the previous day, and being extremely upset about it all, Chris Broad for about a minute went completely barmy. He stood his ground, gesturing 'no' to the Umpire, and protesting his innocence of having touched the ball. Nobody could condone this, and Gatting certainly didn't. He took the view that it wasn't right, and it isn't how cricket should be played, because if you're given out, no matter how unfairly, you walk. But when one side is stretching the rules to the absolute limit, you surely risk having no game at all.

Broad's personal protest earned him a very severe reprimand. Gatting made it perfectly clear, and so did the England management, that if the Umpire gives you out, you can't turn round and say, 'I'm not going, sorry, I didn't hit it', and then just walk out to square leg and stay there, as Broad had done. Gooch had gone over to him and said, 'Come on, Chris, you've got to go – you've been given out. Don't be such a fool.' But unfortunately Broad had simply gone off the rails, as some sportsmen do when faced with the most intolerable pressure.

England lost Tim Robinson after tea, to quite a good decision, Gatting thought, after a delivery from Qadir came back a long way. This brought the captain to the wicket, to join Gooch. Abdul Qadir licked his fingers, his black hair flopping up and down as he skipped in, and down came another googly (he was bowling three an over at one point). Again, Gatting was well outside the line, but Qadir threw out his arms in a huge appeal, and when the batsman was given not out, Abdul spun round towards Gatting and said something about that having been his wrong 'un. Another heartfelt yell was turned down against Gooch, and a big argument broke out between Abdul and the Umpire as to how it was.

Even though the batsmen may not have understood the lingo, it was fairly apparent to them what was going on. Qadir was trying to convince the Umpire that even if the batsman was a long way forward, he could judge that it was going to hit the wicket, and the Umpire was telling Abdul that he couldn't deduce anything of the kind. Abdul, however, got so exasperated at this news, that he decided to take further steps, and he appeared to the batsmen to be saying, 'Right, that's it then. I'm bowling up the other end where I'm more appreciated.' And that's exactly what he did, evidently hoping the other Umpire might be more sympathetic to his appeals. Gatting was convinced that's why Qadir changed ends, because he'd got his haul from the end he was on, and if a man gets nine wickets bowling from one end, you'd normally need a crane to get him off it.

The Pakistanis didn't put Qadir on at the bottom end immediately. England were treated to a spell of Qasim first, and he bowled a very good ball at Gooch which Graham couldn't get a bat on – and then in a nightmare repetition of the Broad dismissal, he was given out, caught behind. As Gooch went off he was shaking his head in disbelief, but there was nothing he could do – he'd been given out. Off he trudged, an older and wiser man. Gatting felt that his teammate missed the ball quite comfortably. He stood up the other end, stunned. Comfortably, in cricketing terms, is a very long way indeed. It's not just a little mistaken judgement.

The two cornerstones of England's rearguard action, Gooch and Broad, were gone. The rest of them clung on defiantly, but then Athey was out caught behind, and French the nightwatchman and Gatting himself had to see it through to close of play. Back at the Pearl Continental Hotel, England went into emergency session. The Press had been poking their heads round doors saying, 'What about this? What about that?' and Gatt and the England management had been telling them, 'Watch the TV replays – see for yourselves'. But the Press wanted quotes.

Now, the manager Peter Lush had said, up until this point, that they couldn't comment on the umpiring while the match was in progress – which is a policy Gatting happens to agree with because in the normal way, it's bad for the game, full stop. But a unique sort of crisis had now arisen, and the newspapermen wanted to know where the players stood. Mr Lush told Mike, 'Well, we've got to issue a statement', so on the third day of the Test Match, the England manager went on record explaining their position and making a formal protest about the umpiring.

At the same time, there was an emergency meeting of the players, because many of them were unhappy with the situation. Mutterings to the effect were heard, 'If this is going to continue, there's no point playing here. There's no way we can compete on a fair level.' Gatting thought they certainly had a point but, in the wider interests of the game of cricket, he and the management team had to tell his team-mates something sensible. 'Hold on, lads. We've got to try and do the best we can. We can complain to the authorities, but we must play on. We've got two more Test Matches to get through. Besides, the Pakistanis think they're going to grind us down like this; we've just got to go out there and beat them on the field at cricket. We can't give in – that's exactly what they want us to do. So just go out and do the best you can.'

It was a very short, sharp meeting. Peter Lush had said his piece, and explained to them that it was necessary to go through the proper channels, and he and Gatting tried to give the team some reassurance and peace of mind, to make them feel they weren't just being walked over.

Despite these efforts to calm everybody down though, the next morning, out on the field, things deteriorated. Bruce French was given out lbw to a big googly that may well have missed another two stumps down the leg side, and matters had become very annoying and frustrating. So when David Capel was given out, caught off his arm, it must have seemed to Gatting that whatever was going to happen was not going to benefit England. The BCCP had three World Cup umpires sitting on the sidelines, who had been accepted as proficient and fair by all the international players in the competition. Being a Test umpire is a much-coveted job in Pakistan, with a lot of prestige attached. It seemed to Gatting and his team-mates, if not to those unlucky World Cup umpires, that for some reason the best-qualified people had been passed over in favour of giving more Test-match experience to two of lesser seniority.

Well, the sad tale of England's innings drew to its inevitable conclusion, inevitable not because the players weren't trying their best, but because of a quirk of Fate beyond their control. Gatting was given out to a Qadir flipper: whether it would have hit leg stump or not, he doesn't know. DeFreitas played a dubious shot to long off and was caught by Tauseef, bowled Qasim, and after a vain flourish here and a pointless prod there, England were finally all out for 130. Pakistan had 'won' by an innings, 87 runs and five aces.

Abdul Qadir had the incredible figures of 13 for 101 in the match – incredible to the visitors, if not to the Pakistan Press. The *Nation* commented that England had fallen 'to the magic of his controlled *slippers* and googlies', giving the whole episode a fairy tale touch, with magic slippers and so forth. So far as the England players were concerned, they hadn't fallen to Abdul's slippers, his flippers, or anything else, but they had undoubtedly lost a Test match. They knew that Abdul Qadir was a very fine bowler: of course he is, and they acknowledged that he had bowled exceptionally well in this match. But Gatting and his team-mates thought it a great shame that Abdul's figures had been arrived at in the way they had. The man is a class exponent of his art, and he takes a lot of playing because he *can* turn it, and he *can* deceive batsmen, as he was to show in Karachi. Qadir ended up with a phenomenal 30 wickets in the three Test Matches, but Gatting thought he could probably have done that anyway without the help of questionable decisions: that he deserved to.

Even Abdul himself, when he was batting in Pakistan's only innings, showed dissent over one outrageous dismissal – his own! It was fairly obvious to those best placed to judge that he wasn't out; and although Gatting was standing behind Bruce French at the crucial moment and couldn't see when he took off the bails, when he saw it on the replays afterwards, he could understand why Abdul was ranting and raving about it. At the time, though, Gatt found it quite amusing, he had to admit, because as he and Qadir were walking away from the middle, he remarked, 'Abdul – how can you complain after what happened to us in our first innings?'

Not at all appeased, Qadir snapped, 'I just wasn't out!'

'Well,' replied the England skipper sardonically, 'a few of us could say that!'

But Abdul wasn't prepared to see the funny side of it at all. 'Disgraceful!' he muttered as he stomped away.

Poor old Abdul. Poor England. Poor cricket – because cricket was undoubtedly the biggest loser in Lahore.

At the Press Conference afterwards, Gatting broke a rule that he had always tried to observe, and criticized the umpiring to the Press. He felt that he must show some sort of solidarity with the team after what they had had to put up with. His opposite number, Pakistan skipper Javed Miandad, went on record as saying he felt all the umpiring decisions were 100 per cent correct. If he'd said nothing, Gatting could have thought, 'fair enough', but when Javed openly supported what had been done to England, he sank even lower in Gatting's esteem than he had that day he tried to throw a punch at the England captain in the World Cup.

Gatting thought that had been a totally shameful incident, yet Javed was not even reprimanded by the BCCP. In fact, they had wanted an apology from Gatting himself – perhaps for having his face in the way of Javed's glove – saying Gatt had sworn at their player. They also wanted an apology from Chris Broad for showing dissent on the field. They didn't ask for an apology for Abdul Qadir's outbursts – these were evidently considered perfectly acceptable shouting, screaming and bawling at the umpire. And they didn't want an apology from Javed Miandad for trying to punch the England skipper in the mouth on the field of play, or for hoisting his bat menacingly in the air.

It wasn't the first time Javed had been involved in such an incident, either. He'd claimed a catch off a half-volley at Headingley and swore blind it was clean, and when his appeal was turned down, he had shouted and hollered at the England umpires and kicked the ball down the wicket. If that had been an England player, Gatting felt sure he'd have been banned from the next Test match, if not from the side altogether. To say nothing of Javed's boring little spout with Dennis Lillee in Australia, when it looked as though one of them might go flying.

Ah well. On to the biscuit factory. That was the next venue for most of the England lads after the 1st Test, up at Sahiwal. Gatting stayed on in Lahore with Graham Gooch, Neil Foster and their manager Peter Lush, though, because Gatt and Fozzie had played in every match so far, and it was quite important that they had a break. In fact, they managed to relax a bit, and fit in the odd game of golf and squash. Gatt played the British Under-23 squash champion Sohail Qaiser – who happens to be Pakistani as well. He ran Mike ragged.

The England players had thought the 1st Test had been quite eventful enough, with perhaps 9 of their 20 wickets, in their view, lost through questionable umpiring decisions, although some journalists thought 3 or 4 of these might be considered 'marginal'. In any event, the *Observer* correspondent seemed to voice the majority verdict when he wrote: 'Had Job himself been batting, he might have smashed down his stumps.' So the team were looking forward to putting all this behind them, and starting afresh in Faisalabad. They were in good heart and ready to do their best to win the 2nd Test and draw level in the Series. Little did they know what black clouds were gathering on the horizon . . . .

The hairy journey to Faisalabad, along narrow roads where all the drivers leave it until the last second before giving way, was made in the team coach, with the manager sitting in the front and the rest of them playing cards amid the occasional squeal of brakes. Driving in these parts is a test of bottle and there are many serious accidents. In fact, the rest of the team arrived having had an even worse journey, very upset about the facilities they'd enjoyed (or rather not enjoyed) at the biscuit factory. A meeting was hastily convened by their entertainments committee – Dilley, Athey and DeFreitas. The three lucky beggars (Gooch, Foster and Gatting) who had stayed in Lahore with their manager were heavily fined, and it was decided to hold a court case on the matter, similar to the Spanish Inquisition. Because of events arising from the 2nd Test, this trial never took place, otherwise the manager who had approved the biscuit factory might have been severely reprimanded, and possibly hanged.

They had a couple of days' practice in Faisalabad. They found the wicket was a turner, which wasn't surprising and which would, in any case, suit them as well as the Man with the Golden Gun, Abdul Qadir. England felt it gave them a chance of winning. They saw the practice nets, though, and they immediately had their first to-do. There were two nets: one good one and one dangerous one, where you bowled fast at your own and the batsman's peril. England had the dangerous one. So as soon as the Pakistan team had finished, the England players nipped over into their net, and the following day they were up early and in it before you could say Tim Robinson. They'd had a leg spinner bowling at them the first day, and no sooner had he begun then he was removed by England's hosts, which the players felt was rather cavalier. The following day, this happened again, and because England had managed to get in the decent net, there was a huge argument between the teams' respective liaison officers over why the good net wasn't saved for Pakistan for their practice. Much better was the brand new hotel where the players were staying, with swimming pool and tennis courts

– so new that the shale hadn't yet settled. The accommodation on previous trips to Faisalabad had been on a par with the biscuit factory, so they were surprised and delighted. It gave them a lift and showed that people had made an effort, for which the players were very grateful. They had some new video tapes coming, the rooms were plush, and they were happy, and looking forward to the cricket. At the team meeting on the eve of the Test, because they'd learned a few lessons from Lahore, it was clearly stressed to everybody that whatever happened, and however peculiar the decisions, they were to say never a word about them, and just get on with the job. They were already one down and they had to try to win this match.

At Iqbal Stadium, the great day dawned and Gatting won the toss, so they decided to have a bat. They had got off to a very good start, when Gooch was given out caught Aamir Malik, bowled Iqbal for 28, and Bill Athey, having played well with Broad, was also given out caught Aamir Malik, bowled Qadir for 27. Unfortunately these two bat-pad catches didn't seem the best of decisions, but never mind – on they pressed. 124 for 2. Gatt went in with Chris Broad, having decided that after what happened in Lahore, it was better to attack the bowling than hang about, no matter what the score. They needed to seize the initiative early on. Gatting managed to get 79 from 81 deliveries but then played a bad shot and got out to Qadir, and Tim Robinson followed 8 runs later, caught behind off a glove. Broad, though, was on a fine, undefeated 101 not out. So England were in a very good position at the close, 254 for 4, and with some batting to come. They felt they had a good chance here.

The following morning, though, they added only another 38 runs to their overnight score and they were all out for 292: a bit disappointing, Gatting thought, but still a decent total. Then when the opposition went in, the England bowlers struck early, one of their victims being the Pakistan captain, Javed Miandad, who had come down the strip and had a wild swing at Emburey. Gatting put down a slip catch to reprieve Salim Malik, but generally things weren't going too badly, and approaching close of play Pakistan were 106 for 5, having also lost Mudassar, Ramiz, Shoaib and Ijaz. There had, however, been a few niggling incidents. The main one concerned a very simple bat-pad catch against Ijaz, which had been turned down. It was this decision that led to Gatting saying, 'One rule for one and one rule for another', and Bill Athey was heard to mutter, 'The sooner we get out of this f—ing country, the better', which was very unfortunate because on television it came across as though the pair of them were calling down the wicket at Shakoor Rana, the umpire. According to Gatting, this was not the case.

Bill Athey made his remark under his breath, and Gatting's was intended for his team-mates round the bat, out of earshot of Mr Rana who was walking away down the other end of the wicket and apparently didn't hear a thing. What had happened, though, is that Gatting and Athey had been picked up by the microphone just behind middle stump, and the Pakistan television technicians had turned the volume on maximum to catch what was being said – quite contrary to normal practice. There is *always* commenting and muttering going on on a cricket field, and players have sworn and uttered cheeky asides since the year dot: it has always happened, and it is always going to happen, especially when they've got chronic tummyache and they're worried and upset about the state of play. It isn't necessarily directed at umpires, or at anyone in particular; the players are just letting off steam. So although the incident may have looked and sounded appalling, especially on the foreshortened television screen that made the two England fielders appear just behind the Umpire, it really wasn't as unusual or as dramatically rude as it seemed.

What *was* unusual was the way in which the microphones were being used, turned up full blast. This was not at all in keeping with the unwritten code of practice concerning mikes on cricket pitches. They are intended simply to pick up the sound of the ball bitting the bat. Even in Australia, where producers are nothing loth to use huge television screens to bring the action into sharp focus, they turn off the microphones as soon as the ball has gone past the bat, or at any hint of an 'incident' – otherwise they would be continually having to bleep out the comments that arise in these situations.

Pakistan had installed on-pitch mikes only comparatively recently, and it seemed to the England team that they were being used, in this instance, to highlight and broadcast private conversations and comments from the players. The victims of the episode could only think that by turning up the volume, someone, somewhere, was out to get them – and in the event this is exactly what happened. These little voice actuation microphones are extremely sophisticated and can pick up a whisper. In the wrong hands they can be used like any bugging device to eavesdrop and misrepresent. Umpire Shakoor Rana evidently hadn't heard Gatting or Athey at all, but being just two feet either side of the stumps, they were made to sound as though they were shouting abuse and trying to cause a furore. If microphones were to be routinely used in this way, players simply would not permit them on the pitch, and cricket Boards will be chary in future, knowing what trouble they can cause.

There had also been another very minor incident when Shakoor Rana, without any prompting from the Pakistan batsmen, started moving anything casting a shadow round the wicket. This isn't the Umpire's responsibility in any case: the batsman will normally complain, if it bothers him, without the need for interference from the Umpire. It was only a little thing, yet it seemed to Gatting as though Rana wanted to be involved in the action.

But the real trouble came just before close of play. There were about five minutes to go, and Gatting told Eddie Hemmings, the bowler, that they needed to try and get in a couple of overs, as they naturally wanted to have a bowl at new batsman Aamir Malik. So as often happens in the last overs of the day, the England fielders were rushing around a bit.

About four balls of Hemmings' over had gone, and there were now only two or three minutes left, so to save time Gatting told the striker, Salim Malik, 'We're bringing fine leg up to stop the one, Salim'.

'OK', said Salim, 'right.' Gatt had gone down on his haunches and David Capel, who had been at deep square-leg, was coming up to his new position. Once Hemmings was satisfied, he prepared to bowl. The skipper looked round at Capel, and, seeing he had come far enough, gestured for him to stop, and Hemmings, meanwhile, had gone back to recommence his little run-in. Everybody was ready; the batsman tapped once, twice, three times with his bat, the ball left the bowler's hand and was halfway down the wicket – and all of a sudden Rana came hurrying in from his position at square-leg shouting 'Stop, stop!' Fortunately the other umpire, Khizar ('Kitzie') Hayat, had been quick enough to call dead ball.

Said Rana, a railway engineer by trade, 'It's unfair play.'

'What's unfair play?' asked Gatting, puzzled.

'You're waving your hand – that's cheating. You're cheating!' Rana said.

Gatting told him that he had informed the batsman what was coming up, and that he hadn't been 'waving', simply gesturing for Capel to stop moving and stay where he was. Gatting told Rana, 'I'm allowed to move my fielders where I want, and in any case I wasn't moving him, I was only stopping him. As far as I'm concerned it has always been up to the non-striking batsman to keep the striker informed of field changes behind him, and in any case I'd already told Salim myself'. And Gatting finished by telling Rana that since he was the square-leg umpire anyway, there was no need for him to interfere like this when it wasn't necessary, and he should go back to square-leg, keep quiet, and let the players get on with the game.

Rana had already begun walking back when he decided to let Gatting have an outburst. 'You f—ing cheating b—!!' he spat, in the hearing of all the close-in fielders, some of whom thought the culminating noun began with a 'c' rather than the 'b' Gatting remembers. And it was at this point, the England captain very much regrets, that he finally completely lost his cool. Had it been an isolated incident, he could probably have managed to contain himself, although sporting celebrities have frequently let fly in *much* less provocative situations than this, and no England cricket captain had ever been called such a thing in recorded history by an umpire on the field of play. But it wasn't an isolated incident at all. It was the last straw, and it broke the camel's back. It was a culmination of all the little niggles and frustrations that had been going on since the start of the tour, and even before that: Pakistan captain Javed Miandad's attempted assault in the World Cup; and glaring contrast between facilities in the World Cup and facilities on this tour, where non-cooperation had made the England side feel so unwelcome; the decision by the BCCP to allow their more junior umpires to officiate in the Tests, rather than the World Cup umpires – all this suddenly blew up in Gatting's face, and he blew up with it. What he actually said in his fury need not be repeated here. It was infinitely regrettable, and Gatting knows, with hindsight, that it didn't reflect well on himself or on the game he loves. But he didn't think this Series was being played in the right spirit. He thought it was very unfair. He took the view that, even if one is working in a factory, one expects to have the right to complain about unjust treatment without being abused and sworn at by the boss. He didn't think an England captain had ever been accused of cheating by an umpire, let alone called what he was called. And although it shouldn't have provoked him to do what he did, he shouldn't have been provoked in the first place. He would never, ever, allow such a thing to happen again. He felt, and who could blame him, that the England side had been set up. The way in which the BCCP went on to appoint Shakeel Khan to officiate in the 3rd Test, despite what had happened in Lahore, and despite England's official protest, serves to illustrate this. There was a lot of what one might call 'background' to the affair, in any case, probably dating back as far as the 1982 Series in England, and to when the TCCB had refused to replace umpire David Constant in the 1986 Series, after objections from the Pakistanis. Whatever the truth of the matter, Shakoor Rana and Mike Gatting had locked antlers as they were perhaps intended to do, and the 2nd Test now came to a screeching halt.

Negotiations went on that evening to try to resolve the dispute, but the following morning it had become fairly clear that Rana wasn't going out again in this match until he received a written apology from Gatting for swearing. For his part, the England skipper was quite prepared to give this, but only if Rana extended the same courtesy to him. Umpires should not be sworn at, but then neither should England captains. The England manager Peter Lush and assistant manager Micky Stewart did everything they could to bring about a compromise that might seem fair to both sides, but sadly without much cooperation, either from Rana or the BCCP. Indeed, at one point, on the rest day, 10 December, Mr Lush drove 100 miles back to Lahore in the hope of discussing the subject with the president of the BCCP, General Safdhar Butt – who was otherwise engaged. Only the England camp seemed to have the 'wider interests of the game' at heart. Gatting knows that this situation would not have been allowed to happen in this country.

Also, while dissent against umpires on the field is not unheard of (as far back as 1971, for instance, England captain Ray Illingworth had a terrible row with umpire Lou Rowan in Sydney over John Snow's bouncers), it *is* quite unprecedented for an umpire to effectively halt a Test match as Rana seemed inclined to do here. The closest comparison would probably be the Birmingham Test of 1973, when Arthur Fagg refused to officiate until he got an apology from West Indies captain Rohan Kanhai, but he went back after only one over. The game was by no means disrupted. It seemed to Gatting a great pity that the BCCP should allow one of their umpires to hold up a Test match as he thought fit, when reports could quite easily have been submitted and the necessary disciplinary measures taken after the game, so as not to ruin things for the public.

Ironically, on a couple of occasions on the third morning, the two sides seemed very close to getting the match restarted, until Pakistan captain Javed Miandad had his say, and things once again took a turn for the worse. Javed implied that the honour of Pakistan rested on Rana's decision. The England players had plenty of time to call to mind that the New Zealanders once got so exasperated over a decision of Rana's to give Javed Miandad not out against them, that *they* all stormed off the field. England's problem was not storming off, but getting back on again. At 9.30 am, nothing having been resolved, Gatting and his team-mates showed willing by going out in the middle. They at least were prepared to get on with the game as best they could. But Shakoor Rana remained defiantly in the pavilion. Until he got his unconditional written apology from Gatting, they were told, he wasn't coming out to play. He had actually done this before, against India, so the England side were in no doubt about his track record for this sort of thing. It was stalemate, and it was all very sad.

The third day was a rest day but the fourth morning was even sadder, especially for Gatting. After a lot more negotiations, and many hotline phonecalls back and forth between the England management and the TCCB in London, it got to the stage where apologies had more or less been drafted and agreed, but Rana then had to keep going away and thinking about it all, and coming back with his statement radically altered. He kept telling them, 'I probably won't be able to finish this Test Match, you know, because of my high blood pressure', and Gatting and the England management got 'doctor's orders' and 'presciptions and pills' thrown at them, and finally the best one of all: 'Whatever happens, I don't think I'm going to be able to continue now, because I'm not in the right frame of mind'. Gatting's own frame of mind took a distinct dive when, the Foreign Office having interested itself in the affair, the instruction came down the wire from Lord's to get the game restarted *at any cost.* And as everyone likely to be reading this book now knows, that cost was Gatting's own unconditional written apology.

So at 9.20 am on the fourth morning of the 2nd Test Match, Mike walked along the corridor to the umpires' room, sicker than two parrots, with the handwritten note that had been wrung from him under duress, and handed it over to Shakoor Rana. All of a sudden, despite his health problems and high blood pressure, he was as right as rain again, spritely, out to the wicket (after only a 40-minute delay), wicket cut and rolled, and away they went. Gatting had never seen a happier man. He was a national hero, now, of course. The fan mail had come flooding in, and a colleague had handed him a note congratulating him on his stand, and saying, 'I wonder if Mike Gatting is the son of a man – he has the face of a white monkey'.

Gatting felt dreadfully let down. He wished the TCCB had given him a bit more support. So too did the great majority of English cricket lovers, judging by the damburst of expletives that began flooding into the Lord's switchboard. Of course there were two widely differing opinions, one that Gatting should no longer be captain of England, and another that he should be given total support – and indeed, some who thought that the team should come straight home.

The team felt deflated and disillusioned by the events so far. The Pakistan manager Haseeb Ahsan, who the previous season had stated that he thought cheating was part of the game, couldn't understand why the England side should be upset, since they had stayed in some of the nicest hotels in Pakistan. But England weren't complaining about the hotels, or anything else in Pakistan for that matter. They were complaining about the cricket. As a matter of fact, the people of Pakistan themselves had been very kind and sympathetic. A number of them, especially in Lahore, had approached members of the England side to express their disgust at some of the decisions against the tourists.

Privately, Gatting wasn't particularly worried about his job being on the line, despite Press speculation. Because he felt, all the time, that he had just cause for his stand, if not for the finer points of his behaviour. The England side had had enough. Gatting took the view that you can't keep turning the other cheek, getting whacked down, and then getting up and turning the other cheek again. 'Stiff upper lip, old chap' is all very well, he thought, but you can only get whacked so many times on your stiff upper lip before you haven't *got* any upper lip. The metaphor was rather typical of Gatting: a man who had gone straight back into the fray after Marshall smashed his face in, and whose courage had galvanized England on a number of previous occasions. A person of uncommon valour and straightforwardness does not like to be called a cheat, or to see his team humiliated.

The England captain did come very close, not to resigning, but to refusing to continue in the 2nd Test Match. He thought quite seriously of letting John Emburey take them out on the field. But he didn't think the players would have let him do that, anyway. They were just as adamant as himself, and Gatt was afraid that if *he* hadn't resumed, there wouldn't have been any resumption. He knew what this would mean and he didn't wish to jeopardize the younger players' careers. In fact the players were so solidly behind him, that they took the totally unprecedented step of issuing a statement of support, which in theory contravened their contracts with the TCCB. The text was reproduced in the newspapers. Quite apart from this, Gatting couldn't resign as England captain, or refuse to do his job, because he felt himself to be a prisoner of conscience. He thought that if he did resign, the BCCP would effectively have won the battle of principles. But he hoped that things would now be sorted out by the TCCB at Lord's. Hopefully, he thought, no captain would ever have to go through this again. Hopefully, the BCCP would not be given the satisfaction of seeing him give up a job he honoured and dearly loved doing. Hopefully, they wouldn't be allowed that privilege. Gatting didn't feel like playing in Pakistan any more, because for once he wasn't enjoying the game. He was a professional trying to do a professional job and finding it difficult to do so.

Well, England got the game underway again, at whatever cost to Gatting's personal feelings. They managed to get Pakistan out fairly quickly, and then Gooch played a very fine knock to get them into a position where they could try and make some quick runs the following morning and perhaps put the Pakistan batsmen under pressure. But unfortunately that all fell by the wayside, because England really didn't have enough time to bowl at their opponents in the end. Gatting and his management team had requested an extra day to complete the match, in view of one whole day having been lost and the fact that there was a long interval between the 2nd and 3rd Tests. But obviously, their request was denied. There was a feeling that had England been slightly losing rather than slightly winning, the BCCP might have shown more anxiety to press on with the match. Gatting felt that, in the much-quoted 'wider interests of the game', the BCCP might have acceded to their request for an extra day, and initially they were going to consider it and let England have an answer by 3 pm on the fifth day. But England didn't get an answer until 6 pm, and when it came it was 'no'. So the 2nd Test ended in another ultimately boring draw. Soon, the England players were off to Karachi for the 3rd Test.

After Faisalabad and all that went with it, the Karachi Test was something of an anti-climax. It passed off comparatively free from incident – although the smallest sign of dissent, disagreement or 'loitering' after dismissal was seized upon by a hungry Press corps with their pencils sharpened for more sensations. At one point Gatting 'loitered' slightly over a caught behind that was turned down, after he had distinctly heard the nick and seen Bruce French take the catch: he was standing particularly close to that one. But the Umpire in this case had walked over to square-leg, and that took up a bit of time, and when he came back Gatting asked him if he thought the batsman had hit it. The Umpire answered that yes, he had hit it, but as he himself couldn't see whether it had carried, he'd given the batsman not out. Nobody said anything else; DeFreitas the bowler was a bit upset, but Gatting got him out of the way as quickly as possible. The umpires weren't unduly concerned, and when they were asked at the end of the day what they felt about the incident, they said they could quite understand the players' reaction, because it must have seemed very disappointing. So there was no problem about that, and apart from a few minor hiccups, and the business about neutral umpires having been offered for the match when it wasn't feasible for them to get there in time all the way from India, things went comparatively smoothly. England had been offered 'Kitzie' Hayat and Shakeel Khan (who had stood in the controversial Lahore Test), and when they objected, they had a World Cup umpire, Mahboob Shah, instead. And really, Gatting thought, they handled the Karachi Test very well. These umpires even wondered what all the fuss was about, though by then the Press had probably rather brainwashed themselves into seeing dissent where none was intended. There's a very fine line between registering disappointment and showing dissent, and Gatting thought that, in this match, the Press were apt to confuse the two. As for the cricket itself; well, he reckoned there was some pretty good stuff played out there to interest the connoisseur, notably by John Emburey, David Capel, Graham Gooch and Abdul Qadir – who produced another very fine exhibition of the art of leg-spin bowling. Gatting gave credit, too, to Aamir Malik, who came so close to getting 100. But neither of the top orders batted particularly well in the match; it was a very good wicket, flat and true, yet it was left to the middle and late order batsmen to get most of the runs – apart from Gooch's powerful 93 in England's second innings. Gatting wasn't sure why the others failed; he thought that perhaps they were just as fed up and disappointed as he was. At all events, the game ended, so far as he was concerned, in yet another boring draw.

But of course, the last Test, like the Series, had been completely overshadowed by events in Faisalabad, and by the arrival in Karachi, on the eve of the match, of TCCB chief executive Alan Smith, and TCCB chairman Raman Subba Row. They sat down with the team, and listened to the England players' grievances, saw a copy of the videotape of events which had been shot from square-leg, and saw the frame of mind the players were in, which was very, very downcast indeed. A few telegrams had begun to arrive in Karachi, from people in England, expressing support for Gatting's stand, and those tokens of kindness and reassurance had helped him get through the 3rd Test, because he really hadn't wanted to play in it at all. The TCCB delegation took due note of all this, and drew their own conclusions, and then as they were leaving on the Friday, England manager Peter Lush told Gatting, around midday, that he had some good news for him.

Gatting asked what it was; he hadn't had much good news in recent weeks.

'I'll tell you later', said Mr Lush.

Well, it transpired that the TCCB had given the England team an extra payment of £1000 each, and contrary to Press reports, a cheer did *not* go up. The initial reaction of the players was, 'Why are they giving it to us?' It was very nice, but it certainly wasn't a requirement or condition made by the players to recompense them for all the hardship they had suffered, or anything like that. That had never, ever, been mentioned by any of them, and a number were in favour of refusing to accept the perk. All the players had asked for was support. They were, according to Gatting, flabbergasted at the payment. As they told the Press afterwards, it was like a bolt from the blue. Before he left, Raman Subba Row had tried very hard to secure a written apology from Shakoor Rana to the England captain, carefully wording a statement ready for the Umpire's signature. Significantly, this was not returned until *after* Subba Row and Alan Smith had gone home, and when it was eventually delivered to Gatting, he found the crucial word 'apology' had been omitted from it. Mike kept it to himself. It was too little, and too late.

So the TCCB delegation returned to England with their findings, and after Karachi, so did the team. England had lost the Series, and it had been a very long and trying tour. Gatting wanted nothing so much as to get home and see his wife and children again. He knew that, whatever else people might think of him back in England, his little son Andrew would be pointing at him on television saying, '*You!* You should be here, with *me*!'

CHAPTER SEVENTEEN
Appendix
1988

My publishers have asked me to update my book for the new paperback edition and tell you what happended to me in 1988. For various reasons this is hard for me to do. I'm sure you will understand that recent events you may have read about in the newspapers, have caused a great deal of pain and worry to me and my family and I've no wish to relive them here. But I'll try to set the record straight as best I can.

1988 was my benefit year, and a very well supported one at that. My first benefit dinner was early in January at the Porter Tun Room, which is the old Whitbread Brewery in Chiswell Street, London. Having just come back from Pakistan where everything let loose (the Australians toured there this year and encountered similar problems to our own), and having lost the Test series, I wasn't sure how people were going to react. Well, there was such a tremendous atmosphere and such a warm reception, that I felt it was an indication of support for the team, many of whom were present on that evening. This was a great relief after all that had happened. I don't want to gloss over things but all in all, I think the lads had put in quite a good performance in Pakistan and although we lost the Series, we did very well in getting to the final of the World Cup and won our three one-day internationals. If we had come back home after the World Cup, I believe everybody would have been very pleased.

Three days after this heartening dinner we were heading for New Zealand, having had a team meeting and been told to behave ourselves by the tour management. We arrived around 17 January and had a couple of days' warm-up and a couple of matches in Hamilton and cold and windy Wellington. Then we had to hop over to Australia to play in the Centenary Test match in Sydney, which was quite an affair and which had all the makings of an interesting match until we lost over two and half hours for bad light – quite phenomenal when you consider that they have floodlights at the ground and, if the playing conditions had allowed, could presumably have turned them on. The Aussies were keen to get at us after recent encounters, but with a magnificent 139 from Chris Broad and with everybody chipping in, we were able to put together 425, and then having bowled them out fairly cheaply, we asked them to follow-on. Unfortunately for us Messrs Marsh and Boon then steered them through the storm and with the time lost for bad light, they were able to bat the day out. There was also the incident involving Chris Broad, when he tapped his stumps as he got out. He was duly reprimanded. It was a bit silly, and particularly regrettable in the prevailing climate of concern about discipline. Apart from that, the match went off very well.

After an undistinguished day-night match in Melbourne, where I was struggling on antibiotics with a heavy cold and perhaps shouldn't have played at all, we had to go back to New Zealand. The First Test match was played on a result wicket at Christchurch. Unfortunately, we were without Neil Foster, who was hurt, and after the first day the Kiwis were missing their indomitable Richard Hadlee who had a calf injury. We probably had the better of the match; we were in a very strong position but couldn't force home the advantage on account of a few questionable umpiring decisions and some bad weather. Graham Dilley got hauled over the coals for shouting swearwords after a succession of 'not out' decisions. There was an almighty fuss about it and connections were made with the Chris Broad incident and with events in Pakistan, so obviously it got us into trouble and I think people felt that I wasn't strong enough with my team. My response was to try to explain that cricketers are human; that expressing emotion on the pitch has been done since the year dot, and that the only reason it seems so apparent now is that microphones and television cameras have exaggerated it and brought it into sharper focus than used to be possible in the old days (where I believe it went on just as much). Today, TV cameras zoom in for close-ups on the players' faces and study their expressions, and naturally some of the human beings involved, trying so hard to win under the extremes of Test match pressure, are likely to get a bit excited or frustrated. The microphones and cameras are supposed to be there to give the public a bird's eye view of the players' feelings, but very often they are looking for something to pick up otherwise the cameras wouldn't zoom in. I only wish they would allow the players a few moments' grace to compose themselves and quietly vent their frustrations before putting them under the microscope. More often than not, when they pull faces and mouth obscenities, they're just angry with themselves anyway, rather than being rude to anyone in particular. People do this in all walks of life. It just so happens that if you're a professional sportsman, cameras morbidly zoom in to catch your reactions like they do with disaster victims. The Press then seem to take their cue from this and start making a story out of a reflex gesture or grimace. I thought this worth mentioning because I believe it is something people need to understand. I'm not saying cameras or microphones are in themselves bad things, but just that using them to lip-read is slightly unfair.

After a couple of intervening matches we came to the 2nd Test in Auckland, and a boring draw on a very flat wicket. The weather interfered with the 3rd Test and the lads were sploshing about playing football in the rain after New Zealand had crawled to 301 and we'd replied respectably. The last day was totally washed out, with me in the thirties. In the one-dayers we won the first two comprehensively, let the third one slip, and then contested the fourth on an interesting wicket at Auckland, where the New Zealanders won and we squared the series 2-2. Overall, considering the very young side we'd taken out there to meet a very experienced set of Kiwis, I thought the team acquitted themselves quite well, even without facing the full blast of Richard Hadlee. We hadn't lost a Test match and we'd been in strong positions as well. I didn't think our record would meet with too much press criticism, but I was wrong. When we came home, the only thing hitting the headlines was 'discipline' and 'conduct on the pitch'.

Comments were made and appeared in the newspapers. Graham Dilley was fined; Chris Broad was fined; I was criticized for not clamping down on the lads and issuing dire warnings. My answer to this was that Chris Broad *had* been warned, and knew exactly what the consequences would be if he disobeyed, yet still went ahead and did what he did. As for the renewed outcry about Graham Dilley expressing *his* frustrations – and it is the first time I have ever seen Dilley explode like this – I could only repeat what I'd said already: cricketers are human beings, and when someone gets frustrated on the pitch, he lets out a cry of frustration. If onlookers would prefer to watch robots with no feelings at all, well and good, but in my opinion the game would lose something of its vitality and spontaneity. If you had bowlers running in and saying nothing, and batsmen going through the motions with impassive faces, it would be a sad day for cricket, surely? Obviously I don't condone bad behaviour, but if the viewing public want to tune in, in close-up, on our sport, then these things are going to be seen and heard through modern technology. If viewers prefer, they can turn it down, or the media can tone it down, because some of the more excitable players will inevitably express their feelings. You're not going to tell me that men like Dennis Lillee and Jeff Thomson didn't show feelings when they were bowling – or for that matter, Imran, Malcolm Marshall and Kapil Dev.

Middlesex had a very commendable season in 1988, and the start was amazing compared with the previous year's poor opening games. After the first round of four-day matches, Middlesex topped the championship table, topped the Refuge Assurance League *and* reached the quarter-finals of the

Benson and Hedges Cup competition. It was a tremendous achievement for the team, and a great uplift for me. Fortunately, I was managing to get some runs, and so I was named England captain for the three one-day internationals against the West Indies and for the first two Test matches. I was asked the usual question as to whether this would put me under any extra pressure, and as usual my answer was 'Not at all', because I felt that if I did a good job then hopefully I'd be asked to captain the rest of the series. The atmosphere in the England dressing room at the beginning was like the atmosphere at Middlesex – extremely good. England went out and won the one-day internationals 3-0 – which we hadn't done against the West Indies for a very long time and which maintained our good record in one-day cricket. England were playing well and with the team knitting together so effectively, I felt we stood a good chance in the Test matches.

By the end of May and beginning of June, Middlesex's season had started to go slightly off the boil. We lost the quarter-final of the Benson and Hedges, we'd lost a championship match to Worcester and been knocked off the top of the table. But we kept up our challenge in the Refuge Assurance, and in the NatWest competition we were unstoppable, reaching the final against Worcester. The big match was billed as a battle of the season's giants because Worcester were top of the championship table and threatening to clinch that, and we were top of the Refuge Assurance League. This was also to be Graeme Hick's first final, and people were keen to see him unleash himself at Lord's. As often happens on these occasions, there was a slight anticlimax as players who were expected to put on great exhibitions – Hick, myself and Tim Curtis, for example – didn't get big scores, and the battle was won and lost on the efforts of others. Angus Fraser, Norman Cowans, David Leatherdale and particularly young Mark Ramprakash turned in decisive performances; John Emburey and Andrew Needham bowled particularly well, and both sides fielded magnetically, with everything sticking to their fingers. In the end, it all turned on the Middlesex batting. I was run out without facing a ball and obviously felt that if we lost now, I was very much to blame for letting the side down. I was so upset that I couldn't watch the rest of our innings, but at tea-time victory looked on the cards, and we told John and young Ramprakash that if they could stay there we were home. And of course, 'Ramps' did us proud, and we won in considerable style. The Press were all abuzz afterwards over the young man's performance and were keen to make predictions about his future. I told them that he would do fine provided people kept off his back.

Meanwhile, back in the Test arena, the 1st Test match at Trent Bridge marked the rise and fall. From there on, it was all downwards. So far as the match itself was concerned, England came out with a creditable draw, although we were backs to the wall a little bit after the West Indies had batted so well, and the lads had to play *very* responsibly to save the situation. Goochie was very solid. After a fine 73 in the 1st innings he turned in a formidable 146 in the 2nd, just when England needed him to. He's very difficult to shift when he's in those moods, and he was ably supported by David Gower with a splendid 88 not out. We ended on 301 for 3, 98 ahead. It was the first time England had avoided defeat against the all-powerful West Indians since the tour of 1980-81, and ensured that there would be no 'blackwash' this summer. Considering Neil Foster had been ruled out by an injury and Graham Dilley, though he played, wasn't fully fit either, this was not a bad result and we were feeling fairly confident about meeting Viv Richards and his team at Lord's.

As it turned out, all this was fairly academic. It was during the Trent Bridge Test that all hell broke loose following reports in the Press over alleged events at the team's hotel. Oddly enough, Elaine had heard through the grapevine earlier on that somehow I might be set up; it would not have been the first time this had happened – indeed I'd had some intimation myself during an episode in Brisbane when a group of girls were intercepted by the management.

Because of these rumours, when we initially saw the newspaper headlines, our reaction was simply, 'Oh – so this is it'. The thing that really hit us was when the TCCB said that they believed my version of events, and then sacked me from the captaincy anyway. Following this the press laid siege to our home and made our lives a misery for four days and nights, hounding us continually. Even my ghostwriter had to put a cushion over her phone. Reporters are a persistent breed, and with their questions being fielded at the front door by our close friends and relatives, they resorted to various other methods to try to catch us out. Things like scaling our garden wall, climbing onto the garage roof, trying the doors of my car and ringing the door-bell at midnight. One lady reporter stuck her foot in the door at 11.30 pm in her quest for an interview. They all wanted to know if the marriage was breaking up, and pestered Elaine for some weeks afterwards for her 'story'. I don't think journalists have a right to harass people in this way.

The selectors made an announcement about my fate, saying that I had 'behaved irresponsibly in inviting female company to my room for a drink in the late evening'. At that time I had had another Test match to run as captain, and I was told that although Lord's accepted what I had told them about events at the team's hotel, they felt that they must now 'withdraw their invitation' for to captain the side at Lord's for the 2nd Test. The invitation for me to shore up the middle order batting still stood, but with everything that had gone on I felt I should now spend some time with my family. Unfortunately, this was not to be. I attended a benefit day with my family, after which I travelled away with Middlesex for ten days and the support I received from everyone was fantastic, with kindness and sympathy everywhere I went. At the same time, this was hard on Elaine and the children as I wanted to be at home with them. Middlesex were to confirm me in the captaincy, believing my version of events. I'll always be grateful to them, for their support at the time was a great comfort to me and my beleaguered family, as I said in the newspapers at the time. I would also like to say thank you to everyone who wrote to me and my family giving their support – it meant a lot to us all.

Another complicating factor during this period of upheaval was the publication, on 12 June of a preview extract from this book in *The Sunday Times*, edited almost beyond recognition which, as I explained to the TCCB, I knew nothing about. The extract appeared in this particular paper alongside some of the most rampant anti-Gatt criticism anywhere in the press, with the reporter sounding off about what a disgrace I was and saying I should be suspended indefinitely if the book's publication went ahead. The editorial accused me of betraying 'all our young dreams' – which just shows the hypocrisy of some of our press. The book was obviously getting me into a bit of trouble. I'm not allowed to comment about this as freely as I would like, but it's a matter of record that I was scheduled to appear before the full Disciplinary Committee of the TCCB later on. The TCCB took the view that they were trying to patch up relations with the Pakistan Cricket Board and by contract I was not allowed to print anything about my experiences on the tour.

As far as England's fortunes against the West Indies were concerned, changes were obviously now in the offing. I was, of course, omitted from the side for the 2nd Test at my own request, and John Emburey was named caretaker captain. I wished him luck. Greg Thomas and Eddie Hemmings lost their places; Martyn Moxon was brought in to replace me, and Gladstone Small was added to the strike force because although Graham Dilley was back to full strength, Neil Foster was not. I hoped the lads would keep up the good work – I really thought England had a good chance here, having drawn at Trent Bridge. As it turned out, it was a great Test match, and if a few things had gone England's way I believe we could have won. I say 'we', as all England supporters do – I remember being down at Basingstoke, fielding for Middlesex, and being almost unable to refrain from jumping up and down when I heard that the West Indies were 50 for 5.

It was a tremendous thrill – it meant that all the effort we'd put in wasn't a total waste of time. It would have been wonderful if England could have been rewarded with a win at Lord's, but unfortunately this wasn't to be. As for me, I was quietly getting some runs for Middlesex, hoping I might do well for my county and that I might be considered for the 3rd Test.

I won a place in the 3rd Test at Old Trafford, and I tried to play in it. The opening day coincided with the publication of *Leading from the Front*. Publication had advanced too far to be stopped in compliance with the TCCB's objections, so they simply banned its sale from the cricket grounds. The England captain was still John Emburey, but the atmosphere in the dressing room, not surprisingly, was not quite what it had been at the beginning of the Series. There was an air of uncertainty, because the 4th Test was going to be at Headingley, and the selectors were apparently not going to bother playing a spinner there. So there was a lot of speculation and unrest about the leadership. Very few words were said to me, but I could see that a feeling of anticlimax had set in. Every member of the team was trying like nobody's business but enthusiasm and confidence had been dented. My own enthusiasm was dented as well. Apart from everything else, I wasn't fully fit, having had a blow on the instep, and as I hobbled about, Marshall thundered in. England were skittled out for 135 and lost fairly comfortably. The book had started coming to the fore and things were beginning to mount up, I'm afraid. So far as I'm concerned, Old Trafford is best forgotten. Looking back on my mental state at the time, I realize that I should not have played and I felt I let England down. Meanwhile, Ian Botham was getting bored in his hospital bed after his back operation and telling the press that the TCCB should stop trying to suppress my book, because his Dad fought in the Second World War for freedom of speech.

Chris Cowdrey was appointed captain for the 4th Test, at Headingley, and he too had the same baptism as I had had two years previously: a Test match loss. The press conference after a match is always quite testing, especially the one prior to the rest day, and particularly when things aren't going too well. Chris's reign was short-lived as he was injured, and so the fourth captain of the year was appointed, Graham Gooch. The selectors' choice may have been complicated by the fact that Graham had declared himself unavailable for the scheduled winter tour of India (eventually this was called off amid yet another row), and mention was made in the press, too, that both Gooch and Emburey had been banned for three years in 1982 for going to South Africa, and that these recent captaincy honours represented a change of fortune for them. This was true; if they hadn't joined the rebel tour, one or the other of them might well have been captain before; Emburey would certainly have captained Middlesex.

I didn't play at the Oval, despite Chris Cowdrey having a chat with me and trying to persuade me to join up. I felt that it was crucial for me to spend time with my family. There was a great deal still to be talked through at home. Through my solicitors I gave the Press a statement explaining that I wasn't in the right frame of mind to do my best in Test cricket, and that I intended to play for Middlesex, and to make myself unavailable for the scheduled winter tour. I'd only had one winter at home in the last ten years; I was awaiting the hearing on my book, and I had intended to have a winter off in any case at some stage – originally this was to be the West Indies tour of 1989–90. So what with all the fuss and goings on, I felt my family must now come first. I needed to remember what it was like to be a father again.

Twenty–four hours before the full Disciplinary Committee hearing on my life story, I took Elaine and little Andrew to Buckingham Palace for the investiture ceremony, where Her Majesty the Queen pinned the OBE on my chest, for services to cricket on the triumphant tour of Australia in 1986-87. It was a very great honour.

When the TCCB announced their ruling on the book and fined me a record £5,000, the secretary, Alan Smith, stated that the fine would have been higher but for my previous exemplary record and contributions to cricket. And that's about it really. I am looking forward to getting back into the England side and to letting my bat do the talking again.

CHAPTER EIGHTEEN
Considerations
[1989]

I hope you've enjoyed this book. Even when I was a kid, I found it quite hard to put my thoughts down on paper. I find it a lot easier to talk to somebody, or into a tape recorder, because then things seem to come out spontaneously, whereas when you're writing it down, you tend to lose your train of thought. I have tried to keep it sensible, the same as I used to do at press conferences.

As far as I was concerned, it wasn't particularly important for me to tell the Press everything I felt. And I gave standard replies, not because I didn't have any original opinions, but because I wanted to keep a low profile. I didn't want them to start building things up out of what I said. I didn't want to get into any hot water, or put anybody else under pressure by saying the wrong thing. So they gave me a lot of stick because I wouldn't tell them anything. I wouldn't tell them the sort of things I've told you in this book.

There have been times when I haven't slept too well, worrying about cricket, trying to have positive ideas instead of negative ones. And now when our fortunes take a turn for the worse I don't worry so much. When I was very young I used to think about ridiculous things in the middle of the night, such as what might happen if aliens invaded the earth, or what might be coming up the stairs after I'd just been watching a vampire film. That's the sort of stupid imagination I had. But then I'm not supposed to have any imagination at all, according to some people.

Peter Roebuck did a big feature article on me a while ago for the *Sunday Times* magazine, in which he said of me,

> He is, in many ways, a man of ordinary tastes, a man of pickle, chips and lager . . . . At press conferences he can be outstandingly obtuse, rolling out clichés as if they were revelations . . . 'Such an obvious chap,' the whisper goes round.

He says I appear to be 'a confoundedly ordinary man. Fantasy plays no part in his character. What you see is what you get.' I suppose to Peter Roebuck, because he's supposedly an academic, I might seem pretty dull. He can talk about things I can't, and admittedly, like most cricketers, I might like a drink in the bar after the game, rather than going to a night at the Proms. I like to enjoy myself, that's all. I think I'm more of a kid at heart than anything. I like playing on pinball machines. I like fantasy stories, like *Jungle Book*, James Bond, the *Wizard of Oz*, and Tolkien. I'm not sure that that makes me dull, though. Perhaps talking to Peter Roebuck simply drags all the dull and boring things out of me.

I do tend to keep a lot inside. Evidently, I disguise it very well. I'm a very emotional person, but I find it difficult to parade my feelings in public. I'm not one for jumping up and down, or shouting and screaming all the time, because I'm very conscious of people sticking labels on me. So if people like Peter Roebuck think of me as a superficial sort of pickle-eating England captain, perhaps that's simply the impression they choose to have.

Whereas what I really am is something of a softie. I can't watch *Born Free* without a bit of a tear, or the *Sound of Music* for that matter. Sometimes 'prosaic Gatting' even likes a candlelit dinner. I'd love to go to the Greek Islands, and just sit out on the beach for a couple of days, looking at the sea, or perhaps get a paddleboat out like I used to do when I was young, and stick a line over the side, and do a bit of fishing, or scuba-diving, or snorkelling. I'm not particularly exotic when it comes to having 40 ft yachts. But there are simple little things that I'd like to do. I like places that are quiet, because I spend a lot of time rushing around.

My ideal setting would be a peaceful valley in Wales or Derbyshire, with nobody about and a river running through on a lovely sunny day. Or a nice Cornish beach (I love Charlestown), or wandering through a bluebell wood with the dog and the kids, enjoying the peace and quiet. I have a sort of reverence for nature, which might sound silly to a lot of people.

Another little throwback to my boyhood days, when I used to be a bit envious of families with dogs, is that I love all sorts of animals (apart from cats – I'm not a very catty person). Horses, dogs, and anything you can stand and stare at in admiration, such as lions, tigers, elephants – I suppose all kiddies, large or small, dream about wildlife and big game.

I also have a sense of wonder about planes and flying (my Dad was an aircraft fitter after all). Planes fascinate me. I think it's quite marvellous that somebody like me spends half his time gliding across the clear blue sky: it's magic the way an aircraft stays up there, as if somebody's holding it in the sky, with no wings flapping or anything, and when you look out of the windows you can see miles of blue reaching out into space, or perhaps an ocean down below, with little specks of boats, and nobody can get hold of you on the phone, or ask you to attend a cricket function. I suppose flying is a sort of sanctuary: flying in Jumbos, that is, not flying in those horrible little planes that go up and down and make you reach for your sickbag.

I have a very well-publicized love of science fiction – I don't know why, but I think I like the uncertainty of it. I'm not above looking up at the moon now and then and wondering what's up there. I'm a great *Star Trek* fan. It's light-hearted and relaxing. What would it be like to travel faster than the speed of light? Interplanetary travel intrigues me. Science fiction has the beauty of being intangible: you can't actually grasp it or get to the bottom of it. I'll sit and watch science-fiction films and be in my element (or elements)! *Star Wars, War of the Worlds, Blake's Seven* (I've got a lot of those episodes on tape), *Dr Who.*

When I'm away, Elaine records all the instalments of *Dr Who* for me. Mind you, it's got a bit silly lately. (*Elaine:* 'He can remember the first paragraph ever written. The first two days after he comes back from a tour, he's usually watching end-to-end *Dr Who* episodes. You can't speak to him or anything.') I suppose that's my way of relaxing – it takes me out of myself; it's an escape from reality.

I'm inclined to think there's life on other planets anyway. If you read things like *Nostradamus* and *Chariots of the Gods,* it does set you wondering about the unsolved mysteries of this world; about strange metals, and long ruts in South American plateaux, and the construction of the pyramids. And it's not a far cry from wondering about that to wondering about the possibility of time-travel and thick perspex for whale-tanks aboard the *Enterprise!* Unexplained phenomena fascinate me so I think anything's possible. I believe in a bit of everything – God, the supernatural, ghosts, superstitions, UFOs. I like to keep my options open.

I suppose it's fairly strange, too, for such a 'down-to-earth' character as me to be hooked on Tolkien. I don't really have any 'favourite bits' though I did read some passages on the kiddies' programme *The Wideawake Club,* filmed with me sitting on a log in my garden. I like the whole world of Tolkien really. I have to admit that when I first read *Lord of the Rings,* I found the first 40 pages fairly hard work with all the genealogy and explanations of Hobbit history, but once the party sets off on the actual adventure, I find it very hard to put down and I just keep reading on and on. He creates these tremendous fantasies that are full of vivid detail, and you never know what's round the corner, whether it might be the Balrog in the Mines of Moria, or Orcs, or trolls, or giant spiders, or something terrible from Mount Doom or Mordor.

I haven't started reading it to my children yet because although it's a great adventure story, I think Andrew might find it all a bit scarey. The Ralph Bakshi film I've got of the first part would be rather strong stuff for him at the moment, and I'd have to keep stopping and explaining about

Ringwraiths and Orcs and what have you. One day I expect we'll all sit round and watch it, Andrew, Jimbo and me, and then we can all be little boys together!

Our Andrew is a very determined little bloke. He's got a temper at times, like I used to have at his age. (*Steve Gatting:* 'He's asking questions all the time, now, whereas he used to run and jump at you and kick you!') He's really very bright, too clever for his own good in some ways, though he's also a bundle of energy. Yet he'll sit watching educational programmes without a murmur, and he'll do his homework, concentrating, with his little round spectacles on. He's fairly inquisitive and picks things up lightning fast. He can operate any electrical gadgetry that comes into the house including video recorders, and he's very articulate now.

I introduced him to a journalist that came to our house recently and he told her, 'At school I'm just making a model wasp's nest out of half a football, which is very complicated work.' And when she was leaving he said, 'You've got a nice car, but you've got rather a lot of flies on the front.'

Our other little fellah, Jimbo, is only a toddler but he seems very active and smart as well. He's worked out that if he pushes chairs into the breakfast room, he can use them to climb up on the table and play with the television. I suppose it's a stage they go through. He's got a bad temper at times. I guess they've inherited it from me, though they're both very lovable little characters really.

As anyone will know after reading this book, my family are always at the back of my mind. Elaine's constantly telling me, 'First there's cricket, and then after cricket it's all the other things people want you to do, like functions, and committee meetings, and dinners, and then *we* come after all that'. But I keep telling her, I *have* to do those things, but in my mind my family are still very, very important. Everybody has an idea what his perfect schedule would be; mine would be two or three days a week at home with the wife and kids, though obviously with Test matches and tours, that's not very realistic. But it would be nice to be able to switch off now and then, and not have to worry about the pressures of the game. I think my idea of heaven would be just being able to live without having to worry too much about money. I wouldn't want to do extravagant things, but I'd like the basics: a nice home, and to be able to go away with the family and unwind on holiday.

What do I do to unwind? Well, apart from falling sound asleep, reading science fiction, watching uncomplicated films and going out in the middle of nowhere with a set of golf clubs (which I love), I also read John Le Carré and Jeffrey Archer (especially in Pakistan where there's not a lot else to do), and I like listening to my music tapes. I've got rather wide-ranging tastes: I'll listen to Beethoven and Holst (I think the *Planet Suite* is magnificent) but I'll also sit round the piano singing Elton John songs if I've had a few, and I like Peter Gabriel, Lionel Richie, Frank Sinatra and Barbra Streisand, and I go back a long way to Diana Ross and the Supremes as well, and Elvis, and Frankie Laine. The only music I positively dislike is punk rock and heavy metal. I prefer 'Champion the Wonder Horse' any day to that racket.

I also enjoy a game of cards with the lads and some of the Press guys, and I'll play Scrabble as well, though I prefer my crosswords. I don't often finish the *Telegraph* one – perhaps I'll succeed once a month and get it all, but there are usually three or four cryptic clues that I can't figure out, and I'll look up the solutions the next day for my own peace of mind. Those are my sedentary hobbies; I also collect wine. I wouldn't say I'm a connoisseur or anything – David Gower's much more of a wine buff than I am – but I'd like to read up and learn a bit more, and I think I will as I get older. Vintage ports are a favourite: I've got quite a few bottles at home that I've picked up on trips to Australia and Jerez and places like that.

Of course, most of the things I do require a lot of energy: that's why I'll flake out when I get home. I love swimming, which is a very fine form of exercise, and though I can't just run and run for the sake of it, if it's in the cause of football or squash or cricket, I'll run till the cows come home, or for as long as my legs will carry me. It's not just that I have to beat people – at squash I'll deliberately seek out opponents who are better than I am, to build up my game. But I think it's a question with me of giving a hundred per cent in all I do. I don't have a motto, but if I did, I think it would be this: if you're going to do something, do it to the best of your ability. I don't honestly know what I'll do when I stop playing cricket, and I haven't thought about it much, but whatever it is, I'll do my very best at it. I'd want to give it a hundred per cent. I don't have my cricket shop any longer but there are all sorts of possibilities.

As I've said in this book, I'm not really the Fat Gatt people take me for, but you have to laugh about it really. Asked to describe myself for a foreign passport or something, I'd probably put, 'Short, wide and hairy!' I'm really not unhappy with the way I look. I'm 5 ft 10 in, I've not got particularly long legs (inside leg on the cricket trouser being 30 in), and I've got short arms as well. Now, if you add to that a fairly broad chest (44 in), and stick a few pads on and then put me on a square screen, of course I come out a bit cubelike. I don't mind. I laugh louder than anybody at the Fat Gatt jokes.

Once, during a Test match in Calcutta, I was fielding at 1st slip, with Allan Lamb at 2nd, and Chris Cowdrey was bowling so we decided we didn't need a 2nd slip any more and Lamby came out. I shouted to skipper David Gower, who was talking to the bowler, 'David, do you want me a bit wider?' And Chris turned round to him and said, If Gatt gets any wider he'll burst!' David fell about on the pitch laughing.

I'm prepared to see the funny side of a lot of things in cricket. Even when I'm upset I don't usually show it, and I try to find some way to get it out of my system, like for example going out and having a run when I was given out in that 1st innings at Lahore. I knew that if I *didn't* get the pent-up feelings out of my system, I'd have done something stupid. I think the only thing to do when you're *really* cross is either to go to a punch-bag or just to get out of the way of everybody.

Still, not a great deal bugs me on the field, really: I think you've got to try to be fairly understanding of most people. I don't think you should lose your temper at the drop of a hat, because we all have to learn in life, and be tolerant, and give people a chance. I suppose Elaine knows my attitude as well as anybody.

Elaine Gatting:

He can't stand the unfairness and the anger in sport these days, or colour prejudice or anything like that. I know when he was leaving Edgbaston that day and he was completely surrounded by Pakistan supporters kicking his car, that upset him, and almost brought him to the point of tears, because he plays cricket purely and simply because he loves it. I think he would have played even without being paid, he loves it so much. And he can't bear to see any other player who doesn't love it, or who's only in it for the money. He's quite a tough captain, I think, because he expects everybody to do his best and not be half-hearted. I suppose that, in a world where a lot of them are ex-public schoolboys, he's been regarded as the rough end of the market and if they still had Players *v.* Gentlemen, he would be a Player, and yet you couldn't have a more gentlemanly man. He's all for the good of his sport and would never deliberately do anything to harm it. If he felt that he wasn't doing the right thing for England, he would give up the captaincy. He's not the type to go on playing till he's 45. I know Mike, and if he felt he couldn't give the job a hundred per cent, he'd stop.

The way I view the game certainly won't change because of the Shakoor Rana incident. That was strictly a one-off thing in which we were in my opinion set up, and we were made to pay for the Pakistanis' feud with umpire Constant which was nothing to do with me, and perhaps, too, it arose out of their frustration at not having done very well in the World Cup. Perhaps their cricket needed elevating – I don't know. Cricket is taken very seriously indeed in the Subcontinent, with rioting and fighting, and their cricketers are national idols. The whole incident, so far as I'm concerned, goes down as experience, and not an experience that I'd care to repeat, or that I'd like any other England cricketer to have to suffer, either.

I intend to go on playing cricket in the right spirit and hope that nothing so explosive ever happens again – I'm sure it won't. I'll be going out there to do my very best as I've always done, and trying to enjoy it again – because that's the way I play it. I feel that sport and life tend to run parallel and you need dedication *and* enjoyment in any job you do. I suppose to a degree you have to have 'tunnel vision' too – because you've got to channel all your efforts into achieving a specific goal, the thing that you dearly want to do, and this is where all the concentration, self-belief and positive thinking come in, and everything that will serve to make you a better player than the next person.

You need to set yourself targets: I think my target these days is about 1500 runs a season. These targets, I believe, are very important. So long as they are realistic (and I don't think averaging 100 *is* realistic for *most* batsmen) they help to motivate and give something to aim at, something to keep struggling towards, something to make you knuckle down when you think perhaps you've done enough in a particular innings.

On the less practical side, I do believe in inspiration. I think strokes really can come to you when you're not thinking about making them. It's rather like the spin bowler following a hunch and saying, 'I've got a feeling he's going to try and whack me over there. So tell you what – I'll put a man there' – and then the batsman hits it to that particular spot. A batsman can be inspired, though, by big crowds: that happens to me sometimes. A full house creates a lot of atmosphere. Like in Perth, when several thousand spectators were on our side, cheering and singing. That was brilliant – you could hear the passion in their voices, and it gave you a lift to think you were being supported and sung to so many miles from home!

Inspiration tends to happen when a batsman is in good nick – when he has spent a lot of time at the crease and he's been getting a lot of runs; when, in other words, he's watching the ball. *Not* thinking where his feet are going, or where his hands are on the handle, or whether his bat is coming through straight or not. Just basically watching the ball, with the mind totally concentrating and focusing on the ball. That is when he seems to have so much more time than usual. His mind isn't cluttered up with thinking about what he's doing.

Then as soon as he sees the ball come out of the bowler's hand, his body's reacting to the stroke he's going to play, even before the ball has pitched. He sees the trajectory; as soon as it leaves the bowler's hand, he knows. He makes up his mind without thinking about it.

Of course, with a spinner, you *do* have time to weigh up the possibilities. You do start thinking, then, what you're doing. But with fast bowlers, it all happens so much more quickly. You notice everything about the bowler and you may even be quite detached about it.

Somebody like Michael Holding had such a lovely run-up in his younger days – and I hope he'll forgive me for saying he's got a little bit older now, though he can still bowl very sharply off a short run. But I remember first playing against him at Old Trafford – I think it may have been in 1981 – and he was running in a long, long way, and the thought struck me how *graceful* it was. That's why it wouldn't be fair to get the over-rates up by forcing bowlers to shorten their run-ups. A long run gave Michael Holding his rhythm and his pace. Fast bowlers like him need to run in. You shouldn't stop them. It might not be very pleasant for the batsman seeing it coming towards him, but at the same time, it *is* a tremendous thrill to watch a great athlete in action like that.

I've never spent much time watching other players, really, because I've always been too involved with playing myself. I used to watch Basil D'Oliveira fairly closely, and Ken Barrington. But I never really had any cricket 'idols'. We're not idols. I don't like people treating me as though I were a superstar – I always try to get that across. One thing I hate is people being big-headed, and I steer away from that staunchly and ferociously. As far as I'm concerned, we're all human beings, and famous cricketers shouldn't be treated differently from anybody else.

If Joe Bloggs and his wife are eating in a restaurant, you wouldn't wander up to them and interrupt their meal. If a stranger buys you a drink in the pub, fine, but we do have a right to a bit of privacy. It's nice to have a few moments with my wife and family – goodness knows, I see little enough of them as it is, and if people see us alone, it would be very considerate of them to leave us alone. On the other hand, people can be very, very thoughtful too, like the chap who saw us dining out and quietly ordered a bottle of wine for our table before leaving, not wanting to disturb us. Elaine and I were very grateful for that gentleman's kindness.

And myself and the rest of the England lads were extremely touched by the support we received from members of the public back home who sent messages to us when our hearts were sinking in Faisalabad. I'd like to tell them here that it was *very* much appreciated by us all.

Index